I Blow My Own Horn

I
BLOW
MY OWN
HORN

by

Jesse L.
Lasky *with*

Don Weldon

Victor Gollancz Limited, London, 1957

PRINTED IN GREAT BRITAIN
BY LOWE AND BRYDONE (PRINTERS) LTD., LONDON, N.W.10

To my mother and sister Blanche

Contents

8

I Blow My Own Horn

A *

Slight Pause for

Station Identification

"Step out of the car!" the cop ordered my driver when he had pulled us to the curb. "And you in the back seat, too!"

I protested.

"I said step out of the car!" he repeated, in no mood to be trifled with as he prepared to write a summons.

Very reluctantly I started to obey.

The officer's eyes bugged out. "Get back in the car and put your clothes on!" he sputtered. "What are you—an exhibitionist?"

I stammered that I had just come from a dinner the Screen Producers Guild had tendered me, and showed him the silver wreath of honor on a plaque inscribed, "To Jesse L. Lasky for his historic contribution to the American motion picture."

"Where's your pants?" he demanded somewhat irreverently.

I explained with as much dignity as I could under the circumstances that I had only half an hour to get from the Cocoanut Grove to the airport to catch a plane to New York and, as I didn't want to greet reporters and photographers at La Guardia in the morning wearing a tuxedo and stiff shirt, I was changing my clothes in the speeding car.

"Wait till I tell my wife I caught a big movie mogul with his pants down," the cop exulted. "And don't do seventy on Sepulveda again unless I'm with you! Come on if you want to make that plane!" And his siren screamed.

On the plane I had more time to savor pleasantly the heart-warming tributes at the testimonial dinner—Adolph Zukor recalling the beginnings of the company that became Paramount under our joint twenty-year stewardship, Sam Goldwyn and Cecil DeMille acknowledging that I started them in the picture business as partners in the company that bore my name, Gloria Swanson and Mary Pickford referring to my influence in their lives and careers as employer and dear friend, others recalling instances when I had played cupid in introducing Sam Goldwyn to Frances Howard, Robert Z. Leonard to Mae Murray, Lou Tellegen to Geraldine Farrar, Elliott Dexter to Marie Doro, Gene Raymond to Jeanette MacDonald, Nicholas Schenck to his charming wife, Pansy.

I pushed my seat back to the reclining position and entertained myself with a long flashback of the events that culminated in this evening's brilliant gathering of film personalities to bestow the first honor of its kind, forerunner of an annually perpetuated ceremony.

If you're beginning to think I'm addicted to name-dropping, I'll have to plead guilty. I've dropped my share of names in more than forty years as a maker of motion pictures. I dropped Rudolph Valentino when he no longer wanted to make the kind of pictures we thought best for him. I dropped Fatty Arbuckle when scandal blighted his career. I dropped Kay Francis, Ruth Chatterton, and William Powell without meaning to when I forgot when their options were due and they were stolen from under my nose. I didn't want to drop Wallace Reid or William Desmond Taylor, either, but I had no choice in those tragic cases.

I could mention a good many more, including some of the celebrities who toasted me at the Screen Producers dinner. The most difficult decision I've ever had to make in my life was to drop my brother-in-law, Sam Goldwyn—and later I also had to agree to drop my best friend, Cecil B. DeMille, from the company we three formed as partners, The Jesse L. Lasky Feature Play Company, which, shortly after producing the first feature-length film ever made in Hollywood, merged into Famous Players-Lasky and eventually changed its name to Paramount.

But I'd rather not talk about the names I've dropped. I'd much rather tell about some of the names I've helped bring to recognition and acclaim in the course of presenting over a thousand motion pictures to the public—Academy Award winners like Fredric March, Charles Laughton, Gary Cooper, Paul Lukas, Bing Crosby, Spencer Tracy, Claudette Colbert, Ginger Rogers, Mary Astor, Emil Jannings, Frank Sinatra, whose talents I've been credited with discovering or developing. Some of those names I coined myself—Mary Astor, Carole Lombard, Gale Storm, Ricardo Cortez, Lila Lee. . . .

If you surveyed the list of the pictures I've helped to make, it might strike you as curious that Metropolitan Opera stars frequently crop up at the head of the casts, even in the early voiceless films—Geraldine Farrar, Enrico Caruso, Lina Cavalieri—and later Nino Martini, Schumann-Heink, and Lily Pons. In one instance I even hired an opera director with no film experience to direct pictures for me. His name was Rouben Mamoulian. Two of my later pictures were much concerned with classical music; *Rhapsody in Blue* and *The Great Caruso*.

There's nothing curious about it, however. I'm just a frustrated virtuoso, as ecstatically moon-struck in the presence of musical genius today as I was when I was old enough to blow my own horn.

That's when this story really begins. . . .

A Pretty Kettle

of Fish

I was pretty good at tooting a horn before I was out of knee breeches. I was solo cornettist of the San Jose Juvenile Band, and I thought I was good enough to be in Sousa's band. I thought if only Sousa could hear me play, he'd leave off waving his baton long enough to wave a contract. But how was Sousa going to discover me in San Jose, California?

I felt sure that fate was playing into my hands when, heading from school toward my father's shoe store on South First Street with my cornet under one arm, I suddenly froze in the attitude of a pedigreed pointer before a window card that announced:

SAN JOSE AUDITORIUM

John Philip Sousa and His Band

with

Herbert Clarke

World's Greatest Cornettist

The words swam and melted before my eyes like those trick movie titles where one list of credits washes out and is magically replaced by another set of names. I'll admit that "Herbert Clarke" went through such a transformation.

There wasn't time to save up for a balcony ticket to the matinee out of my weekly ten-cent allowance, but I'd been hoarding for months to buy firecrackers, come the Fourth of July, and I had over a dollar with which to indulge my eardrums one way or another. Of course Sousa won.

I got there so early the auditorium was empty. My efforts to get a glimpse of my hero backstage were firmly repulsed, but the stage doorman did volunteer the information that show people usually walk around town after a performance.

That was it. The auditorium was exactly six blocks from our cottage on Santa Clara Street. The only place Sousa could conceivably walk after the concert was down Santa Clara Street right past our front porch.

I was, out of the auditorium and racing for home while the bandmaster was still taking bows. I set up my music stand back of the rosebushes that twined around the porch pillars and for three solid hours I auditioned for Sousa. I played *Semper Fidelis, Washington Post March,* and *Liberty Bell.* When I had run through all the Sousa marches I knew, I barely paused for breath before starting over again, because I couldn't chance missing the moment when the leader would walk down Santa Clara Street.

My heartbeat set a new tempo when I heard heavy footsteps stop at our front gate. I didn't dare look up. My lips ached and my lungs were ready to burst, so the effort brought tears to my eyes, but I drew on that mysterious reserve energy that can save the day in times of dire emergency.

Knowing that my whole future hung in the balance, I blew the clearest, sweetest notes since the Pied Piper played a one-night stand in Hamelin. The gate clicked and the footsteps were drawn irresistibly through it and up to the porch.

Not until then did I lower my cornet and turn to face the trustee of my destiny. It was with a distinct shock that I looked up into the irate face of neighbor Johnson. "My wife is sick and if you don't stop that infernal racket," he stormed, shaking his fist, "I'll have the police on you." He wheeled around and stalked off, still muttering imprecations.

I stood alone in the dark, behind the rosebushes, my life blasted to bits—with no hope anywhere in the world for me—because Sousa hadn't walked down Santa Clara Street.

But in the early teens despair is highly perishable. If I couldn't be Sousa's cornettist, I could be his rival. I organized an All-Boys Brass Band and we practiced in our front parlor on Thursday nights.

At the first rehearsal my sister Blanche plopped herself down at the piano with grim determination. In vain we pleaded with her that a kid sister didn't belong in an All-Boys Brass Band. But what she lacked in age and gender she made up in brass. She set her chin and wouldn't budge.

There was no place we could go to keep the masculinity of the band undefiled, since our little group wasn't blessed with another set of parents who would put up with the racket. So we glared at Blanche and she glared at us from her piano-bench citadel.

We tried ignoring her. She ignored us right back, while she bound our individual musical efforts together with strong chords. She was a capable if stubborn accompanist, and we gradually got used to her.

Our father hadn't hesitated to pay for Blanche's and my music lessons even though I couldn't think of any better reason for wanting to play the cornet than that it was shiny. Somehow he knew it was more than a passing whim. My mother was also sympathetic to my attachment for the instrument, though she did make me stop taking it to bed with me.

The lessons continued after my father could no longer afford them, but he never let us find out during his lengthy illness that the Boston

Shoe Bazaar was slowly slipping into bankruptcy without his own friendly presence, which was its best advertisement.

He called me to his bed one night after a rehearsal of our Almost All-Boys Brass Band. "It's funny how music can crop out in a family all of a sudden," he mused, "like a stream that runs underground for a long way and you'd never know it was there until it comes to the surface and bubbles out all over the place. It's all I can do to whistle 'Ta-ra-ra Boom der é.' But you and Blanche have got music popping out of you like a spring. And maybe it isn't as accidental as you might think. Your grandpa, when he isn't imagining things that never happened to him crossing the plains in '48, sometimes talks about his father, your great-grandfather, who was a musician in Prussia for a king!"

"What did he play?" I wanted to know.

"How the devil should I know?" my father said. "Ask Grandpa. He doesn't know either but he'll make up a good story about it."

True or not, Grandpa's tales of covered-wagon days and skirmishes with the Indians along the Oregon Trail enthralled me. He must have spent far more time telling about his westward trek than the trip itself originally took. And the stories improved with age, like any fine cheese. It isn't any wonder that my daydreams for years were peopled with redskins, punctuated with "ughs" and war whoops, and cluttered with flying scalps.

My father's early life, playing on the steps of the Capitol at Sacramento with the sons of the railroad builders, seemed tame by contrast to the conquering of the West. But he found exciting things to do, even in a small town. He was part owner of the San Jose Baseball Club, president of the Athletic Association, organizer of the Bicycle Club, a devotee of walking contests, and the best fly fisherman in the county.

I shared my father's enthusiasm for fishing. I liked to fish as well as I liked to listen to Grandpa's pioneering fairy tales. Fly-casting remained my favorite relaxation even after I grew up. But the first time I went fishing without my father left a scar on my memory.

Fishing was more an art than a sport to him. He schooled me in the fine points of fly-casting in many evenings of front-porch rehearsals before I was allowed to accompany him to Alum Rock Creek, seven miles away, flowing down from the Coast Range.

He had an explorer's zeal for finding new trout pools. Each Sunday, it seemed, we would ride farther on our bicycles and crawl through more underbrush than the time before in order to fish virgin stream.

Getting out on the first and last days of the season was a ritual with him, ". . . the first day because it's the best fishing and the last day because that makes it shorter to the next season."

I went with him on the first day of the season the year I was thirteen. But I noticed he didn't have his usual zest for it. He walked more slowly and once in a while he leaned against a boulder as pain tightened his lips. We didn't get as far up the creek as we had planned. On the way back it worried him.

"I've got a sneaking hunch there's deeper pools than we ever saw before up around that bend," he speculated. "There's big trout in that creek, Jesse. I know it. We didn't go far enough today. Next time we'll start earlier."

But there wasn't any next time.

Before the end of the season he was confined to bed. I knew his other pains were easier to bear than missing the cherished last day, and I carefully avoided any mention of the subject. When he reminded me the night before, I pretended I'd forgotten, but he knew I hadn't.

"I've been wondering what we would have found clear up above where the end of the road is, up above those hills," he said. "It's flat land, but it's high. There's bound to be rocks and pools. If we'd only gone a little farther."

"Nobody goes up that far, Pa."

"A real fisherman would. And a real fisherman wouldn't miss the last day."

It wasn't going to be the same without him. The fun would be gone from it, but my duty was clear.

"I'll catch some fish up above the hills, Pa, and I'll come back and tell you what it's like up there."

"Take my rod and those new flies I got from old man Muller—but if you snag the line or break the tip, *don't* come back. Get out of the country. Make a beeline for Nevada."

"I'll practically be there already, after I follow the creek up as far as you're talking about."

I didn't sleep that night. Alum Rock Creek was slow and tame near the road, but it got wilder every mile into the jungle of cottonwood.

The morning was cloudless and still—a great day for fishing, I thought, until I pedaled up into an excited cluster of men at the edge of town. After listening to a few snatches of their conversation I wasn't so sure.

"If the posse wants to find Evans and Sontag, they better follow the draws on Alum Rock Creek, 'stead of beating the bush farther south," I heard.

"If you was the posse, would you go in those draws?" someone challenged.

"Naw, I reckon I'd beat the bush farther south," the first one admitted with a sheepish grin.

I knew who Evans and Sontag were. Everyone in these parts knew. Their train stick-ups and murders of brakemen, passengers, and conductors had the countryside in a panic. I suppose I could have turned back then. But I couldn't have faced my father. I had his rod and creel and his new two-bit flies that he hadn't even used yet himself, and he expected me to bring back a mess of fish from above the falls.

I started on. One of the men called me back.

"You ain't thinkin' of goin' up Alum Rock Creek, are you, son?"

"It's the last day of the season," I said rather desperately.

"It'll be *your* last day if you run into Evans and Sontag!" he snapped. "They'll kill the first thing they see movin' near them."

I felt embarrassed and out of place clutching a fishing pole there in an atmosphere brittle with anxiety and foreboding. I couldn't explain to myself, much less to a bunch of strange men, why I had to go fishing. But I could escape from their disapproving eyes.

It was horribly quiet above Alum Rock. I had always got a thrill out of wondering what was on the other side of a hill I hadn't climbed before. I kept wondering what lay beyond my line of vision now, but this time anticipation gave way to dread. I walked fast, kept whistling and crashing along with needless noise. If Evans and Sontag were in the vicinity, I didn't want to surprise them. I wanted them to hear me in plenty of time to draw back in the tall, thick snakegrass or behind a boulder until I got past. I climbed around the falls and went farther up the creek than we had ever fished before. My heart pounded and my hands shook so I could hardly tie the fly to the leader. My father was right—there were plenty of trout where the creek ran wild and deep with sudden pools, but they were indifferent to my urgent need.

I fished as though my life depended on it. I had no appetite for the sandwiches I'd brought along. What had to be done I wanted to get done quickly. But what with the distance I had to go, a fly tangled in a tree, doubling back a mile or so because I'd left the creel behind in my nervous haste, and the cruel lack of co-operation from the fish, it was dark before I caught enough trout to call a mess, and was making my way over unfamiliar ground to where I had left my bike.

As I clambered on and pedaled away furiously, I was so startled by two forms that loomed at the side of the road in the moonless blackness that I swerved, lost my balance, and went sprawling in a tangled heap of handle bars, fishing creel, trout flies, and slippery trout. By the time I picked myself up and gathered the fish and equipment, the forms had vanished. Or perhaps they hadn't been there in the first place—I couldn't be sure.

I was too short of breath to say anything when I brought the catch to my father. He looked at me a long time and seemed to examine the fish minutely without noticing that they were dirty from the spill on the road. My mother couldn't conceal her agitation as she went into the kitchen to fix my dinner.

"You're pretty badly scraped up, Son," my father finally said, eying my torn pants and bloody knee.

"I didn't know my way in the dark, and being up the creek . . . alone," I fumbled.

"*Were* you alone?" he asked in a quizzical tone.

"I hope so," I said, which broke the tension and we both laughed.

"Those fellows made a beeline right over here after they saw you start for Alum Rock Creek," he confided. "Your mother wanted to send the Army out to bring you back, but I was afraid they'd scare the fish."

"I hope you don't think *I* was scared, Pa—not really scared," I bluffed, warming to the hero's role in the security of the family hearth.

His eyes crinkled as he cut me down to size in his kindly way.

"Want to know something, Jess? I would've been just as scared as you were. But you sure got a mess of fish to be proud of."

The Horn Blows
at Midnight

I had been born in San Francisco in 1880, and lived the first eight years of my life there, but it was a strange tyrant of a city when we moved back to it. San Jose was casual, undemanding. You could take your time about dreaming your future. I assumed I'd go to Stanford when I finished Santa Clara High School. Then I'd be a great cornettist and write music and possibly some prose. But when I was caught up in the surge of San Francisco, there was no looking ahead, no more planning for the future. It was sink or swim. Life had to be lived right now.

Perhaps the impression was distilled from stresses and economic strains, but it did seem that I crossed the border of childhood somewhere on the trip from San Jose to San Francisco.

We moved back to the Bay City because it would no doubt be easier to get a new start there after the shoe store went bankrupt, and because San Francisco specialists could possibly work the miracles for my father that San Jose doctors had failed to, and because old friends and relatives, including Uncle Mark, were there. Mark Lasky would know what to do. He could always solve a dilemma providing it didn't concern himself. Our situation was discouraging, but we had plenty of feeble straws to cling to.

My father's younger brother and his wife visited us as soon as we were settled in an apartment on O'Farrell Street. They were an inspiring picture of self-confidence and well-being because they believed in dressing up to things that might happen, rather than down to the things that always did. They wore their fortunes on their backs.

As we had counted on, Uncle Mark knew exactly what to do. He was never frugal with advice. He decided that, in as much as my father was still capable of working part of the time, he should seek a job with a wholesale shoe house that had supplied his Boston Shoe Bazaar with much of its stock. Aunt Celia, a packed jury of a woman, brought in the same verdict. My mother also thought the shoe firm should be grateful enough for past business to do my father a favor now.

Uncle Mark agreed with me that the family welfare would be better served by my getting a job immediately instead of finishing high school and going on to college. But he wouldn't concede the cornet as a tool of trade for an honest workingman, even when my mother pointed out that I had been able to contribute ninety dollars to the family fortunes from my earnings with Witherell's Brass Band, a professional group that played at picnics, parades, fiestas, political rallies, Fourth-of-July celebrations, and funerals.

"This isn't San Jose," Uncle Mark noted disdainfully, fingering his flashy watch chain. "In order to play here, you'd have to get into the Musicians' Union and that would be impossible if a friend of mine didn't know an officer of the union. It would be impossible anyway until you're twenty-one."

"Couldn't I have a few birthdays on the way over?" I suggested, grabbing his arm and guiding him to the door.

I got into the union. Sometimes it pays to be big for your age. But I sat around the hall on Post Street opposite Union Square every day for weeks, waiting at first for the golden moment when a hiring man would show up sorely in need of a cornet soloist for a name band at a time when there was luckily no one in the hall but me . . . later on, waiting for one night's work so mean and lowly and so poor-paying and far away that no one else would want it . . . then simply and forlornly waiting for anyone to notice I was there, for a passing shark to swim close enough to my desert island to bare his teeth in a friendly greeting . . . finally, just waiting . . . waiting. . . .

In the meantime my father had taken a drummer's job at token wages which the shoe firm offered him with elaborate apologies. It must have been heartbreaking for my mother to watch him aggravating his ailment to such little purpose by carrying the heavy sample cases from shoe store to shoe store. Each morning she saw her two men off to "work," and welcomed them home in the evening. But both of us were only going through the motions of earning a living.

I was long since resigned to waiting my life away in the union hiring hall, when a stranger came in to hire a second cornettist for a traveling medicine show. It was late in the day and a scant half-dozen men remained. The good musicians had jobs or had given up hope and gone home.

I knew I had no chance when an experienced horn player was available and up to now there had never been any crumbs left over for a greenhorn. But this time I was the only cornettist in the room, so I breathlessly offered my services.

He looked around and saw he had no other choice.

"I can give you $18 a week," he said, significantly laying three fingers on his lapel. I knew this stood for the kickback he wanted.

"I'll take it," I almost shouted, without thinking to inquire any of the details and intent only on getting the job before he could change his mind.

"You're hired!" he almost exploded, intent on filling the vacancy before I could change *my* mind. "It's an eight weeks' tour. You open in Vallejo day after tomorrow."

He gave me a contract, and, arriving back home, I handled the paper as reverently as though it was the Declaration of Independence, which in a way it was. I objected to Blanche's touching it. I didn't want it desecrated with grimy fingerprints. Blanche wasn't impressed with the document's import, but my father showed proper regard and pride in my accomplishment. My mother of course expressed a degree of concern that would have been more appropriate if I had announced I was off to play in a waterfront dive in Singapore instead of a tent show in Vallejo, thirty-one miles across the bay. She complained that I had never been away from home before. I reminded her that I had definitely been away from home before—what about the time I had slept in the woods for two nights after Calvin Moran and I skinned a skunk? And, what's more, she hadn't objected to my leaving home then.

The two tents of the medicine show had attached themselves barnacle-fashion to the edge of the bay town. I met the leader of the ten-man band, who doubled on clarinet and violin, a bloated bass-drum player who looked as though he'd swallowed his instrument, and other members of the troupe outside the tents. Then Dr. Silas Crabtree, the medicine man, staged a grand entrance by majestically tossing back a tent flap like an Inverness cape. He wore his black hair long, flowing over the shoulders of his buckskin coat in the manner of Buffalo Bill, and topped with a huge black hat. He had a silver-buckled belt on his leather trousers, which were stuck into tall boots.

"Mighty glad to have you with us, my young bucko," the great man boomed. "I can see you're a smart pinto so you'll appreciate what I'm going to do for you as a gesture of welcome." He withdrew a bottle of murky fluid from a pistol holster.

"You're looking at Dr. Crabtree's Cure-All Indian Herb Medicine, son. Cures aches. Kills pains. Can be taken externally or internally. This elixir of health sells regularly for one dollar and fifty cents, but as proof of my friendship I'm going to make this bottle available to you for only one dollar. Don't ask me why. . . . I guess I'm just in a generous mood."

"That's very kind of you, sir, but . . . but couldn't I wait till I feel unhealthy?" I stammered, chary of biting the hand that fed me but also reluctant to feed the hand that was putting the bite on me.

"Don't worry about the dollar, son," the benefactor of mankind assured me affably. "I'll take it out of your wages."

The agent's commission had already shrunk my poor salary to $15 a week and here was another precious dollar taking wing.

"Wait, son!" The potion vendor postured dramatically, as though in tune with a message from the infinite. "I can't welcome you with such a measly token of hospitality. Never let it be said that Dr. Crabtree does things by halves. I know you won't believe this, son, but instead of letting you have one bottle of Dr. Crabtree's Cure-All for one dollar, I'm going to make you a present of two whole bottles for only a dollar and a half! No, no—don't thank me. Thank Crawling Bear, chief of the Pawnees, who whispered the secret formula of this ancient Indian remedy to me as he died in my arms."

I blinked my eyes in disbelief as he thrust the bottles into my hands. I was rapidly developing some aches and pains that Dr. Crabtree's Cure-All couldn't relieve.

We shortly piled into a carryall which served as an animated billboard for the bilge Chief Crawling Bear must have inopportunely run out of, because if he had gargled a few drops of such a miracle panacea or even rubbed it in his hair, he would undoubtedly have got up off his deathbed and danced for joy. We rode into town playing Sousa's marches, not exactly as I had pictured myself playing them, but at least it was show business, I told myself. The "parade" wound around town and enticed a cloud of kids and a sprinkling of weak-willed townsfolk back to our tents. We gave a "band concert" outside the main tent to attract a bigger crowd, then doubled as an orchestra inside while two Indian braves did a "genuine Pawnee war dance" to tom-tom accompaniment, and Dr. Crabtree hawked his elixir.

After our evening appearance the trombone player, a youngish fellow with an air of sophistication and patent-leather hair parted in the

middle, invited me to have "a glass of steam" with him. I had no idea
what he was talking about, but I was flattered that such a worldly person would request my company, and gladly followed him as he steered
me across the street and around the corner. The shattering realization
that I was in a saloon staring into a big five-cent mug of frothy beer almost unnerved me. I had never tasted spirits in any form. My mother
considered alcohol the root of all evil. She had imbued me with her
conviction that divine punishment is meted out in subtle but swift
and certain fashion to all who imbibe. She was as rabid and voluble
about the curse of liquor as my father was with his insistent counsel
that I must never vote the Republican ticket or marry a foreign girl,
and by foreign girl he meant a pitiable creature who had placed herself beyond the pale by being born outside the state of California.
There were forewarnings of the dire afflictions of the flesh attendant
on trafficking with the wrong kind of women who abounded in forty-
seven of the states and territories.

I gave lip service to these parental principles because it was the only
way to stem their monotonous tide, and because, so far as I was concerned, none of the vital issues had ever entered the present tense.
Now one was present and I was tense. I remembered well my mother's
taboos, scrambled together with my father's alarming accounts of the
afflictions of the flesh. But after all, I asked myself, how could she be
an authority on liquor, never having touched a drop herself? I was
pathetically anxious to merit the respect of this man among men who
of the whole troupe had bothered to make a friendly overture. Besides, my mother was thirty-one miles away and needn't ever know
about my fall from grace. I quickly downed the "steam."

"How's that, kid?"

"Fine!" I said stoically.

I don't know how many beers I had or how I got to my room in
the boardinghouse. I woke up in the unfamiliar bed, which was doing
a genuine Pawnee war dance to the tom-tom throbbing in my temples.
I had been sick. I was sick again. The darkness outside was nothing to
the darkness in my soul. I had sinned, and vengeance had swiftly over-
taken me, even as my mother had warned.

I couldn't know the entire extent of the vengeance inflicted on me
until the light of day revealed red welts all over my body. I recoiled
from my own flesh. How could I conceal my guilt from my mother
now that I wore the scarlet letter of my dissipation for all to see? Would
I be marked for the rest of my days? Was I already beyond medical
help, a hapless victim in the last stages of the disease?

Remembering that Dr. Crabtree's Cure-All could be taken externally or internally, I rubbed some of it on the afflictions of the flesh and the angry welts seemed to get even angrier at this indignity. I was a sorry object lesson a little later as I confided to my partner in vice that I had contracted beer poisoning and showed him the red welts. It was several minutes before he stopped choking with laughter and explained the facts of rooming-house life to me. "You'll learn about bedbugs," he said.

That day we pitched tents in a different section of town and went through the same routine as before. After the show I avoided the trombone player because I couldn't face another glass of "steam," avoided the other musicians because I didn't know how to play poker, avoided the boardinghouse because I wasn't hungry and was nauseated at the thought of spending another night at the mercy of the little visitors that had caused me so much mental anguish and the trombone player so much merriment.

I walked aimlessly up and down dark streets until I couldn't stand that, either. The precious contract I had wanted to frame and wouldn't let Blanche touch lest she get it dirty was revealed to me in its true colors. It bound me hand and foot to eight weeks of unbearable torment. And I was certain that I would have to collect my weekly salary with a bushel basket in the coin of the realm, Dr. Crabtree's Cure-All.

There's a tradition in show business that the show must go on when your heart is breaking. You'd be amazed how silly that tradition seems when you're a homesick youth. Of course I'd be cast out of the Musicians' Union and probably go to jail if I broke my contract. But going to jail was a small price to pay for freedom.

I packed my suitcase and at dawn slipped away to the railroad station.

At home I was a prodigal son returned and at the Musicians' Union nobody cared that I was back ahead of time or, for that matter, noticed that I had been away. The only one it made any difference to was me. Safely severed from the nightmare, I began to feel splendidly professional: "Just in from a 'med' show in the sticks." At last I had a background, such as it was, of trouping on the road, and I could do my bench-warming on equal terms with other *experienced* musicians.

Gradually I began to pick up leftover jobs for picnics across the bay. I liked to watch the athletic German-Americans, members of the *Turn Verein* and *Schuetzen Verein*, dancing waltzes, polkas, and schottisches in their uniforms of marching teams and shooting clubs:

they sported drooping or upturned Kaiser Wilhelm mustaches, often glistening with beer. Sometimes there were band concerts in Golden Gate Park, with my family in beaming attendance, accompanied perhaps by Uncle Mark and Aunt Celia or Cousin Edna. I substituted twice at the Orpheum Variety Theatre, as it was known before B. F. Keith used the word "vaudeville." And once I filled in for two performances of *The Mikado* at the Tivoli Opera House when the cornettist was taken ill. My mother and sister were so proud of me they attended both performances.

Then the Spanish-American War headlines began exploding in the San Francisco papers. *"Remember the Maine!"* was on everybody's lips. Teddy Roosevelt was enlisting his Rough Riders in the East. The Presidio was teeming with activity. Parades were being organized on short notice; troopships began leaving from the docks, sailing through the Golden Gate. This meant an increased demand for bands, which escorted marching regiments down to the docks, played while the soldiers embarked, then went back to the Presidio for the next contingent.

Twice I stopped in front of the enlistment tent on Market Street and hoped the war would last until my father's health improved. I practiced the bugle calls of the U. S. Army until I knew them all by heart.

The jobs I was getting didn't pay much better than the ones with Witherell's Brass Band in San Jose, but they were becoming more and more the mainstay of the family budget.

There was one job I didn't talk about at home. It was at the Bella Union, a name that couldn't be mentioned in Blanche's presence or in my mother's parlor. I never would have had nerve enough to walk boldly up to the portals of this palace of forbidden pleasures on Kearny Street and buy a ticket to see Little Egypt "straight from her triumph in the 'Streets of Cairo Show' at the Chicago World's Fair." An eighteen-year-old boy from a respectable family didn't do such things in that circumspect era. But on the other hand, if the eighteen-year-old boy was hired to perform certain offices, he didn't shirk his duty—not even if duty required him to tootle for the seductive wiggling of a notorious cooch dancer.

I was in a transport of anticipation all day. And when I arrived in a delicious state of goose pimples to fulfill my obligations, the Bella Union's prominently posted proclamation only lathered my excitement. It read:

Full Grown People
Are Invited to Visit The

BELLA UNION

If You Want to Make a Night of It
The Show Is Not of The Kindergarten Class
But Just Your Size
If You Are Inclined to Be Frisky and Sporty
It's Rather Rapid, Spicy And
Speedy
As Sharp as a Razor
And as Blunt at Times as the Back of an Axe

The trombone, first cornet, and bass-drum players were draped listlessly around the stage door. I identified myself. They nodded glumly. I couldn't understand their lack of agitation over the approaching adventure.

"When do we start?" I asked.

"Any time," the trombonist replied indifferently.

"Well, let's get going," I urged, practically leaping for the stage door.

"Stay away from there, kid," he cautioned, "if you don't want to get tossed out. You're supposed to be working."

"But aren't we playing at the Bella Union?" I protested.

"That's right—*at* the Bella Union, not *in* the Bella Union," he emphasized. "They've got a real smart band inside. We blow here in front —drive 'em in off the street. It don't matter what we play, just so it's loud."

"But when do we get to see Little Egypt?" I wanted to know.

"We don't!" the other cornet player informed me, snubbing my hopes and grinding them under his heel. "There aren't any rests. When I get out of wind, you keep blowing. If the boss catches us all taking a breath at the same time, he'll sack us."

I couldn't have been safer from iniquity in my own parlor!

It was one step from the Bella Union to Brown's Comique in the Barbary Coast—one step down—playing in a five-piece orchestra all night in a packed, smoky dive—walking home miles in the foggy dawn to air out my lungs and save a nickel carfare, meeting my father limping down the stairs to start his rounds with the heavy suitcase of sample shoes.

I learned a lot at that fetid music hall. How to carry my wages in my shirt for safety, how to make the music sob slow for bleary drunks. How to follow and vary the warm, repetitious rhythms of the South or the off-beat ragtime endlessly improvised by the piano player. But the main thing I learned was that I wasn't getting anywhere as a cornet player.

As an avid student of Horatio Alger and Oliver Optic, I wanted to take that suitcase of sample shoes away from my father and throw it in the river. I wanted to make enough money to buy his store back, give Blanche a real musical education, hire a carriage every Sunday, and dress as well as my second cousin, Jack Morris—but the notes I was getting out of the cornet weren't good at the bank.

Jack Morris had recently moved to San Francisco from Reno and already had given me a new slant on life. He wanted to be an actor. He couldn't get jobs on the stage, but that didn't prevent him from acting. With unsuspecting strangers he'd be an engineer just back from five sweaty years of mining in Mexico . . . or a fugitive from justice . . . or a rheumatic mountain climber.

If Jack could conjure up such a colorful individuality out of nowhere, I didn't see why I couldn't add a few tasteful trimmings to my own limited horizon. Necessity might force me to blow cornet in unmentionable joints during the late hours, but this left me free all day long to be a famous composer.

Jack Morris, of course, aided and abetted this whim. He altered his personality to fit into the scheme and became a playwright of distinction. It appealed to his dramatic sense to be the colleague of a famous composer.

We would dress up like dandies in loud shirts, high choker collars, and puff ties and stroll down Market Street every Saturday night to the bandstand in the center of the Emporium department store and discreetly eye the pretty girls who seemed always to be promenading there just for our pleasure. Even though my eyesight was becoming a problem and my teeth crowded my mouth badly, I fancied some of these eyefuls took notice of me. This was a matter requiring quick perception, for exploratory glances were fleeting in 1898.

My romantic dreams suffered a crushing blow when it was decided I had to wear glasses. In those days a boy who wore glasses was considered effeminate. Corrected vision was the badge of a sissy, just as a wrist watch was a few years later. I submitted to the indignity of pince-nez "cheaters" in a pall of gloom. But they did have one redeeming feature (aside from enabling me to see). They made me look more grown-up. And in as much as I was actually teaching one or two music pupils, I promptly had a business card printed identifying me as "Professor J. L. Lasky—Piano and Cornet lessons—50¢."

With glasses I also looked more in character for the role of famous composer I played with my distinguished playwright companion, Jack Morris, as we took in a matinee at the Tivoli Opera House. I particularly remember seeing Edwin Stevens in *Wang* and Paul Hartman's father, Ferris Hartman, in the big New York hit *The Idol's Eye*. On alternate Saturdays we could be found at the Alcazar, where we were ecstatically thrilled by such stars as the lovely new ingénue, Laura Hope Crews, and Blanche Bates in Francis Powers' great play of Chinatown, *The First Born*.

Eager and intoxicated with our synthetic importance, we'd rush home from these matinees and launch projects that were to make theatrical history.

The projects varied with the inspiration of the moment. They were glibly woven from enthusiasm and mutual admiration and had a glorious texture in the talking stage, but something seemed to happen to them as soon as we tried to commit them to paper. Setting down a song title invariably turned the process of composition into decomposition. The title became its own epitaph. Ideas came so easily that each one was abandoned as we were caught in the surge of some new fancy.

We made an appointment one evening to write an operetta. In ten minutes we had a title, *The King of Mum*. The opening chorus took ten minutes more.

After due consideration you'll agree
(We agree, we agree, we agree)
That there never was another king like me—
(King like he, king like he, king like he)
I accept your felicitations, they're my due—
(They're his due, they're his due, they're his due)
And if anyone disagrees, he will rue.
(Oh, he'll rue, how he'll rue, how he'll rue!)

By a strange coincidence we had seen Gilbert and Sullivan's *The Mikado* at the Tivoli that afternoon.

Once I did actually finish a composition by the simple expedient of not writing down the title until I'd completed the tune. It was a march, and I called it *At the Steeplechase*. We had been at Steeplechase Park that day, still playing our roles of dilettante geniuses.

Having a bona fide composition under my belt complicated the business of being a composer. It was something of a shock to face the brutal fact that, once a piece of music is written, it doesn't automatically get published and win acclaim. But I knew there must be ways to prevent a masterpiece from lying unhonored and unsung.

The acclaim was easily arranged for. *At the Steeplechase* made its debut before a select assemblage of relatives, with a piano rendition, followed without interruption by a cornet version, and reprised so many times in various keys and tempos that an irreverent cousin asked if the steeplechase was being run on a merry-go-round.

Uncle Mark was impressed not so much by the merits of the march, I think, as by the opportunity it afforded him to pose as a patron of the arts. He got a special rate through a friend and raised the money to publish one hundred copies. He even inveigled somebody into putting copies in Sherman Clay's music-store window.

I launched an intensive sales campaign, but unfortunately soon ran out of relatives and philanthropically inclined neighbors. There were plenty of copies left over to strew carelessly about the Musicians' Union.

I had a real taste of glory on my second out-of-town assignment. The Cloverdale Citrus Fair needed a cornet soloist. No cornet soloist worthy of the name needed the Cloverdale Citrus Fair, so the lemon fell to me. To that tiny excitement-starved community ninety miles north of San Francisco anyone from the Bay Area was a visiting celebrity, and I had a chance to play my role of nationally renowned composer to the hilt.

The local newssheet must have been frantic for copy, because a cub reporter was meeting trains and recording for posterity the reactions of total strangers to Cloverdale's civic virtues almost before they had set foot on the station platform. He had little choice of "celebrities" among the flotsam deposited from the chair car of my train, but he certainly made the most of what he didn't have. He unearthed with no great difficulty the sensational "scoop" that Cloverdale was playing host to the gifted composer of *At the Steeplechase* and splashed it on his front page, which I suspect might otherwise have displayed a large white gap.

I had arrived in town early in order to locate a boardinghouse, and this blather of publicity preceded me to the fairgrounds. The Citrus Reception Committee dripped orange honey and the band leader greeted me with a bow from the hips.

Naturally I ate it up. I read and reread my first interview and strutted grandly about the grounds in my rented band uniform. I blessed the name of Jack Morris for revealing the secret of success in one easy lesson. All you had to do was convince yourself you were somebody and other people took your word for it.

The fair opened officially with the Cloverdale Band playing *At the Steeplechase* conducted by the composer, "Professor Lasky." I expanded with the applause from the packed pavilion, scarcely able to believe that this was happening to me and not the hero of a paper-backed novel. In a novel, at this point, the hero would gaze out on the sea of attentive faces and suddenly his eyes would rivet on a vision of such unearthly loveliness that he would instantly know he couldn't live another hour without learning her name.

I had a little trouble locating the vision of loveliness in such a sizable crowd, but I finally spotted her, and managed to get an introduction as soon as I could leave the bandstand. As we walked together and munched popcorn, I overwhelmed her with a lavish account of my musical attainments and aspirations, not clearly separating the two, I'm afraid. Her name was Cad Graham, but I don't recall that she told me much more about herself. She didn't have a Chinaman's chance.

Our romance flowered in the shadow of an Eiffel Tower built of grapefruit, lasted that day until she had to join her parents for the Cakewalk Contest, and was continued every afternoon and evening. I was discovering life, and I was numb with the wonder of it all.

The week passed in a gratifying whirl. What tales of conquest the family would hear on my return. I wouldn't be slinking back like a whipped cur as I did from the medicine show. This time I was coming home with honor and new stature. I had a pocketful of newspaper blurbs and a head full of lofty plans for adding to these laurels as I bounded up the stairs to our flat.

Aunt Jenny met me at the door and I sensed something wrong.

My father had had another bad stroke. After a consultation with the doctor as to whether he could see me I went in.

He looked at me a long moment and the words seemed to cost him great effort. "How'd you make out, Jesse?" he asked.

My triumph was crumbling to rubble, but I tried to salvage a little bit of it for him. "Fine, Pa. I had a great time. I'll tell you all about it in the morning."

His eyes flickered with interest, but his voice was tired. "I want to hear all about it," he sighed. "How was it above Alum Rock?"

To Alaska

in a Breadbox

A funeral leaves the taste of ashes suspended in the air for months, like a volcano that erupts unexpectedly and stills the happy movement of life within range of its blighting breath. The thick atmosphere shuts out the sun and casts an eerie light on familiar objects—on wrapped fishing poles in a closet, limp-hanging clothes, photographs that preserve the stillness.

There was some of the life-insurance money left after my father's funeral expenses and debts had been paid. We knew it would be foolish to let this nest egg lie idle in the bank when we sorely needed what little income it could bring to reinforce my uncertain earnings.

"If Ike were here, he'd know how to invest it," Mother fretted, quite illogically.

We cast around for a profitable small business which could be financed with limited capital. Three lines in the personal column of the classified ads seemed to read our minds.

> WANTED $500 to be invested in amazing new home process for manufacture of maple syrup. Unlimited possibilities for large profits.

We couldn't have wished for a sweeter investment. We hastened to answer this enticing invitation lest some other opportunist should get in on the ground floor ahead of us.

Two brothers arrived on the double with their maple syrup factory in a suitcase. They were faultlessly turned out from gleaming shoes to gleaming diamond stickpins—and the gleam in their eyes. More diligent demonstrators might have lugged in a maple tree to set the scene, but my mother and I only regarded the scanty equipment as evidence that the syrupy brothers had reduced the mechanics of their process to incredible efficiency.

They talked engagingly of the corporation which would be set up to control world rights to this exclusive process. They promised that I would be a full partner. I could see myself in a few years sitting on the board of directors of a national chain of factories. What more could one want for $500?

But my mother wasn't satisfied to taste destiny. She wanted to taste maple syrup. The brothers delicately but firmly declined to reveal their secret procedure until we gave proof of our integrity. We showed them the integrity in a neat green bundle, whereupon they discarded their coats and flew into furious action with a flanking movement on the kitchen. Commandeering all the pots and kettles in the place, they measured ingredients, dissolved powders, stirred concoctions, and tested samples. A Peeping Tom would surely have wondered whether we were operating a still.

The boiling, bubbling end product of this hocus-pocus was indistinguishable from genuine maple syrup. We were too amazed to question whether one of the ingredients was indistinguishable from maple sugar. For due consideration the brothers gave us a contract assuring us a respectable share of the corporation profits as well as the paraphernalia we needed to give "Home Sweet Home" a more saccharine significance.

My mother and I exchanged gloating glances.

"A little business like this was just what we needed," I observed.

"And now for $500 we got the business," she agreed.

We wouldn't admit for several weeks that the maple syrup brothers had sticky fingers. At first, when the home manufacturing equipment didn't arrive, we feared our new business partners had met with an accident. Later on we could have gladly furnished the accident.

We solemnly vowed never to snap at such bait again. Avarice had been our undoing. Being greedy for quick, excessive profits without working had made us natural prey for slick operators. We realized what we should have sought as a safe niche for our minute capital was a good, solid, established business that returned a steady if humble income on an honest day's toil.

After moving to an inexpensive boardinghouse on Golden Gate Avenue, we turned to the ads again. Like an answer to a prayer, there was a chance to purchase a *Bulletin* newspaper route. No fly-by-night scheme, this. Newspapers were a proven, indispensable commodity.

Each delivery represented so much profit . . . no suppositions or guesswork. It could all be itemized in conclusive figures.

The figures, when we contacted the owner of the route, were most refreshing. He had a thousand customers who were paying twenty cents a week. And one of the subscribers was Jack London!

I couldn't contain my excitement at this disclosure. To have the immortal Jack London directly dependent on me for enlightenment on world affairs . . . such an association could lead to great things. . . . I pictured our doorstep exchanges . . . he might ask me if I had ever considered writing as a career . . . there were those English essays in high school that I got good marks on and compliments from the teacher . . . to be a protégé of Jack London's . . . I had never realized that carrying newspapers was such a glamorous profession. And between stimulating chats with Jack London the dimes would keep rolling in. Best of all, the $1000 purchase price of the route could be paid off in installments, out of the profits. Mother was as delighted as I was with the prospects.

The route took in Oakland, Alameda, and Fruitvale. Sometimes after playing the cornet on a late night job I could get home, undress, and crawl into bed, but there wasn't time to turn out the light before I had to get up, dress, and go to the *Bulletin* plant for my papers. I took them across the bay on the ferry, changed to the train, and tossed off bundles at each station for the local paper boys.

Even so, I liked the ferry rides in the salt-tanged dawn—watching the fishing fleets escorted out to sea by clouds of gliding gulls—and I labored under the delusion that I had a fine job, until I started making my collections. Subscribers had moved away and their papers were piling up on the deserted doorsteps. Others didn't have the change or didn't answer the door, or claimed they had canceled weeks ago. Only three hundred ever paid their bills. And I never did see Jack London, though it's a wonder I wasn't arrested for loitering on his doorstep.

Again I stubbornly clung to the illusion that it wasn't money down the drain. I told myself I was weeding out the deadwood and putting the route on a firm basis. But I finally had to face it. I was supposed to be paying the installments out of the profits. There weren't any profits. I was paying the installments out of the bureau drawer and paying my carriers the same way.

I was working hard and not expecting too much. What was the matter? Was it my fault? Could someone else have done better? Obviously millions of people could do better. All around me people were living and working and earning money. Why had I failed? What should I do?

My gaze drooped with my sinking spirits—and I found the answer at my feet. A stack of the undelivered, unwanted papers that were slowly draining away what funds we had left—and every one of them shrieked, "NEW GOLD DISCOVERIES!" "CAPE NOME!" "BIGGER THAN THE KLONDIKE OR YUKON!"

Suddenly I knew why I had the paper route. Its sole function was to tear the veil from my future, to reveal my true purpose in life. Fate intended that I cast my eyes down in this despairing moment and read my destiny in the headlines. It didn't matter any longer that no one would buy those headlines. The headlines belonged to me. They were there to guide me.

News of the fortunes being scratched out of the frozen dirt in the Klondike and along the Yukon, and of the more recent gold strikes in Alaska, had been heralded in the papers for some time, but I had been blind to what they were trying to tell me—that rich deposits of gold were beckoning at Anvil Creek and on the beach of the Bering Sea, waiting to be shaken out of the roots of the tundra.

I soon made up for lost time. I bought a little book about the Klondike and read till my eyes smarted. I began to haunt the wharves and stores where mining equipment was sold, straining my ears to pick up the flying fragments of rumor and conjecture that filled the tense air. The gold on the beach at Nome, I heard, was flour gold. Its fineness presented difficulties in wresting it from the sand, and much of it was lost through the sluices. This matter weighed on my mind for some time until I ran into a brand-new invention that, its backers claimed, would revolutionize placer mining.

I became hopelessly enamoured of the Aurn Electrum Depositor at first sight. It was a mammoth gadget of virginal allure that seemed capable of magnetizing gold out of the sand by the sheer personality of its sixty silvered copper plates, four-horsepower engine, dynamo, outsize boiler, and water pump. A display of its virtues completely enslaved me to its wiles. The man in charge started the machine, and with ten rockers shaking like spaniels just out of the water, he took a handful of sand from his pocket and dropped it into the machine. In a moment he switched it off to point out that the copper rockers were now covered with a fine powder of gold!

The demonstrator introduced himself as W. H. Orr, president of the Triumvirate Mining Company and controller of the manufacturing rights to the mechanical marvel. He had me shake hands with his partner, Frederick Vroom, a rawboned miner who might well have given the inventor of the Aurn Electrum Depositor the basic idea for his device. Vroom's handclasp could shake a deposit out from under your fingernails.

The two men, it developed, were looking for another partner, one who could put up $1200 and be on the first boat through the Bering Sea to Nome as soon as the ice broke. They would send one of the machines with him to work the beach, while they remained behind temporarily to put the machine in production and organize a sales force.

I had made up my mind to go to Alaska anyway, and here was a golden opportunity to make a real killing. The gold dust that could be taken out of a placer claim by the slow, crude, hand-rocker method was nothing compared to what could be done by improved mechanical means.

There was just enough money left from the insurance to swing it. We'd struck out twice. But we had one strike left, and it was going to be a gold strike.

My mother was shaken when I broached the subject. She dropped the sewing she had in her hands and spluttered that she'd never heard of such a thing.

"The gold is *there*, Ma!" I pleaded. "The first people up there will get it, and the people who have the best equipment will get the most gold. It's up to me to make the money now. I've got to for you and Blanche—and you know I can't do it with the paper route and the jobs I've been getting at the Musicians' Union. This is the biggest chance I'll ever have to make money in my whole life. You've just got to let me take it!"

"How much is it going to cost?" she asked finally. I knew when she put it that way that I was going to Alaska. The resigned way she said it didn't mean that she was convinced it was the right thing to do, but it meant that she knew I'd keep at her until I did convince her.

At the inevitable family conference bedlam broke loose when the venture was aired. They said she should be declared incompetent if she'd let a minor become a miner—take every cent of the family funds and go thousands of miles from home where there wasn't any law and nobody but ruffians and murderers and gamblers.

"You won't think it was such a bad idea," I said with some asperity, "when I come back and send Blanche to the Boston Conservatory of Music and Mamma has her own carriage and I have an office here and maybe one in San Jose."

"I'm sorry you all think I'm crazy," my mother told them defiantly, "but if Jesse isn't on that first boat up to Cape Nome, he'll think as long as he lives that I deprived him of his chance to find a fortune. I don't care what any of you say—I'm going to let him have the money."

Since there was no stopping us, Uncle Mark grudgingly consented to witness the contracts with Orr and Vroom for me, and he also helped me to pick out the outfit I'd need. He told me before we got home, "If the rest of your pa's insurance money isn't enough for what you need, I've got a few dollars I could invest. But don't let on to your Aunt Celia. She has a high opinion of my intelligence."

I booked second-class passage on the first boat sailing north, the S.S. *Zelandia*. The Aurn Electrum Depositor was crated, ready to follow on a slower freighter, the S.S. *John S. Kimball*.

As we left the house for the dock, my mother advised me that it was cold in Alaska and I must keep warm and not let my feet get wet. She had put plenty of woolen socks in my huge canvas bag and she admonished me to use them.

"Don't worry," I reassured her. "I'll use 'em to carry gold dust. What'll we do with all the money, Ma?"

"Oh, we'll find a way to use it," she said practically. Then she stopped abruptly. "Jesse, don't you want to take your cornet?"

"Gee, Ma, I can't carry anything more," I complained.

"You'd better take it," she decided, and went back into the house to get it, carrying it to the dock herself. At the last minute, to my discomfiture, she thrust it into my hands with a loud entreaty to remember to do some practicing. Dressed as I was in the working clothes of a miner, with trousers stuck into my boots, a wide leather belt, and feeling kin to the rough, tough specimens who were to be my shipmates, I was in a mood to renounce such civilized refinements as music forever. It was as though I had been handed a brass toy or submitted to having my nose wiped in public, with Orr and Vroom looking on, and I blushed to the brim of my sou'wester as I made haste to conceal the unwelcome article in my bag.

A final, smashing backslap from Frederick Vroom and a last-minute flurry of kisses and handshakes helped restore my ego. But it suffered another setback after I was caught in the tide of embarking passengers, shoved up the gangplank, and found a spot at the rail where I could wave to my mother's white face, Blanche's transfixed stare, Uncle Mark's cane, and Aunt Celia's fluttering handkerchief. The *Zelandia* was pulling away, pulling me away from all the people and all the things I had ever known. As the familiar faces on the dock grew smaller and smaller, a sudden sense of loneliness assailed me . . . and I wondered whether gold was worth it.

I stood at the rail a long time. Gradually I began to feel that my father was standing there with me . . . his insurance money was making the trip possible. How he would have loved such an adventure! This time I was really exploring untamed waters. I was going *way* up above Alum Rock Creek. And my father had given me fishing tackle for the biggest catch of all.

As these emotions flooded over me, I wanted nothing but to find my berth and lie down in it. I waited my turn in the long line at the purser's window. He looked at my ticket and dismissed me curtly with, "You don't have a berth!"

"But it says right on my ticket, 'Berth 370,'" I argued.

"Can't help it—there's no such berth on board," he insisted, and brushed me aside. Others crowded in and cut off my protests. In desperation I found a blue-coated officer and told him my troubles. He inspected my ticket and confirmed my predicament.

"We're overcrowded with baggage this trip," he explained. "You've got one of the twelve berths that were knocked out for storage space."

"What am I going to do?" I said wildly.

"I don't know," he said, "but if you want to eat you better start fighting your way into the dining saloon. There's a lot more people on board than are going to get any food—let alone a place to sleep!"

I had no appetite, but self-preservation propelled me toward the dining saloon. A mass of crushing humanity aided the process. Everyone seemed to have the same idea at the same time. By now the rough waters of the Golden Gate were playing snap-the-whip with the ship, and I no sooner got seated at a table than I discovered it was the last place in the world I wanted to be. I groped my way out to the deck through crowds still pushing their way in.

I clung to the rail as the ship reeled and slid from under me. The cold spray caught me full in the face and I tried to hunch down back of some huge breadboxes lashed to the railing. Then I discovered that one of them was empty. I crawled into the coffin-like refuge and lay huddled, shaking with cold.

Either I slept from exhaustion or shock and wretchedness numbed my senses for a few blessed, unconscious hours.

A slosh of icy water woke me up. The breadbox was deluged. I was sure that the ship had foundered while I slept and that the horde that had rushed the dining saloon was now swarming the lifeboats, leaving me abandoned on the sinking ship. I clawed feverishly, barking my knuckles and bumping my head, not sure which way was up. As I crawled out of the breadbox like a drenched rat, three sailors stopped swabbing the deck to roar their amusement.

"If you're a stowaway, son," said the one with the hose, "we've got to report you. And what happens to stowaways shouldn't happen to a dog!"

It couldn't be worse than what happens to a passenger, I thought, fumbling in my pocket for my soggy ticket. I showed it to him.

"That's different," he said. "You can go back to sleep in there if you want. We're through washing down."

"I'm through sleeping!" I said, wringing my sodden clothing.

One of the officers was moved by the story of the waters cast upon the breadbox and fixed me up a makeshift berth. With my plight somewhat eased I began to take notice of my fellow voyagers. They were a curious collection—bookkeepers who had given up security and the comforts of a home and family for a golden will-o'-the-wisp . . . an old prospector with an unbroken fifty-year record of failure . . . another grizzled desert rat, equipped for the desert . . . gamblers prospecting only for victims . . . a group of squabbling theorizers who nearly came to blows every night over the vital issue of whether the Cape Nome gold washed up from the Siberian shore or was carried out to sea by icebergs floating down the Yukon and washed back to the beach by the Japanese Current.

I listened in a mounting fever of excitement to tales of holdups and murders in the mad scramble for wealth in Chilkat Pass, White Horse Rapids, and the Klondike.

We docked a day and night at Seattle, which had the feverish activity of a booming mining town itself, being the provision center and gateway to the gold fields. I went ashore with a young ship acquaintance named Wilson and sucked in the tingling excitement that filled the air.

The three weeks' trip to Dutch Harbor, Unalaska Bay, in the Aleutian Islands, was almost continually rough and stormy. As we progressed northward, the chill air became noticeably more penetrating, the sunsets tardier, the nights a lighter shade of dark, until barren, snow-streaked mountains rose abruptly from the edge of the sea. A cluster of small houses, some ancient Russian buildings, and a mixed breed of people from Russian, Japanese, and Eskimo stock was Dutch Harbor, a whaling station almost completely landlocked at the mouth of the Bering Sea. Tundra or Russian moss was the only form of vegetation.

With my friend Wilson I walked around the town, looking at the shacks, inspecting the Russian church, until there was nothing more to see. Then, for lack of something better to do, we rented a rowboat from the natives. More ships were arriving by the hour, the dock space was filling up, and late-comers were forced to anchor out in the harbor. As we paddled around among the anchored ships, one of the anxious, stranded passengers who jammed the rails yelled, "How much to take us ashore?"

I set a five-dollar tariff on shore leave and four days later we had cleared over $500—definitely proving that there was gold in Alaska. Ever since then I have believed in ferries!

The Revenue cutter *The Bear* guarded the entrance to the frozen Bering Sea and no boats could leave Dutch Harbor until the ice broke and the sea was declared navigable. Restlessness tightened nerves.

There were no set charges for washing shirts or for a fish dinner. Natives who had the monopoly gauged the gouge by the customer's look of desperation and the thickness of his wallet. Prices and tempers soared. Fights broke out.

When *The Bear* issued the bulletin everyone was waiting for, we rushed to our ships. The *Zelandia*, being in a choice position against the wharf, and ready to sail at a moment's notice, got a good lead in the furious race up the Bering Sea. But other ships were straining close behind. All the passengers kept day-and-night vigil on deck, staring back over fog-wreathed cakes of ice as if they could ward off pursuing vessels with anxious eyes. Once we were caught for hours in an ice floe. It was as though we had crept into a pocket of dead winter. The air was freezing. The ship's carpenter crawled far out on the chunky carpet and took a picture of the ship. I was pressed so far forward in the tip of the bow I looked like a carved figurehead on the prow.

We were fearful that another ship might have stolen our lead, but the ice floe stopped the whole fleet. On our way again the *Zelandia* made steady progress up the choppy sea. As we neared Nome, relationships cooled with the lowering temperature until they were as fragile and brittle as frozen rubber bands. Those who had bragged loudly about their plans and methods now became secretive and suspicious. Friendships and partnerships shattered at a word as the tension mounted.

I had expected Nome to be a sort of glacial cathedral, a majestic mountain of ice rising out of the sea, with a picturesque harbor. It was a low, dark line of uninteresting coast, but it had one feature of unsurpassing beauty—there wasn't another ship in sight.

Wilson and I piled into the lighter that came from shore. A few whaleboats, canoes, and boxes of equipment cluttered the sand. Other vessels were arriving; tents began to sprout up around us even as we stood there. We had to wait for the lighter to return with our own luggage, which we decided to carry up the beach, and we looked around for some means of transporting it. Wilson spotted a man trundling a narrow pushcart, ran after him, and started negotiating for its rental. The man shook his head and Wilson turned away with a shrug of defeat.

"If you won't rent it," I called after him, "would you consider selling it?"

"I should say not!" he blustered. "This cart is worth a hundred dollars to me!"

"It's a deal!" I said, overtaking him and stuffing the money in his hand. Wilson thought I was crazy—I was aghast at such folly myself, but it was too late to unbind the bargain. The man, at first speechless, had come out of his trance and was already fleeing with the money as though fearful of pursuit.

I was vindicated after we had hauled our own pile of luggage and were mobbed by others for the same service. At $10 a load, we made our second fortune in the North in the few hours before the overburdened cart broke down.

Gold was not lying on the beach, waiting to be scooped up, all previous rumors to the contrary. In fact the more impatient prospectors were starting a trek to Anvil Creek, in the interior, where reports had it that the real discoveries were being made. Wilson's imagination was caught and pulled into the outgoing tide. I probably would have joined him, but I had to wait for the Aurn Electrum Depositor, so we parted company, promising to join forces when we had both made a strike. I felt alone again, as I had when I saw the San Francisco docks fading away.

There is only one thing worse than being forsaken on a dismal beach in a far corner of the world, and that is being forsaken on a dismal beach with a ten-ton pile of complicated apparatus that you haven't the slightest idea of how to put together or operate. When the *John S. Kimball* steamed in the next day and unloaded, I didn't at first recognize the crated apparition as my own. It hadn't seemed so cumbersome when viewed in San Francisco, a city of skyscrapers and hills. But, deposited on the barren Alaskan wastes after much lifting, hauling, shoving, and cursing, it looked monstrous and terrifying. I felt desolate.

Everyone has his own way of bucking himself up when his spirits hit bottom. Some women go out and buy a hat. Some men get drunk. I left my crated enigma on the dock and went to my tent for a talk with a boy's best friend.

Dear Ma: Nome is wonderful. There are hundreds of people here by now but I was one of the first hundred to set foot on shore. I haven't seen any gold yet, but it won't be long. The Aurn Electrum Depositor has just arrived, so get ready to be rich.

I was telling myself these things. The letter was just an excuse to put them down in black and white, so they would seem reasonable.

And Ma—don't worry about the kind of people I'm with. You'd be surprised what nice people are in this gold rush. . . .

Her presumed surprise was interrupted by my own surprise—as three shots rang out close enough to smell the gunpowder. A thud in front of my tent flaps was followed by running feet, excited voices, the shoving and pushing of a curious throng. I sat frozen, the pencil clutched in my fingers. The corpse lay in front of my tent for a long time before someone wearing a revolver and badge of authority got a cart and hauled it away. I had planned to stroll around the camp when I finished my letter, but I changed my plans. The letter didn't get beyond the point of what nice people there were on every side. Also, it was too nice a night to sleep, so I didn't go to bed.

It was a night for cowering in a corner.

Gold Is Not Where

You Find It

So I was in a hotbed of murderers and, no doubt, thieves. But that might have its advantages. It might solve a few weighty problems. In the morning I rather hopefully made my way to the spot where I had left my mechanical nightmare—but the weighty problem was still there.

Making inquiries about the best place to stake a claim, I learned from an old sourdough that, the beach had been staked for several miles to both north and south. The best claims were farther north, up the beach. He offered to lease me one of his claims, a few miles north of Snake River, long enough for me to get started, in as much as he hankered to prospect for a month up Anvil Creek way. We got a pail, miner's pan, small shovel, and courage for the long walk from the Northern Lights Saloon and started a three-hour hike, passing groups of disappointed prospectors with crude sluice boxes and improvised rockers.

The beach was unoccupied and dreary when we reached his claim. He picked a likely spot, handed me the shovel, and commanded, "Dig till you hit the black sand."

Tingling with excitement, I dug furiously for the pot of gold at the end of the rainbow. About two feet down I reached the black sand. Scooping a shovelful into the miner's pan, my companion manipulated it with a circular motion, washing the white sand away with water from the pail. Then with great care, sitting tautly on his haunches, he swirled the black sand around until some fine colors of gold particles appeared at the very bottom of the pan.

"I reckon that's about $5.00 worth of flour gold," he commented. It was the first gold I had seen in Nome. His terms were $250 ad-

vance and 25 per cent of all the gold I took out. Quick calculation
told me that if one pan of black sand yielded $5.00, the 10 rockers of
my flour-gold sifter could shake out 10,000 pans of gold in a month's
time—$50,000. I signed the lease on the spot and took from my money
belt one $10 and twelve $20 gold pieces.

We trudged back to Nome together, where we parted with a genial
handshake, and I went immediately to survey the Electrum Depositor
and speculate on how to transfer it to the claim. In a few short hours
the crates of machinery had lost the aspect of bugaboo and assumed
the guise of benign benefactor. What a difference a thimbleful of
gold makes!

A short, sandy-haired Scotsman I remembered as a shipmate
watched me knock out some of the crating slats. He had small, ex-
citable blue eyes which blinked continually and large, efficient-
looking freckled hands which couldn't keep from poking and tapping
about the levers and gears as though they had a way with machinery.
He proved to be an old-time miner with a passion for tinkering.

"I'd sure like to see it work," he confessed.

It seemed to me that a kind providence had handed me Jim Douglas on a golden platter and that if I didn't cater to his curiosity to
see the darn contraption work, I wouldn't be likely to see it work
myself. I offered to furnish the machine and the claim and split profits
with him if he'd take over the mechanical operation. This apparently
wasn't sufficient inducement for him to give up his own prospecting
plans, so I suggested a straight salary of $25 a day, and he agreed.

I bought a dory and a ton of coal, and with some help from by-
standers we loaded the machinery, my tent, shovels, and grub and
rowed to the new location. We drove the dory hard up on the bleak
bit of beach and spent the rest of the day unpacking and assembling
the machine. I wasn't much help putting it together, but Jim seemed
to know instinctively where each part belonged.

"It'll take more than two men to keep the rockers full," Jim observed, looking it over.

"Then I'll hire some more men," I said grandly.

We found two stranded prospectors to help, and all of us worked
hard digging down to the gold-bearing black sand as long as the machine puffed and scraped and shivered. But we were losing a lot of
time by having to stop every few minutes while one of us waded out
and pulled seaweed out of the intake pipe. At the end of that first
twelve-hour day we had a thimbleful of gold.

I thought the yield would be better after we hired still another man to stand in the water and keep the pipe from clogging up, and dug into the richer areas of sand that were strangely evading us. So we kept on shoveling sand into the rockers and coal and driftwood into the boiler. In a week we shoveled away the rowboat and pushcart profits. The whole proposition was taking on a horrible resemblance to the newspaper route.

I saw I couldn't hang on much longer. After taking inventory one evening I told Jim I was nearly broke. I couldn't understand it. When I leased the beach, I had panned more gold with a tin plate in half an hour than the five of us dredged up in a whole day.

Jim sucked on his stubby pipe. "Ever hear of salting?" he asked.

The cold truth hit me hard. Of course I had heard, aboard the *Zelandia,* of the common swindle worked by firing gold into a hillside from a shotgun or planting it in the sand and then guiding the prospective buyer of a claim to dig in the one spot where it would do him the most good. But I had been so grateful to the old bunko artist for telling me what I wanted to believe that I believed it.

"But there's gold here—we're getting some!" I insisted.

"You could buy gold cheaper than it's costing you to mine it, kid," Jim said. "If I were you, I'd call it quits. I'm thinking of going back up the creek anyway."

He was going up the creek. I was already there.

There was nothing to do but let them all go. Then I fried some cold mush left over from breakfast, made some coffee, and tried to figure out what to do. Could I get anything for the equipment? Not likely, even if I had it in Nome. The long arctic nights would soon be setting in, a bad season for mining even with a paying claim. I wouldn't be the first casualty—a glance up and down the beach made that obvious. Mounds of rusted equipment and machinery marked the graves of abandoned hopes.

The money I had left, $150, would buy no more than a pair of boots or a couple of dozen meals in Nome. . . . It would be easier to think in the morning. I took off my boots and hung my trousers on a nail in the tent pole by my cot. My frustration was monumental. Things always look darkest before dawn, I tried to console myself.

Dawn brought a change in the situation, all right, but one that made things look much, much darker. As daylight crept over the horizon, a strange sound awakened me. I was jolted into fascinated horror by a sharp, gleaming knife stealthily slitting the back wall of my tent. I watched in a sort of cataleptic state as the knife finished its work and was withdrawn. Then a hand snaked through the slit and felt its way around. It found my trousers with money belt attached and they disappeared through the opening.

I fumbled for my revolver, which I always kept loaded under my pillow, and rushed outside. The man was running about fifty feet away. I knew I should fire at him, but I couldn't pull the trigger. I could only stand there and watch him run away.

The wind was beginning to rise and the waves swept higher up on the beach. The approaching storm sent me scurrying to move my tent as far back against the marshy tundra as possible. A northern windstorm can last for weeks, carve away whole beaches. This one lasted all that day, through the night, and all the next day. The breakers crashed on the beach, battering away at my machinery, and I spent much of the time hanging on to the tent with all my strength to keep it from taking off like a kite. When the wind relented somewhat, I tried to vary my diet by figuring out a different way to cook mush. The words "Mush! Mush!" don't call up the usual mental picture of dog teams in Alaska for me, but they are associated in my mind with a dog's life in Alaska.

When the sky cleared, my efforts to save the tent seemed rather futile. It was whipped to rags. My dory had been carried out to sea, the machinery was rusting beyond hope of salvage, and I was still marooned, the tundra being too marshy to walk on. But by the third morning the waves had receded enough to leave a thin stretch of beach, so I left the whole sorry mess behind and started the ten-mile trip to Nome, wearing my spare pair of pants and carrying my big canvas bag with the ridiculous cornet inside. Recalling my mother's concern over keeping my feet dry, I tried to remember the last time they had been dry!

Even during my short absence Nome had changed appreciably. New ships had arrived with more people, wooden shacks were going up, and the seacoast was jammed with more tents, boxes, lumber, and impedimenta.

It was already getting dark. I went in the Northern Lights Saloon and asked the good-natured Irish proprietor if he knew of any place I could sleep. He gave me a meal and told me I was welcome to bunk in a shack he used as a storehouse. It was a few hundred yards out on the tundra. A plank walk that creaked under my weight led over the swamp to a small wooden structure that lacked even a door. The lights of Nome, blinking on in the distance, seemed miles away.

The bartender had told me there was a candle on a shelf somewhere, but I didn't bother to hunt for it. I could make out the form of a cot, covered with a piece of old canvas sail against the back wall. I pulled off my boots and coat and trousers and climbed in under the sail. There was something cold and stiff in the cot with me. I leaped out of bed with a cry. Groping for the candle, I lit it and threw back the sailcloth. A human skeleton grinned up at me.

It was him or me—there wasn't room in the cot for both of us—and I was too tired to be superstitious, so I gingerly picked up the bones and placed them under the cot. But I was no sooner settled, with the sailcloth pulled over my head, than a fusillade of shots rang out, mingled with unearthly shrieks. I sat bolt upright. Was the killer of the other evening on the loose again? A horrible thought crossed my mind. Was this shack his hideout, the skeleton one of his victims? Would he return here now? I waited, scarcely breathing. But nothing happened.

The skeleton, it turned out, was that of an old Indian, left in the shack to discourage prowlers. The saloon keeper had neglected to tell me about his superannuated watchman. I waited for him to mention the shots, but he didn't. Such occurrences were evidently so commonplace in a mining camp as to be hardly worth making conversation about. But I had to satisfy my curiosity, so I tried to bring it up in an offhand manner, without appearing too much of a tenderfoot.

"By the way," I asked casually, "who was murdered last night?"

When he caught on to what I was talking about, he laughed loudly and told me a Malemute sled dog had broken his leg and had to be shot, but the men who undertook the task were so liquored up they fired half a dozen shots before they hit him.

The Irishman helped me get back on my feet by loaning me a shotgun and a box of shells to hunt back in the tundra. I bagged quite a few ducks and ptarmigan—selling them for $5.00 apiece. It was a good livelihood until I used up all the available shells.

By this time Nome was roaring. Ships were bringing in a different type of gold-digger, along with roulette wheels and other gambling devices, foodstuffs, clothes, and medicine. Dance halls and saloons sprouted up along the main street like weeds. Some had tiny stages and were obliging enough to furnish a facsimile of entertainment along with rigged dice games, adulterated whiskey, and light-fingered ladies. As I loitered in one of these places, The Sourdough, listening to the orchestra, which consisted of violin, piano, clarinet, and drums, I remembered the cornet still reposing in the bottom of my big canvas bag. I hadn't thought of it since I left home.

When the number finished, I went up and asked the leader, who was playing violin, whether he could use a cornettist.

"You just find me one!" he replied. I was hired at $20 a night, and blessed my mother for forcing my cornet on me the moment before I embarked. It suddenly seemed like a horn of plenty.

A throaty contralto, enchanting to my youthful eyes, was the main attraction of the place, which reminded me of Brown's Comique. I fell under her spell, as did many others. Miners showed their appreciation by tossing coins on the stage for her and even, in some instances, if they were drunk enough, pokes of gold dust. Some of the contributions fell into the pit and I would take personal charge of this overflow as an excuse to visit the charmer backstage. I kept on working there until the end of the season.

I remember a celebration on the Fourth of July, 1900, in honor of the first white child born in Cape Nome. Watching the parade go by, I stood in front of the Lucky Baldwin Saloon. It was distinguished by the studded door from San Francisco's Baldwin Hotel, salvaged and preserved from the disastrous Baldwin Hotel fire and later shipped to Nome and grafted onto the saloon. Years later Rex Beach told me that he and Jack London must have been standing very close to me, because they likewise watched that same parade from in front of the Lucky Baldwin Saloon. For a second time I had barely missed crossing Jack London's path!

There was plenty of time during the days for exploring, and I nosed around Anvil Creek but couldn't find a spot anywhere that hadn't been staked. I cast covetous eyes at a miner who billboarded his good luck with a watch chain of gold nuggets and another dazzling chunk in his necktie. I bought a small nugget for $25 and had it mounted in a tiepin. What did it matter that I had dug it up with a cornet instead of a shovel?

By October days were short and biting cold. Defeated fortune hunters, destitute and sick, booked passage home by the hundreds. Men marched up and down the crowded streets carrying big banners announcing ship sailings. I stayed until the last steamer was ready to sail, before the Bering Sea froze again and locked the remaining fortune hunters in till spring. For all the heartaches, it had been exciting. I was reluctant to leave the vital, raw turbulence. I was also reluctant to go back home and admit failure, but I knew I had better do it while I had the price of a steerage ticket.

The voyage back was torture. The steerage was one huge room, its bulkheads lined with berths for the sixty beaten, discouraged men who overflowed the reeking, airless dungeon. With winter blasting over the sea and constantly raging storms there was no thought of going on deck. There was nothing to eat but a nauseous mulligan stew. There was nothing to talk about—all were broke, depressed, wrapped in the gloom of their failure.

The first thing I did on reaching Seattle was to spend most of what I had left to phone my mother that I'd be home in a couple of days. It was the first long-distance call I ever made. She used up a large part of the time regretting the expense and when I asked to say hello to Blanche, shouted, "I'll say hello—it's cheaper!" and hung up.

They were both at the docks in San Francisco to meet me. My mother sized up my miserable appearance and didn't have to ask questions. I hadn't shaved off my beard—after all, it was the only thing I had to show for my high adventure except the stickpin.

"I told everybody you struck it rich in Alaska, Jesse," she said defiantly, "so don't tell them anything different."

"I don't have to tell them anything," I said. "They can see for themselves."

"Nonsense!" she snapped. "Everybody knows you were among the first hundred men in Nome, so how could you help but find gold?"

"I don't know, Ma, but I did help it."

"That doesn't matter. Did you have a good trip?"

"Ma," I said earnestly, "as long as I live I'm never going to set foot on a ship again!"

I kept that promise for a month. And the ship I set foot on was the same one that took me to Alaska—the *Zelandia*, reoutfitted and transferred to the Hawaiian run. The best job that had turned up on the Musicians' Union bulletin board was for a solo cornettist at $25 a week in the Orpheum Theatre in Honolulu.

I read a book on Hawaii while waiting for my sailing date. The warm Pacific sun, the flowers and coconuts and pineapples sounded like paradise after my arctic expedition. Big plans filled my mind. The job was only a means to get there and set them in motion.

"Hawaii is just teeming with music," I told my mother and Blanche. I was saturated with facts and figures from the book. "And do you know the only thing Hawaii hasn't got?"

"Maple syrup?" Blanche suggested.

I gave her a withering look. "There's no conservatory of music in Hawaii," I informed them. "Professor Jesse L. Lasky's Polynesian Conservatory of Music," I added explicitly, already taking in more than the Hawaiian Islands.

"Jesse," my mother said wistfully, "couldn't you just concentrate on blowing the cornet for twenty-five dollars a week for a little while?"

"Don't worry, Ma," I assured her. "From now on you're not going to have to worry about anything! And after I get settled Blanche can teach piano in the Conservatory," I added magnanimously.

She sighed and resumed her crocheting. She had found it prudent to stretch our thin resources by making worsted slippers, which sold at $5.00 a dozen pairs to the same wholesale shoe dealers who had supplied my father's San Jose store in more prosperous days.

Blanche Horns In

on the Act

The cruise to Hawaii on a blue velvet and sequined sea, with first-class passage paid by the theatre, was such a contrast to the grim Alaskan trip that I decided to spend most of the rest of my life on shipboard.

In addition to playing in the pit at the Orpheum we gave Sunday-night concerts on the stage. Several nights a week I walked over to the park in the center of Honolulu and watched the Royal Hawaiian Band, conducted by Herr Berger, a local celebrity who had toured Europe and played for nobility.

Each week I sent part of my salary home, keeping only what I needed to live on. As the tourist season came to an end, instead of being given two weeks' notice, we were given a final two weeks' work without pay and then sacked! With nothing but dreams in my pocket I called on Herr Berger. He would be quite an asset to my Polynesian Conservatory of Music. He had an even better idea. He asked me if I'd like to become a Hawaiian. There had never before been a white man in the Royal Hawaiian Band, but Herr Berger, bless his soul, had no racial prejudice. My light complexion, in contrast to the dark skin tones of the other band members, caused a good many double-takes. Sometimes I overheard the puzzled conjecture among the park strollers.

"I tell you he's white," one would say.

"He can't be! It's an all-native band!" a companion insisted.

"Maybe he's an albino!"

"He must have some kind of tropical sickness, poor thing!"

I was invited to the homes of some of my new Hawaiian friends in the band, and learned to eat poi and native delicacies. There wasn't much to do in the daytime, so frequently I hung around the docks, fascinated by the rhythmic grace of mahogany-skinned divers checking the rotting piles, or I occupied myself admiring the exquisite native and half-caste girls. I saved enough from working in the band to get second-class passage home. Once again Blanche and my mother received me as though I'd conquered the world instead of lost every cent I had.

While I had been in Honolulu, my mother and sister moved to a small hotel. On my first night home, having dinner in their room, I sensed an undercurrent of excitement not related to the tales of my latest adventures with which I was regaling them. Then, as we were having coffee, Blanche mysteriously left the room. Suddenly from the next room a crystal-clear cascade of trumpeting melody burst forth. My mother exultantly threw open the door and there stood Blanche, who couldn't blow a note when I left for Honolulu, playing the cornet brilliantly. It had been staged as a surprise for me, and I was dumfounded. They explained that Witherell—now living in San Francisco —had been so impressed with Blanche's talent that he had given her lessons for nothing.

Now we began to play duets together, and someone asked us to appear at a charity performance in the small concert hall at the Sherman Clay music store. Blanche wasn't at all eager to perform in public. I think she learned the cornet just to prove she could do in a few months what it took her big brother years to accomplish. But she gave in to my mother's and my urging and soon found herself enmeshed in a career she hadn't bargained for.

We finished our number at the music store, ran off stage, and looked at each other breathlessly, bewildered, not knowing quite what to do as we heard rounds of enthusiastic applause. Fifty-six years have passed, but that first applause for my sister and me still rings in my ears.

A sleek little man pushed us back toward the stage. "Take your bow," he commanded, "and then I want to talk to you." He was an agent named Maurice Levy, and after following us to our dressing room he offered us a booking for $50 a week at Shoot-the-Chutes Park. I was thrilled, Blanche was confused, my mother was surprised, pleased, and worried all at once—but she consented.

The excitement of preparing for our debut as professional entertainers on a bill of professionals was almost unbearable. The light opera *Florodora* was currently the biggest hit on Broadway, and I decided we couldn't go wrong with its smash tune, "Tell Me, Pretty Maiden, Are There Any More at Home like You?" As we made our entrance on the stage and began playing together, I experienced again the elation of knowing we were "over."

After our number we joined our mother in front and watched the rest of the show. There were comedy acrobats, two brothers who punched punching bags in rhythm, and Clinton Montgomery, who sang maudlin songs illustrated by a series of lantern slides of postcard lovers paddling a canoe into a yellow-faced moon or poised high in the air on a garden swing or cooing over a gate adorned with candy pink roses and a crowded nest of doves.

This was show business! I was entranced with every second of it— except a trivial novelty which plainly had no future and served only as a poor substitute for exit music. At the very end of the program a quick passage of moving pictures was thrown on the lantern-slide screen, depicting a running dog, a running man, a woman convulsively brandishing a handkerchief, and carriage wheels whooping away to the left while the spokes spun slowly to the right.

A brief review of the program in one of the dailies noted that "the Laskys in a refined, musical act rendered efficient selections on the cornet which showed them up as being clever musicians." It didn't find the flickering screen novelty worthy of mention.

We set to work at once to round out our act and make it really professional. Obviously the first step was to dress it up with a change of costumes. Our mother quickly ran up some military costumes for us, timely because the Spanish-American War was still an exciting subject in the public consciousness, and we themed our presentation around the extensive repertoire of army bugle calls I had learned while playing in the parade bands for departing soldiers. We insured applause at the finish by the lowering of an American flag in front of us as we stood stiffly at salute.

The following week we played at Fisher's Music Hall, opposite the Orpheum, in company with a Tyrolean quartet, a globe-balancing and contortion act, a mezzo soprano, a baritone, and a pair of quick-sketch artists. We were evidently worth our share of the ten cents admission, for the booking agent said he'd get us two weeks at $75 at Baker's Theatre in Portland, Oregon, but we'd have to have a complete change of act for the second week. We embellished the military routine by opening in Russian Hussar uniforms, which had capes that could be underdressed with two other costumes, and the resulting bulky effect seemed appropriately Russian. After a lightning change we reappeared as Tommy Atkins soldiers, then, peeling off one more layer, we closed in the familiar guise of Teddy Roosevelt's Rough Riders, finally dispensing with the cornets to sing the most popular marching-off-to-war song of the era:

He don't belong to the regulars,
He's just a volunteer
He's only one of the rank and file
But his mother holds him dear.

I then grabbed up a gun and walked sentry post while Blanche played.

We chose a colonial theme for the second week, and I got valuable ideas and advice for costuming and staging it from Bothwell Browne, a well-known female impersonator who was on intimate terms with towering powdered wigs and crinolines. Our salary jumped to $90 a week. Baker's was a "class" theatre, with a fifty-cent top.

We also played an engagement on the very spot where my father had had a shoe store when I was a small boy. The store had been replaced by Grauman's Unique Theatre, the first continuous vaudeville house in San Francisco. I had met the manager, D. H. Grauman, in Nome, Alaska. We did six shows a day and eight on weekends. A bushy-haired boy named Sid Grauman brought in our meals.

I decided vaudeville was our future. I decided for Blanche, too—I knew better than to let her decide for herself.

We had a letterhead made showing all our different costumes—which took practically the whole sheet—and we sent it with our pictures to leading theatres in the country playing vaudeville. We obtained their addresses from the *New York Clipper*, the *Variety* of its day. My mother wrote the letters, sixty of them, prodigal with descriptive adjectives. The only offer we got from this onslaught was for a week at $100 at the Boston Music Hall. It didn't include transportation.

After having toiled endless hours on the letters to bring this about my mother now began to be afraid that the Boston Music Hall was a dive and that we shouldn't accept. But she was reassured when I learned at the Musicians' Union that it was one of the finest theatres in the country. And when the family opened up with both barrels as usual, she faced them down with tight-lipped resolution.

"If the children leave San Francisco and go into vaudeville as professionals, they can never live in California again," Aunt Jenny decreed.

Mother thought she meant we would be pariahs if we planted our feet on such a disgraceful path. The lower fringes of show business didn't have too savory a reputation in those days.

"Look here, Jenny!" my mother exclaimed. "My children will never play any place where your children would be ashamed to be."

Aunt Jenny made her point clearer. "Vaudeville people live on trains," she contended. "They're gypsies without homes. They can never have permanent friends. They aren't in one town long enough to learn the names of streets. They forget the taste of home cooking. There aren't enough theatres on this coast to keep the children busy, so it means giving up California forever."

My mother brushed aside all objections. "If the children want to do this," she stated flatly, "they must do it!"

I'm sure Blanche didn't really want to, but she knew it meant a lot to me and she was a game sport about it.

The tourist train had facilities for passengers to brew their own coffee, but no dining car. Stops were made along the way for meals during the seven-day trip East, which also afforded the ideal opportunity for swaggering and posturing with gloves, cane, and roll-brimmed hat.

In Boston, my mother, Blanche, and I stayed with some cousins, the Cobes. It was the first time I knew we had any wealthy relations. We were overwhelmed by the size of Cousin Eva's home and her hospitality. The Cobes had heard through the family of our success in San Francisco and Portland and were very proud of their talented relatives. They entertained for us, praised us to their friends, and even arranged interviews for us at the Boston Conservatory of Music. They invited many of their Boston society friends to our opening.

I began to have faint misgivings when I saw the elegance of the

Music Hall, which was Boston's leading theatre, and the huge, smartly dressed audience. I was really worried when the act preceding ours went on. Rauschle, a brilliant master of mimicry, slipped from one characterization to another—President Theodore Roosevelt, the late President McKinley, Prince Bismarck, Napoleon III—then drew crackling vollies of applause with impressions of Admirals Dewey, Sampson, and Schley.

We followed him and worked harder than we ever had before, but it was no use. Almost from the first moment on stage we knew we weren't making good. It was an agonizing ordeal on both sides of the footlights, and when it was over, we could almost hear the separate beating of hands of the Cobes and their friends in a vast sea of silence. This audience was accustomed to the greatest two-a-day acts in the big-time. It took more than singing, playing, and changing costumes to entertain them.

The manager was exasperated. "You're rank amateurs," he said with cold constraint. "I ought to pull you off altogether!"

But he let us play the week out, since we had made such a long trip for the engagement. He probably blamed himself a little for booking an act without knowing more about it. He made us do three shows a day from then on, and spotted them so that we always played to a virtually empty house. We went on as soon as the theatre opened in the afternoon, filled a gap during the dinner hour, and closed the show at midnight.

It was horrible, having to face the Cobes after our flop, but they were charmingly resentful that Boston was too stuffy to appreciate us. We kept our appointment for auditions at the Boston Conservatory, and afterward the director offered us both scholarships. Cousin Eva arranged for my mother to get a job in one of the big department stores so that we could stay on in Boston and go to school. Mother was jubilant about such an opportunity, but neither Blanche nor I wanted her to have to work (as if ministering to our endless needs on tour wasn't the most drudging kind of work). Despite my sister's hatred for the trouping life she was just stubborn enough not to give up when we faced a challenge. I know she would have loved to go to the conservatory. But she said, "Why should we study music? We're not musicians. We're entertainers. We're not good ones, but we can find out what's wrong with the act and *make* them like it!"

I never again thought of my sister as a little girl.

I went down to the vaudeville booking offices on Tremont Row the next day and got an offer for us to play the Flynn Circuit of summer parks for three months at $40 a week, less 5 per cent. These New England "railroad parks," run by the streetcar companies, featured free shows on small outdoor stages. It was the dregs of vaudeville— broken-down entertainers playing to audiences who sat on benches munching sandwiches.

"We are joining a summer theatrical season," my mother wrote the relatives in California, "after a very satisfactory run in the Boston Music Hall. Everyone loves the children. . . ." They must never suspect that Aunt Jenny's predictions had begun to come true.

When I first saw the weary, battered, unappetizing lot of has-beens we would be forced to associate with for the next fourteen weeks, I was heartsick. Danny Simmons, billed as a hobo clown, had more the appearance of a tramp pretending to be a performer than the other way around. Manuel Romaine was a faded tenor. A heavy-set, ghoul-ish acrobat in a patched costume and a tired circus girl in wrinkled tights billed themselves as Brian and Nadine instead of by their married name. A withered spinster pianist named Sabra Dobson served as accompanist for the troupe.

But unexpectedly this tour was a completely happy period for us —even Blanche liked it. The audiences, perhaps because they didn't have to pay, were uninhibited in their enjoyment and extravagant with their acclaim. Some of the aging performers had, indeed, been headliners who should have saved their money when it came easily. They were all kindly people, of abundant if tarnished talent, who took delight in showing us tricks learned from years of experience on the road. Danny Simmons helped brighten the introductory lines for our bugle routine, Sabra Dobson hunted through her sheet music, with the others looking on and advising, to find a more stirring en-trance march for our opening. Brian showed me how to pull applause with a flip of the hand, signify Blanche and pull applause for her, and pass her in front of me before we bowed together. We rehearsed these new bits of business during the day, changing and improving and tightening the act from show to show. Two curtain calls on our first day lengthened to six by the end of the week.

After the late show the whole troupe would sit around and swap wonderful stories of engagements they had played in their heyday. We loved them all, and as the weeks flew by and our act acquired polish under their deft, friendly guidance, it seemed we had always known them.

Flynn came back to our dressing rooms when the fourteen-week season was over. "I saw your act at the Boston Music Hall," he said as we shook hands, "and you had a lot to learn. But you're not amateurs any longer. You can come back to my circuit any time, but you'll never need to." He gave us a letter of recommendation to the William Morris theatrical agency in New York.

It was like being graduated from college.

We had held our living expenses down by staying in boarding-houses where meals and room could be had for $5.00 a week, so we had saved about $200 with which to conquer New York. Brian and Nadine had recommended Simmons' Theatrical Boarding House on Fourteenth Street, and we went directly there. Fourteenth Street, with Tony Pastor's, Keith's Union Square, and the Academy of Music, was the dream of all variety artists. The Simmons' rates were a little stiff—$10 a week for board and room—but we figured it would be worth it in convenience to the theatres we would undoubtedly be playing. We'd only have to walk a block to Tony Pastor's!

Our $200 was almost gone before a telegram came from the Morris office club department offering a one-night engagement at $20 in the Atlantic Gardens, a beer hall in the Bowery.

"The Bowery!" my mother protested. "If anyone ever found out!"

"Ma, it's no worse than the parks!" I argued.

But we all knew it was.

Blanche and I were no longer uncertain in front of an audience. Our friends on the summer park tour had helped us perfect every movement, every nuance of timing. But it was all lost in the clatter of fifteen hundred beer steins and the babble of liquid-loosened tongues. As we went back uptown, rain beat against the windows of the street-car, and the reflection of the drops slipping down the panes of glass shown on Blanche's face like the shadow of tears. We couldn't speak to each other. This was New York, the mecca of all theatrical hopes. We had traveled a long road to get here, and the road had taken us to a beer hall in the Bowery!

"Anyway, we *are* in New York, and it's a start," I finally had the courage to say. "Don't you think so, Ma?"

"I don't know what I think," she answered. "When I saw the two of you up there among all that beer drinking, playing to people who weren't even listening, I just couldn't believe it. It was like a bad dream. Sometimes I think Aunt Jenny was right. We never should have left California. But of course I'd never let on to *her*."

Our next booking was a Sunday concert at the Lion Palace Music Hall and Roof Garden at 110th and Broadway. After that a one-day engagement at 142nd and Third Avenue, followed by a single appearance at another beer garden, on 175th Street in the Bronx, then one-week stands at typical vaudeville houses in Syracuse, Utica, Youngstown. Blanche had a birthday while we were playing Buffalo and my mother got up a little surprise party for her in our dressing room at Shea's Theatre, inviting another devoted backstage mother with whom she had become friendly, and her gifted daughter, a child star billed as "Little Elsie." Years later, when I went backstage on opening night of *The Vanderbilt Cup* at the Broadway Theatre to congratulate its star on her triumph, Elsie Janis reminded me of that dressing-room party.

We steadily got better engagements, but every step of progress seemed to take us farther away from the goal of every vaudevillian—Fourteenth Street. When we finally did make Keith's Union Square, my mother was so exultant she raised my allowance from $1.00 to $2.00 a week.

We were held over a second week at Keith's and followed that with a week at Tony Pastor's, at $60, commencing February 23, 1903. The prestige of appearing in his theatre was so great that Pastor could afford to pay smaller salaries than his competitors! We knew we had really arrived when we had this contract calling for only two shows a day. We had previously invested in impressively long Conn triumphal trumpets to feign a display of versatility and now we bought still more instruments on the installment plan, mellophones which we used as French horns. I hadn't had a chance to see a bill at Pastor's, and came to rehearsal with an orchestration I had made up for fifteen men. I handed it with a flourish to the piano player, who was Burt Green, king of ragtime pianists and later the husband of vaudeville headliner Irene Franklin. He informed me crisply that he was the entire orchestra. We never had better accompaniment.

A little man in a black silk hat came backstage after the matinee and complimented us. Then a clever young juggler on the bill told us that Tony Pastor liked our act.

"Did he tell you?" I asked, puffing up with pride.

"No—he told *you*—that man in the black hat is Tony Pastor," wheezed the juggler, whose name was W. C. Fields.

Hermann the Great, who road-showed a spectacular presentation of legerdemain and magic, saw us at Tony Pastor's and engaged us for a forty-week season's tour, as a curtain piece between his sleight-of-hand tricks and grand illusions. It was our first steady employment. We joined the impressive entourage at $90 a week, transportation paid for three. Hermann wore high heels to add three inches of prestige to his small stature, and he was accompanied everywhere he went in public by a little colored boy named Boomsky, in a page's uniform. Hermann's wife carried a frizzled poodle that had to be hidden when we entered Pullman cars. Both Hermanns had enchanting accents. We liked the little French couple immensely. They were equally fond of us and called Blanche "Lady Lasky" because of her fastidious ways.

Hermann always ended his performance by borrowing a hat from a spectator in the audience, ripping it to shreds, sticking the pieces in a cannon, and shooting them to the top of the proscenium. The hat stayed there until he shot it down with a pistol and handed it whole and unscathed to the astonished owner.

We carried three or four trunks of every kind of hat for this trick, and Hermann was always careful to borrow one that could easily be duplicated from the trunks. He made the substitution without anyone being aware of it, and then tore the prop hat to bits. The stage manager, as the cannon was fired and attention was on Hermann, raised the borrowed hat from the wings to the ceiling on an invisible black thread—and broke the thread when the magician fired his pistol.

We played in Coffeyville, Kansas, the kind of rip-roaring Western town where cowboys and drunks took over on Saturday night. It was Saturday night and Hermann had the imprudence to separate a drunken cowboy in the front row from his Stetson. The dapper Frenchman must have been thinking only that he had a hat in the trunks exactly like this one, or intuition would have told him how a saturated cow poke might react to seeing his brand-new ten-gallon pride and joy being desecrated before his eyes. The fellow let out a howl and lunged toward the stage with his hand on his six-shooter.

Hermann, somewhat shaken, stuffed the felt remnants in the cannon and fired it with incredible dispatch, pointing frenziedly to the restored hat overhead. With the outraged cowboy clamoring for his sombrero Hermann fired his pistol. The hat didn't budge. He fired again and again in sheer distraction, which of course didn't help matters any. The stage manager had nervously jerked the thread too hard and broken it in the wrong place. The hat was irretrievably moored to the ceiling.

The curtain came down with a thud and the audience was immediately in an uproar, with the cowboy's threats trumpeting above all the rest. The house manager told us to run for our lives.

I had often pictured myself averting a panic while a theatre was in flames by constraining the audience to orderly rout with soothing selections on my cornet. I grabbed my cornet, but one look at the angry mob through the peephole in the curtain changed my mind. I fled with the rest through the stage door to the hotel, pursued by a gang of the cowboy's impetuous friends. Townsfolk joined the melee and soon there was a sizable swarm besieging the hotel. Those members of our troupe who reached their rooms ahead of the thundering herd were more or less blockaded. The others went directly to the train rather than brave the unpredictable crowd. But those in the hotel were sneaked through the kitchen and back doors to the train, and we all vanished from town in a mystifying manner that did credit to the master of disappearing acts.

We played San Jose in the same auditorium where I had watched Sousa's band, and where the stage manager had told me that show folks usually walk down Santa Clara Street after a performance. After our performance I walked down Santa Clara Street past the little house where I had blown my heart out behind the rosebushes. Suppose Sousa had heard me that night . . . suppose he had even put me in his band . . . would I be any better off than I was right now? The local-boy-and-girl-make-good angle rated us more space than Hermann himself in the San Jose newspaper write-up. I felt pretty good.

San Francisco was even more of a triumph. Our dressing room was a mass of flowers and all our relatives turned out on opening night. I swaggered around town all that week, lavishly passing out cigars at the Musicians' Union. We were the guests of the Hermanns in a box at the Morosco for a matinee performance of *Ben Hur*. Backstage afterward I was delighted to shake hands with William Farnum, engaging young star of the play which was his first big success.

The family gave us a dinner at the Cafe Zinkand, and with reprehensible memories proudly vied with each other for the honor of having originally encouraged us to go into vaudeville. No one recalled having said anything about troupers being gypsies who lived on trains and became estranged from a normal life. But the truth of that homily was forced on me during the week we appeared in San Francisco. We had played such a long series of one-night stands, doing all our sleeping in swaying berths over rolling wheels, that we had grown entirely unaccustomed to ordinary beds. We all complained of sleepless nights.

This strange experience intrigued me so much that I wrote a story based on it. I frequently had ideas for stories, and sometimes actually started them, but this attempt was exceptional in that I finished it and sent it off to *Argosy* magazine. Several weeks later, while we were in Montreal, I got a check for $25. No thrill before or since has ever measured up to that one. I precipitately joined the ranks of Dickens, Mark Twain, Bret Harte—and Jack London, on whose doorstep I had once very nearly established squatter's rights. Flowery rhetoric took form in my mind; elegant prose came alive under my pen. I vowed to develop an unmistakable literary style, a style that would be Lasky, as Hawthorne was Hawthorne. But all the stories I submitted after that returned as unerringly as homing pigeons. In one last ambitious effort I began a novel. I remember the first line: "A storm, sudden and fierce, swept over the Bering Sea and when it passed it left in its wake an upturned boat."

I remember the first line because that's as far as I ever got with the novel.

One night at the Columbia Theatre in Washington, D.C., as Blanche and I were putting on our Rough Rider costumes for our military number, Boomsky shouted through the dressing-room door that President Theodore Roosevelt and the First Lady were in the audience. Even Hermann was excited, having played before seven kings but never for a President of the United States.

Blanche took it in stride, but I ran around in circles, endlessly brushing my coat and smoothing out wrinkles and inspecting my shoes and looking in the mirror. When our cue came, I almost went to pieces entirely, and Blanche had to drag me to the wings. We marked the time to the blare of our entrance music to get in step, then marched out smartly, heads up, stomachs in, halted at center stage, and snapped to left-face, heels clicking in unison. The brass of the pit orchestra swelled up and dropped to a crashing silence for my opening bugle call. I filled my lungs and lifted my white-gauntleted hands to play the air. And that's all I had to play—just a handful of air.

I had forgotten my cornet!

As the tour neared its end, Hermann's manager began to lose a prolonged battle with the bottle. Sometimes he was in no condition for the discharge of his routine duties, which included collecting the receipts and checking them by keeping a watchful eye on the box-office and counting the house, to make sure the company wasn't cheated on its percentage. The magician thought I could handle these auditing details for the few remaining weeks. When I realized the show was taking in as much as $600 and $700 a night, I thought that made prettier music than my cornet. I asked Hermann to let me take over his management for the next season, while continuing our act.

But I was scared to death when he agreed. I didn't know where to begin. Even my mother had qualms about it.

"Hermann thinks I can do it," I assured her.

"Hermann thinks rabbits come out of hats," she remarked dryly.

But being manager of Hermann the Great automatically opened the necessary doors. I booked the following season, getting a route through Klaw and Erlanger, ordered lithographs, acted as advance man and planted publicity, then came back and toured with the company, collecting each night's receipts, paying the salaries, and still performing our musical act.

Toward the end of the second season Blanche and I walked out on the stage of the Majestic Theatre in Utica to our entrance music, *The Gladiator March*, and were both startled by the virtuosity of a cornettist in the pit. His brilliant pure tones dominated the whole orchestra. I was ashamed to follow such technical perfection. I shot an embarrassed glance at my sister and looked down to find the source of this prodigious talent. The handsome young man behind the cornet smiled blithely. We met after the show as I was going down to find him and he was coming backstage to look for me.

His name was Ben Rolfe, and he informed me that his wife Nellie also played the cornet. That meeting marked the blossoming of what I regard as my own two most negotiable abilities—a Geiger-counter instinct for spotting potential star material when it is just talent in the raw, and a knack for making other people believe in me when I only half believe in myself.

I saw in the Rolfes a heaven-sent opportunity, since Blanche had already determined to leave the stage at the end of the season. Vaudeville was still expanding as the standard and popular entertainment of the nation, and I quickly convinced Rolfe that I could get bookings for him and Nellie in our ready-made act. We sold them the act for $500, which included rehearsing them in the routines.

Then I talked Hermann into cutting his big show down to a thirty-minute headline vaudeville attraction in order to reach new audiences. Percy Williams gave me bookings at $900 a week for him in the Colonial Theatre at Sixty-second and Broadway, the Orpheum in Brooklyn, and the Alhambra on 126th Street. After teaching the Rolfes our act I had no trouble getting them a tryout week and soon had them booked for forty weeks at $100 a week. As my 10 per cent agent's commission for the two acts I had $100 a week rolling in at the cost of very little effort. Where to go from there? If only I had four Hermann the Greats and ten Rolfes . . .

I rented office space from Arch and Edgar Selwyn, who had a play broker's agency in the Broadway Theatre. Immediately I had a sign painted on the door:

JESSE L. LASKY
Manager of Hermann the Great

The office contained Blanche and a typewriter and a telephone. That's all the office contained because I was outside, admiring the sign.

It soon occurred to me that Hermann should play the leading theatres on the Continent. Possibly the fact that I had seen Alaska and Hawaii but had never been to Europe had something to do with this brainstorm. I would, of course, have to go abroad immediately to book him in advance while he was playing out the three weeks in New York. He fell in with the scheme and even agreed to furnish my passage, but I was to take care of my other expenses. My mother thought rushing off to Europe just when I was getting a good start here was the wildest idea she'd ever heard of, and she'd heard some lulus. I gave her my gold watch and told her to pawn it if I ran out of money and cabled home. She flatly forbade me to announce publicly in a cable that I was broke. But she agreed to rush to Simpson's with the watch and her own jewelry if I sent the message "Miss you both."

Madame Hermann was having tea with my mother one afternoon and listening to the reading of my latest letter from Europe. I had booked Hermann at the Palace Theatre in London for eight weeks, and then at the Alhambra in Paris. I had gone to all the big theatres and been dazzled by the Continental musical shows. Europe was years ahead of America in theatrical *divertissements*. My head was pounding with ideas for bringing America up to date. I would myself create those four Hermann the Greats and ten Rolfes I needed to put the Lasky Enterprises on Easy Street.

The doorbell interrupted my mother's proud reading of the letter. It was a messenger with a cablegram which said, "I miss you both very much."

"What a devoted son you have!" Madame Hermann marveled. "Think of it—sending a cable just to tell you how much he loves you!"

On with the Shows

My imagination sharpened and fed by the European productions I had seen, I began thinking in bigger terms—groups instead of individuals. If our military and colonial musical acts had been good with two of us, why wouldn't they be even better as production numbers, staged in the Continental manner?

We expanded the simple colonial idea into a tuneful confection for four girls and three boys including the Rolfes, and called it "The Colonial Septette." Blanche selected and supervised the preparation of costumes and three set changes. It was no problem to get men trombonists, but girl cornet players weren't easily come by. We finally lined up exactly what we wanted through the Boston Conservatory of Music—three beautiful, cultured girls without professional experience but with excellent musical training. Rolfe's help with the orchestrations and rehearsals was invaluable.

The costumes and scenery were to cost $3000—when we could raise the money to pay for them! Even though we wangled them on a deposit, our money ran out before dress rehearsal, and managers wouldn't book the act without seeing it. They offered to let us showcase it for them one night in the Bon Ton, a burlesque house in Jersey City.

Blanche and I were crushed. We had a chance to sell the act to the managers, but we didn't have money enough to get the scenery and props across the river, and we were afraid if we did get there our Boston society buds would balk at going into a burlesque house.

Miraculously, when we dragged ourselves back to the boarding-house the night before the tryout, ready to throw in the sponge, Uncle Mark was there. He couldn't have chosen a more propitious time to visit New York. He arranged for delivery of the scenery and we spent all the next day going back and forth to Jersey City, loaded with costumes, props, and instrument cases. Then, while the rest of us fidgeted at the theatre, he waited for darkness before collecting the girl cornettists, and was careful to approach the Bon Ton from the rear. All stage doors look alike. For all they knew they were being unloaded at Keith's. Uncle Mark remarked later, "I always wanted to walk through a stage door and today I even carried scenery."

The managers liked the presentation and I started booking it the next morning at $700 a week, which gave me a profit of $300 above expenses. Two months later we launched "The Military Octette," using the same quick costume changes Blanche and I had found effective—Russian Hussars to Tommy Atkins to American soldiers. I added a Girl with a Baton, who blew a bugle in the back of the theatre, then marched up the aisle in a spotlight to lead the pit orchestra. That act brought $1000 a week, and was immensely successful.

I went through the ideas Blanche and I had incorporated into our two original acts to see if there was anything I'd overlooked. Of course —the herald trumpets. Negro acts were popular, so I planned "The Black Hussars." They opened on a dark stage with the long trumpets protruding through the curtains, playing a stirring march. The curtains parted and ten handsome young colored boys and four dusky beauties performed solos, duets, and ensembles, switching to fourteen bass drums of graduated sizes for a rousing finale. This act rang the cash register for $1200 a week and later was a sensation in Europe, but I never had such trouble trying to keep an act together. One by one I lost my tan lovelies in Berlin, Vienna, and Paris. They all deserted to marry white men of considerable prominence and remain in countries where there is no color barrier.

Having squeezed all the inspiration I could from our original acts, I had to venture afield. But I still stuck to music. The Lasky Quintette was composed of four girl cellists and a male string-bass player, ensconced in a giant sea shell, which acted as a sounding board for their Victor Herbert selections, and was bathed in changing rainbow lights controlled from a special switchboard.

Now I *had* the equivalent of four Hermann the Greats and ten Rolfes. And I was getting the producer's profits instead of an agent's commission. It seemed to me I had found the mother lode that had been so elusive in Alaska.

I kept Rolfe with The Colonial Septette a year, then found a substitute for him and pulled him in off the road to become my partner, managing the musical end of production. I shouldn't have done it. Brilliant cornettist that he was, he couldn't abandon his instrument

c

as lightly as I had. It was almost an anatomical part of him. He did his thinking on the cornet. He rehearsed the players quickly, the music endlessly, and frequently the music he rehearsed wasn't even in the production. He was never around when you wanted him, but he was easy to find. You just listened for the sweet tones of a cornet and followed them to some obscure dressing room.

"Ben," I asked him one day, "what do you want to do most in the world?"

"Play this thing in my hand," he said simply.

That was the end of our association.

I needed more money to produce some of the grandiose ideas I had. Through Ted Bendix, a composer and musical director, who also roomed at Jones Boarding House, on Forty-fourth Street, I wangled an introduction to Henry B. Harris, who leased and managed the Hudson Theatre. In a cloud of cigar smoke, without which an up-and-coming vaudeville entrepreneur wouldn't have felt properly dressed, I called on the distinguished play producer. He had seen some of my acts and liked them. I described the even more elaborate things I wanted to do and asked him to loan me a lot of money.

"How much?" he asked.

"I don't know," I answered.

"I won't loan you a cent," he said after a long moment. "But I'll join with you as a silent partner, putting up my share of the backing, and you can take over offices here and use the theatre for rehearsals."

I was drunk with the power of the Harris backing. It was a golden chance to outdo myself, but my imagination was still tethered to musical instruments. What was the biggest thing I could put on the stage? I went to Harris as soon as I thought of it.

"Henry," I said, "I want to build the biggest phonograph in the world—with a box large enough to hold a twelve-piece brass band, including a trap drummer. The music will be orchestrated to have that squeaky, unreal sound of a phonograph, but blaring out a dozen times as loud. We'll even reproduce the effects of a phonograph getting stuck in one groove and slowing down when it needs winding."

Harris tried ineffectually to bridle my runaway enthusiasm. "But, Jesse, do you realize how big a box you'd need to hold twelve men— and how big the horn would have to be?" he challenged. "Who'd build such a monstrosity? And have you any idea how much it would cost?"

"No," I admitted, starting for the door, "but I'll find out from the people who make the best musical instruments."

"Where are you going?" Harris asked.

"To the Conn factory in Elkhart, Indiana," I flung over my shoulder.

I drew plans on the train. In Elkhart the Conn people looked at them and shook their heads at first. But they figured out a way to build the horn in sections that were compact enough for traveling and still could be quickly swung into place for the stage presentation. Twelve musicians packed the box so full that we had to cut the bells off some of the instruments, and the players must have been black and blue from elbow jabs before the unit had been out two days. "Sardinophone" would have been an apt name for that instrument of torture, but we christened it "The Immensaphone," and it was a whopping success. It played four weeks at Hammerstein's Victoria and then took to the road.

Ideas bred other ideas. I thought them up and planned them on the streetcar, in bed, at theatres, at lunch. I made a bet with Blanche once that I could pull a vaudeville act out of anything in the room she named. She pointed to a table holding a stuffed bird under glass and a faded leather-bound copy of *Robinson Crusoe*. We produced an act called "Robinson Crusoe's Isle" and another named "Birdland." Those were the lush days of vaudeville. Everything succeeded. Nothing failed.

I sent out about forty acts from 1906 to 1910, and squeezed extra mileage out of them after they had run their course on the United Booking Offices circuit by disguising them under different names, trimming off the frayed edges, and offering them at bargain rates to the opposition, Loew's circuit, booked by Joe Schenck. That way they stayed on tour and kept producing income for three or four years. We were eating cake and chewing it twice.

In addition to designing the costumes my sister was becoming indispensable as a production assistant. She was greatly attracted to the stage as long as she wasn't on it herself.

"Blanche," I called through the door one day, "how do you like this title: 'A Night on a Houseboat'!"

"What's it all about?" she called back.

"I don't know yet," I said, "but it must be about something or I wouldn't have thought of it."

Blanche appeared in my doorway. "Can you come off your houseboat long enough to look at someone who says she's a dancer?"

"Not now," I said. "I want to get on this idea while it's hot. Tell her to come back next week."

"I told her that *last* week," Blanche said.

"Oh well—my train of thought is broken now anyway. . . ."

A pale face strangled by an enormous boa drifted into the room. "I'm Miss Ruth St. Denis," the lithe young lady said. "I've been studying dancing."

"Where have you danced?" I asked impassively.

"Everywhere—all my life," the girl said earnestly. "Everywhere except on the professional stage."

My mind was plucking at "A Night on a Houseboat," and this interruption annoyed me. "Miss St. Denis," I said somewhat impatiently, "I'm a busy man, and I couldn't possibly use an amateur dancer. Our acts are built around new and unusual ideas and we have to have talent of the highest caliber."

"My act is already built," the dancer interposed. "It only requires presentation. I had hoped that you would at least see it."

"All right," I said indulgently. "Come back next Sunday and I'll take a look at your routine."

"I'm sorry," she said, "I never dance on Sunday."

"Then ask Miss Lasky to arrange another appointment for you." I dismissed her and tried to concentrate on "A Night on a Houseboat."

Blanche stuck her head in the door. "The appointment is arranged," she said dryly. "Miss St. Denis will dance for you in half an hour, as soon as the stage is prepared."

I sighed. I was trapped.

I bumped into Harris on my way downstairs to the theatre. "Blanche says you've got an idea for a new production—something about a night on a houseboat," he said. "I'd like to hear about it."

"Later, Henry," I said. "I've got a little audition going on right now."

"Anything interesting?" he asked.

I shook my head. "Amateur dancer from Jersey, I think. One of those things I just couldn't think up an excuse for not seeing."

"I'm glad you didn't," Harris said, "because there never is an excuse. Producers should see everyone. You never know when something important is going to drop into your lap. It might not show up for a month—or it might be tomorrow—but when it does, you want to be there. The person you turn away from your door may be tomorrow's star. The song you don't have time to hear may be a potential hit."

"Henry," I chided, "after a lecture like that, the least you can do is take your own advice. And while we're suffering together, I'll tell you about 'A Night on a Houseboat.' "

He flinched, but he came with me. We sat in the dark theatre and I heard a large woman breathing heavily behind me. I turned and addressed the intruder brusquely, "Madam, this is a private audition."

"My daughter insists that I accompany her to auditions," she stated severely, implying that managers were not to be trusted. I shrank into my seat, uncomfortably aware that under those chastening eyes I couldn't let my attention stray from the stage. I couldn't use the interval to tell my partner about "A Night on a Houseboat."

The curtain rose on a resplendently dressed stage. The oriental scene must have taken a carload of scenery. We stared unbelievingly. Natives peddled spices from beautiful urns. Weird music permeated the Hindu temple setting with Old World imagery. Incense burned.

For twenty minutes we watched in complete enchantment as Ruth St. Denis performed for the first time on a theatre stage her inspired conception of the Hindu goddess, *Radha,* which was to be hailed as one of the great dance classics of its generation and bring international glory to its creator.

Harris turned to me, his eyes aglow. "Jesse, you're a genius!" he cried. "To prepare and stage this masterpiece for me without a word. Leading me to think you didn't know a thing about it. But how did you keep it under your hat? You're usually bursting when you've got something as big as this. As big as this—what am I saying? You've never *had* anything as big as this."

I felt a little sick. I excused myself and found Blanche. She started to apologize, "I made this appointment for her a week ago and forgot to tell you, Jesse. When she came with a truckload of scenery and costumes and her whole company, I couldn't put her off. . . ."

"Never mind that," I said hurriedly. "Get me a contract quick. I've got to get her signed up before Harris finds out I haven't."

Ruth St. Denis was a sensation from the start. I booked her at the New York Theatre and then sent her upstate to break in her gem of an act and polish it. Harris was so thrilled he asked to take personal charge of her management, booking her on a tour in legitimate theatres. I went ahead with rehearsals for "A Night on a Houseboat."

Successes continued and money rolled in. We were now living at the St. James Hotel on Forty-fifth Street, opposite the stage door of the Hudson Theatre, where our acts were prepared for their out-of-town tryouts. I had a wardrobe that would have made Jack Morris mad with envy, and a suite of offices with my name on the door. I was getting known as one of the most astute vaudeville producers on Broadway. Of course vaudeville was booming and astuteness in that field consisted largely in having more acts to sell than the next fellow. I didn't quite know why I was so prosperous, but when I considered how many useful ideas for our productions had been picked up while I was booking Hermann in Europe, I thought Europe undoubtedly held the clue to my good fortune.

"Let's go to Europe," I proposed. "All three of us!"

"I knew something was brewing," Blanche observed. "You've been too quiet lately. What's the big idea this time?"

I tried to explain what had been going through my mind.

"Without realizing it, we've been building acts with a Continental flair—that's why they go over so well. They were inspired by what I saw in Europe on my last trip. By admiration more than design, I've been injecting a foreign flavor into our productions—it's that little extra something that gives them distinction."

"When you've got a golden goose," Blanche said, "why do you have to analyze it to death?"

"But if vaudeville audiences like a Continental flavor in their entertainment, how would they react to an act that's European through and through—ten times more European than Europe itself!"

"They might choke on it," Blanche said skeptically. "Just because your grandmother likes the flavor of garlic, you don't go out and buy her ten pounds of it. And how are you going to build an act more European than Europe could conceive?"

"I'll have to cast and put it together in Europe, of course, and bring it back to the United States as an importation. A European production, produced by an American for American audiences. It's never been done before."

"I don't know," Blanche said, unconvinced. "Just because a thing has never been done doesn't make it sure-fire."

"This idea is," I insisted. "I'll call it 'The Stunning Grenadiers.' Gorgeous Amazons in tights and magnificent costumes, and a tremendous saber-fencing number."

"That should give it a European touché," Blanche gibed. "Do you think you can pick up a star in Europe you could build the show around?"

"We could," I said confidently, "but I won't chance it. Maude Meredith has a lovely soprano voice—and she's six-feet-two—just what I want. We'll take her over with us and bring her back as our European discovery."

"Fine," said Blanche, "but 'Maude' sounds anything but Continental."

"Suppose we change her name to 'Meredith Meredro,'" I suggested. And I've been changing names ever since.

Looking for colossal beauties who could fence was like searching for the Holy Grail. The combination didn't exist. We ended by selecting eight girls in London and four in Paris and then hiring a fencing master to spend weeks with them. The wonderful London costumers were the one bright spot amid production difficulties on unfamiliar ground that had us tearing our hair. The undertaking was finally pieced together and became the most glittering jewel in our string of hits. It opened at London's Tivoli Theatre and stayed for two months. Its subsequent reception in the United States seemed to confirm my theory that American audiences were predisposed toward the European type of entertainment.

On my return to New York I was having a Tom and Jerry with Bat Masterson, columnist on the New York *Morning Telegraph*, in the Knickerbocker Hotel bar, when he said, "There's a man who has had more champagne hoisted to him than Edward the Seventh." I looked and saw a slight figure sitting alone at the end of the bar. Bat told me he was Tod Sloan, one of the greatest jockeys of all time, with an imposing collection of other talents as well: a record pigeon shot, a champion billiard player, a phenomenon at checkers and bridge, a race driver who could hold his own with Barney Oldfield. But the world had passed Tod Sloan by. He had been down on his luck for a year or so, ignored if not forgotten by those who had idolized him. Bat introduced us; I bought him a drink and asked him to come to my office in the morning. He did.

"I think you could be a winner again, Tod Sloan," I told him, offering him a cigar.

"My racing days are over," Sloan said, smiling regretfully.

"I'm talking about vaudeville," I said. "People paid a lot of money to see you race and they'll pay a lot of money just to see you stand up on a stage and tell how you did it."

He twisted his hat awkwardly. "I couldn't stand up on a stage and face a big crowd. I wouldn't know what to say."

"A race track is a bigger stage with a bigger crowd than you'll ever find in a theatre," I told him. "And as for what to say, leave that to George M. Cohan. He can write the best monologues in town, and I've just asked him to do one for you."

"I wish you'd call it off," he pleaded. "I just don't think I could do it——"

"Too late," I said. "I've already arranged a booking for you at Hammerstein's Victoria. I'm betting on you, Tod. What do you say?"

He spread his hands in a gesture of resignation. "What can I say?" he answered helplessly. "When a person's got a big stake on me, I wouldn't want to let him down."

Blanche came in after Sloan left. "You look worried," she said.

"I ought to be," I admitted. "I told Tod Sloan I'd got George M. Cohan to write a monologue for him and that I've booked him into Hammerstein's Victoria. I've never even met George M. Cohan and Hammerstein may think I've gone berserk when I tell him a broken-down jockey would be a drawing card in vaudeville."

"What are you going to do?" Blanche asked.

"Find someone who can introduce me to George M. Cohan," I said, "and sell Hammerstein on the idea. I don't think Tod Sloan's public has forgotten him."

It was a good hunch. His opening at Hammerstein's Victoria was jammed and he took a dozen curtain calls. George M. Cohan, always generous with show folks, refused to take payment for supplying a sock monologue, and at $1500 a week Tod Sloan recouped some of his dwindling fortune and popularity.

William Morris and the United Booking Offices were locked in a vital struggle for supremacy in the vaudeville booking business in 1906. United controlled Keith's theatres and booked the vast Orpheum circuit. Morris booked numerous independent opposition theatres. The letter Flynn had given me to the Morris office when we left his summer park circuit years before had introduced me to some of the Morris booking men, and we had obtained playing dates through them, but I had never met the great man himself. It took the bitter rivalry between the two powerful agencies to bring me face to face with him.

When I answered his summons, I found a pair of piercing black eyes boring into me from a rather pale face. He got to the point at once. He was going to launch an offensive against the United Booking Offices, he told me, by invading their Chicago stronghold. He asked me to go there and open a branch office for him, sign new talent, and make as big a noise as possible. He would in the meantime keep my own acts playing. It didn't mean severing my connection with Harris—it meant, rather, aligning ourselves with influential interests—and as Harris was agreeable to the arrangement, I eagerly accepted the challenge. Morris gave me $5000 as a starter, and a drawing-room ticket on the gleaming, newly introduced Twentieth Century Limited.

In Chicago I selected offices around the corner from the Majestic Theatre, hired an office staff, and an agent who knew the Middle West, and we started to scout for new acts. We covered all sorts of theatres, even burlesque houses and dives, hoping to unearth budding talent. One day in a small theatre the voice of a singer caught my attention. It was neither a good nor a bad voice, but it had incredible sincerity. It was stirring, pulsating. The slender young man, who looked to be about nineteen, worked in blackface with a partner in whiteface, and whistled between his songs. I sought him out backstage and asked him to come to our new offices the next day.

I had just had a fine new checkered suit delivered from my tailor, and it was lying uncovered in the box when the singer came in. I had a contract ready for him, but the suit seemed to interest him more. He ogled it, felt the material, and wondered how he'd look in it. I got his attention long enough for him to sign the contract. Then I contemplated the signature for a moment and tested it verbally.

"Al Jolson . . . not a bad name. I won't have to change it," I decided.

"I sure do like that suit," he said. "Couldn't you sell it to me and have your tailor make you up another one like it?"

"Oh, all right—take it," I said. "It cost me $60."

"I'll send you six sawbucks out of my first week's salary," Jolson promised.

I got him his first New York booking right away, but I never saw the money for the suit. I reminded him of it years later, while we were playing golf at the Hillcrest Country Club.

"Forgot it completely," he said, but offered to play a match for it right then and there. And so I lost my suit for the second time.

Although I never got the $60, in 1944 Al Jolson made an unqualified gift of something I needed very much and which would have cost me $25,000 on the open market. I wanted him to sing "Swanee" in *Rhapsody in Blue,* which I produced independently at Warner Brothers Studio, his brief appearance in the picture depicting his own actual introduction at the Winter Garden of George Gershwin's first song hit. When it came time to pick up his check, he refused it. "I did this for Jesse," he told Jack Warner.

William Morris lost the battle of the theatres to the United Booking Offices. I went back to Manhattan after six gusty months in

Chicago, and plunged into producing with more fervor than ever. Wanting a spot to break in new acts away from New York, I leased a dark theatre in Yonkers, had it remodeled, and changed the name from the Doric to the Orpheum. We opened it in December 1907 with my latest hit, "The Pianophiends," a musical novelty featuring a concert pianist at a grand, flanked by two uprights on each side, on which four boys and four girls played duets and ensembles. The scene of the miniature musical comedy represented a piano salesroom on Fifth Avenue, and it was rounded out with singing, dancing, and live poodles. My name appeared *seven* times on the program. I was proficient at persistent product identification long before radio and television.

From then on our acts leaned more heavily on good taste and smart presentation than on gaudy costumes and ostentatious scenery. And as usual, when I embarked on a trend, I got carried away. I yearned to trespass on Quality Street. I realized that, no matter how many headwaiters and bartenders knew my name, there was no theatrical prestige in producing musical acts for vaudeville—not the kind of prestige, say, that clung to the name of Charles Frohman, who controlled Sir James Barrie's plays, among others. The monarchs of legitimate drama looked down on vaudeville.

I had seen a one-act play by Barrie, *The Twelve Pound Look*, which Ethel Barrymore used as a curtain raiser for *Alice-Sit-by-the-Fire*, and I concocted the idea of booking it as a headline vaudeville attraction. A tidbit of genuine literary merit might startle the customers, but I was sure they would love Barrie and also take Barrymore to their hearts if we could make a substantial enough offer to overcome whatever prejudices she might have against stepping on a variety stage. If not Barrymore, we could try to get another top-flight actress from the legitimate theatre.

Several times I walked up and down in front of the Empire Theatre, where Frohman had his offices, without working up the courage to go in. Finally I made it to the elevator, went up to his suite, and sent my card in with a request to see the producer.

A large man came out and introduced himself as Alf Hayman. "Mr. Frohman is busy," he said flatly. "You may talk to me."

"I want to make arrangements with Mr. Frohman," I told him, "for performance rights to *The Twelve Pound Look* in a chain of theatres."

Hayman smiled faintly as though my avowed object was not quite fantastic enough to be amusing. "Mr. Frohman would not be interested."

"May I come back when he isn't busy?" I asked.

"Mr. Frohman is busy all day, every day," Hayman said with finality. He retreated back into his office.

The insulting brush-off rankled in my mind. I couldn't leave it alone. I wanted more than ever to be associated with a serious and worthy production. So I went back to the Frohman office a few weeks later and stipulated that I didn't want to speak to anyone except Charles Frohman. Alf Hayman came out.

"You can't see Mr. Frohman and you can't put Barrie in vaudeville—is that clear?" he said by way of greeting.

It made me mad clear through. But there was nothing I could do about it—except change my tailor and outfit myself in more conservative clothes!

Always on the prowl for a fresh idea or a tune worth whistling, I went uptown to Columbia University one night to catch an undergraduate show called *The Ides of March*. It was pretty good, so I referred to the program credits—"Music by Deems Taylor. Book by William Le Baron." After talking to the two seniors I decided that Taylor had no particular talent, but hired Le Baron to write my next vaudeville sketch. He proved an invaluable and dependable collaborator. I would dream up a title and the embryo of an idea for a new production, mull it over with him, and in a few days he'd be back with a finished act, branded with his own sparkling originality. In rapid succession he wrote and we produced "The Red Heads," starring James B. Carson, "In a Music Box," "The Song Shop," "The Antique Girl," starring Mae Busch, "At the Country Club," and "The Trained Nurses," starring Clarke and Bergman. With each one his royalties went up $25 a week.

We went together to a performance of *The Merry Widow* and the "Merry Widow Waltz" enthralled me.

"I wish we'd thought of that!" I declared, swinging into a brisk walk.

"If we work fast, maybe we can," Bill bantered, shoving his hands into his tux pockets and jogging along to keep up with me. He didn't share my enthusiasm for furious marches down wind-blistered streets after the theatre.

I got hold of a new waltz that was enjoying a vogue in Paris, renamed it "The Love Waltz," and built an act around it, with Robert

Hood Bowers' music, and starring the fragile beauty Audrey Maple, a tenor named Alfred Kapler, and John Bunny, who some years later became the first great popular comedian of the silent screen. "The Love Waltz" lived up to its romantic title by having the dance partners kiss from one end of the stage to the other, a rather broad Continental touch which no doubt helped the show to break vaudeville records all over the country.

For once I was stumped for an idea to top the last one, so I decided it was time for a vacation. I went to Long Lake in the Adirondacks with my mother and sister, and there at the Sagamore Hotel I got the best idea I ever had in my life. Nearly always when one project was nearing completion, it touched off a new idea, chain-smoker fashion. So perhaps this one caught fire from "The Love Waltz." It was a conflagration!

The Love Waltz

It was the first time I had money in my pocket and set aside time to do nothing, and I couldn't turn the tempo off. I rushed to the lake, hired a canoe, paddled furiously, scanned the mountains and wondered what was on the other side, inquired about the fishing, paced the grounds, ran back, and changed to white flannels and blue coat for dinner. In two hours I was tired of my vacation. I had picked a place to do nothing where there was nothing to do. Already I was hopelessly bored.

I stepped into the dining room with my mother and Blanche, wondering how I was going to stand the strain of an idle existence for two whole weeks. The orchestra leader recognized me and signalized our entrance with the strains of "The Love Waltz." Heads turned curiously and I found myself looking into the most lustrous, distracting eyes I'd ever seen in years of appraising feminine pulchritude. They were set in a face without make-up, under a towering aureole of

auburn curls. There was about the face such a spiritual air of innocence and sweetness that I lost consciousness of everything else.

All through dinner I kept meeting those melting eyes. Two weeks
suddenly seemed all too brief an interlude to spend in this heavenly
retreat. But I had altered my plans about spending the time doing
nothing. After dinner I made haste to learn from the manager that
the girl was Miss Bessie Ginzberg from Boston and the two people at
her table were her mother and a Mr. Lewis of Gloversville. I hadn't
noticed there was anyone else at her table.

I didn't see her do it, but Miss Ginzberg learned from the manager
that my name was Jesse Lasky and the young lady with me was not
my wife. The manager wasn't slow in recognizing his duty. He introduced us before the dancing started.

I asked her to dance—to her escort's visible torment. He swept
Blanche out on the dance floor, where he could follow us around with
baleful glares. Miss Ginzberg was a charming dancer, and I learned
that she had studied at the Boston Conservatory to be a concert pianist. If Blanche and I had taken the scholarships we had been
offered there, I reflected, I might have met this vision several years
earlier.

Before the dance was over, I asked her to climb a mountain with
me the next morning. She promised she would if her mother gave her
consent. I devoted the rest of the evening to subtle attentions to
her mother's comfort—a glass of lemonade, a fan, an extra cushion for
her rocking chair . . . And for once I didn't mind my mother's inevitable bragging about the brilliant accomplishments of her two children. I even had Blanche play for me while I bravely sang "The
Rosary," after Bessie confided that her mother was fond of the song.

The strategy worked. Mrs. Ginzberg gave permission for her daughter to accompany me the next day, thereby putting me in such a lofty
daze that it was almost superfluous to climb a mountain.

Bessie made the mistake of wearing high-heeled shoes for the hike
—but how can I call it a mistake when it gave me an excuse to steady
her elbow practically all the way? We talked for hours, our initial shy-
ness gone, about our families, the theatre, mountain-climbing, music
. . . the myriad things two young people in love talk about when it
doesn't matter what they talk about. We climbed to the top and were
back down the mountain before I realized I hadn't taken my eyes off
her to see what was on the other side of the mountain! By the time
we returned, her Mr. Lewis had fled back to Gloversville in pique.

We had a picnic under the trees at the lake's edge and then went for a canoe ride. I thought how dramatic it would be to rescue such a lovely, slender girl from drowning. The wish must have been father to the thought. There is absolutely nothing easier to arrange in a canoe than a rescue at sea. The production was on less than heroic scale, however—as it turned out, the water didn't come up to her waist. Years later Theodore Dreiser wrote *An American Tragedy* and I made a picture from it. I have never claimed he plagiarized the idea from our American Farce.

I couldn't go back to New York without knowing whether she felt as I did. Walking to the village hand in hand on the second day after we met, I said, "Bessie—do you think you could ever be true to one man?"

She said, "I don't think so—you see what happened to Harry Lewis."

But I didn't mean Harry Lewis. I asked her to think it over some more and tell me the next day.

A woman has a right to change her mind. So the next day she thought she could be true to one man. With that settled we kissed and considered ourselves engaged. She hadn't realized the first time I asked her that I was proposing. But her mother could tell it a mile off and telegraphed an S O S to Bessie's father. He took the next train from Boston.

Bessie's mother was reminding her darkly that I was a theatrical man from New York and she was answering that that's what she liked about me—I wasn't prosaic and conservative like all the Boston men she knew. Blanche and my mother were asking me if I was sure it wasn't just the lake and the vacation and not having enough to do. The hotel was vibrating with the romance.

Bessie's father arrived after a sleepless night on the train and in no mood to trifle with an unproper non-Bostonian of suspect occupation. But we all settled on having a big, embarrassed lunch together before getting down to particulars, and it must have come as quite a disappointment to Mr. Ginzberg that he liked me. He was a remarkable and courageous man who had smuggled himself out of Russia at the age of fourteen, come steerage to America, and sold matches in Maine as the first step in building a considerable fortune. After lunch he took me aside and asked me why I wanted to marry his daughter and I said because she had beautiful hair and mentioned some other reasons. Evidently they were satisfactory.

"If you haven't done anything about the ring," he confided, "I can be of some help to you. I'm in the diamond business."

We were married in Boston the following December. Just before we left for Atlantic City on our honeymoon, Bessie surreptitiously implored her father to give her some money. He quite naturally wanted to know what she needed money for the minute we were married. I had represented myself as being able to supply lavishly anything her heart desired.

"If I want to buy something, I just couldn't ask Jesse for money," Bessie insisted. "I think I'd rather die than ask him for one penny."

"You'll get over that," her father promised, peeling off a twenty.

She was very young, and had never known any city except Boston.

I know now that I was the blindest and most inconsiderate of husbands in those first years of our marriage. I truly wanted to give Bessie everything she could wish for, but I didn't give her what she craved more than anything else—a home of her own where she could have a domestic routine and time alone with her husband. And, true to the inborn timidity that prompted her to ask her father for money as soon as we were married, she never once told me what she wanted.

I lived in a well-ordered home—a factory would be a better name —and I saw no reason to disrupt its smooth schedule and set up a wasteful duplication of effort just because I had got married. My mother handled the household like a field marshal. Besides, Blanche and I were so wrapped up in our theatrical projects and worked so closely together that neither of us could have stood it to leave off business when we left the office. We talked, ate, and slept vaudeville. There was plenty of room in the large apartment for one more, so I simply brought my wife home to the family, and then was immediately swallowed up in the frantic turmoil of my work.

My poor Bessie had absolutely nothing to do. And nothing to talk about, since she didn't understand a word of the stage vernacular that flew above her head. She was left out of everything, just a bewildered spectator. I wasn't even aware that anything was wrong. In fact I took pride in being such a good provider and so indulgent with my new bride that she could spend the whole day at the piano. That annoyed my mother for some reason, so Bessie gave up her music entirely. I suppose my mother thought her daughter-in-law should be trying to advance my career by spending her time at bridge parties with the wives of my associates. But Bessie never did care for the social game. She still doesn't, although she learned to be a charming hostess when occasion demands.

All of New York was a new experience for her, and I could have shared her delight at discovering its many facets for the first time— a chance that could never come again. But I was always too busy to take her places. I did promise to meet her at the Waldorf for lunch when I could spare the time, and I made it after changing the date three times. She was in a dither of excitement over planning what to wear for lunch at America's most famous hotel. But even that small pleasure was denied her. Blanche, an expert whose word was not to be questioned in any matter of costuming, told her exactly what to wear.

At last we were alone together—in a public dining room—for the first time since our honeymoon. But this rare moment of intimacy didn't last long. Unwittingly Bessie spoiled it herself by musing rapturously, "Imagine *me—lunching at the Waldorf!*"

My fist hit the table so hard it startled her. "*At the Waldorf!*" I shouted. I couldn't wait to get back to the office.

Incidentally, "At the Waldorf" was the biggest hit we ever had.

My frightened little convent-bred wife didn't admit until many years later that she spent a good part of that first year staying in her bed, crying her heart out. And when our first child was on the way, she begged her father to let her get a divorce and come home. He wouldn't hear of it. He told her gently that she had married a good man, and that if she were patient, things would eventually work out and she would have a happy life. But her ordeal was far from over. After the baby was born, she was scarcely allowed a fleeting glimpse of him. My mother hired a nurse for him and took complete charge of his schedule with the irrefutable logic that she had raised two wonderful children, whereas Bessie was hardly more than a child herself and had no experience whatever in such matters.

But Bessie *had* picked her baby's name, and no one raised a word of objection to her choice of Jesse Lenard Lasky, Jr. It was the only way she could be sure of keeping a Jesse around the house. After fulfilling my paternal obligations by attending the premiere of that production I had sailed for Europe with Blanche the day after Jesse, Jr., was born!

The Folly
of the Folies

On my two previous trips to Europe I had been dazzled by the intimate but lavish cabarets and the magnificent music halls in Vienna, Berlin, and Paris. They represented the ultimate in catering to sophisticated pleasure seekers. The Alhambra and Empire music halls in London featured gorgeously costumed show girls, along with exquisite ballet productions, and boasted pit orchestras of sixty to seventy-five men, whereas our best vaudeville theatres had only twelve to eighteen musicians. An elegant decorative touch was supplied by the most luxurious courtesans of London parading all evening on the promenades of those rival English music halls, as though at a fashion show, for the benefit of the London Johnnies in white ties and tails, who could watch the ballets at the same time, thus combining pleasure with pleasure. Men in tuxedos were considered only half dressed and weren't allowed on the promenade for closer inspection of the merchandise.

America had nothing to compare with the opulent entertainment of Leicester Square or the fabulous Folies Bergère and Casino de Paris in Paris. But it seemed to me the public would welcome a theatre-restaurant where they could dine superbly while watching a superlative show, welcome it as avidly as it had endorsed other Continental conceptions, such as my psuedo-importation of The Stunning Grenadiers.

I told Henry Harris that I was convinced that if we built a Continental type of music hall in New York City and offered revues comparable to the Ziegfeld Follies, in combination with a cuisine in a class with Delmonico's, the achievement would remain a monument to both of us for the rest of our lives. Moreover the elaborate shows we produced for the theatre would provide a steady stream of traveling units as well. He conceded it was the most extravagant idea I'd ever had, and possibly the best. He agreed to put up his share of the backing.

We got a long-term lease on a site on Forty-sixth Street just off Broadway, an ideal location in the heart of the theatrical district. Charles Dillingham's Globe Theatre was right across the street and the Gaiety, managed by Sam Harris and George M. Cohan, abutted on our property but fronted on Broadway. Since we were frankly inspired by Parisian éclat, we had no hesitancy in making the first cabaret in America a namesake of the original Folies Bergère. Blanche took almost complete charge of the interior decorations and, later, the costuming.

I could hardly hope to have a Continental music hall without Continental talent, so as soon as the building was designed to our specifications and plans approved, I waited only long enough to be told that I had a son before sailing for Europe to seek stellar attractions. In Paris I picked a renowned soubrette, Janette Denarber, and Martha Lenclud, justly famed as the most beautiful woman in Paris. At the Wintergarten in Berlin I found The Pender Troupe, eight acrobats on stilts, including a ten-year-old boy whose stilts were so high that he had to be put on and taken off them from a ladder, and bend down to show his head under the proscenium. The lad's name was Archie Leach. In later years when we were both working at RKO, Cary Grant reminded me that the ladder on which he started his climb to fame in this country was the one he used on Forty-sixth Street to mount his stilts.

From the Alhambra in London I brought over the ballet *Temptations* intact and commissioned its celebrated ballet master, Alfredo Curti, to do all our choreography. I also discovered a talented mimic performing under the name of Muriel Harding in London. I engaged her with the understanding that she'd use a foreign-sounding name when she embarked for New York, and talk with an accent to the newspaper reporters. I didn't want anyone to get the idea that my importations had come over from Brooklyn.

She asked me what kind of accent I preferred, and modeled a few for me—British, Scottish, French, etc. We settled on Russian and the name of Olga Petrova to go with it. When the New York press met her, she spread the accent on as thick as caviar, with a questioning look at me to see whether it passed inspection. I approved thoroughly, as did all of America. And such a peerless mime was Muriel Harding that she kept up that pretense all her life. After the Folies Bergère engagement, she appeared in a Henry Harris play, and then I booked her in a vaudeville tour. Years later I gave her a picture contract at $3500 a week, but in all the time I knew her after she stepped off that boat as a Russian she never dropped her phony accent for a minute. She actually became the thing she was imitating!

In our advertising for the Folies Bergère we called it "more Parisian than Paris," and in at least one detail it was. Instead of merely having nude murals on the boxes, we had three-dimensional nude murals *in* the boxes. When a bugle sounded in the rear of the theatre (There's that bugle again!) lights disclosed Jean Marcel's Living Statues, another high-ranking group from Europe, posing gracefully in little more than make-up, which lent them the appearance of having been dunked in a flour barrel.

Of the "200 artists" our opening bill boasted half were chorus girls, but the other half included such names as Ethel Levey (ex-wife of George M. Cohan), who was starred, Otis Harlan, Kathleen Clifford, Laddie Cliff, Ada Lewis, Taylor Holmes, and Grace La Rue.

I should have counted the performers before we had the theatre built. While it was being completed, the ballet groups, chorus, and other entertainers rehearsed simultaneously on stage, in the lobby, in the balcony, and on the stairways of the Hudson Theatre in the liveliest medley since the Tower of Babel. When we moved to the Folies Bergère Theatre, we realized we had provided only enough dressing-room space for a normal musical-comedy house, and we actually had the full complement of a two-act musical revue, a complete vaudeville bill, and a ballet company. We had to lease a couple of adjacent brownstone houses and renovate them into spill-over dressing rooms. The traffic back and forth across the alleyway was like a buffalo stampede.

We did have enough foresight, however, to insulate thoroughly the kitchens underneath the theatre against food odors wafting upward.

A week before the opening night we had a scenic rehearsal on the stage and discovered we couldn't strike a big set in time for the following number. We'd have to put in a song or something using a drop curtain to cover the set change. In those days, when you needed a song for a show, you had only to drop a casual hint on Thirty-eighth Street, better known as Tin Pan Alley, and you'd have song writers in your hair like a flock of pigeons. I sent the word, and in about as much time as it takes to get from Thirty-eighth to Forty-sixth Street, a dark, dynamic twenty-three-year-old kid burst in with his pal, another song writer. He had never had a song in a show, but he blustered eagerly as all song writers do about every number they write.

"I've got a great song," he said. "It's new and different—just what you want."

His friend, Ted Snyder, backed him up. "It'll be a terrific hit," he insisted.

The dark-haired boy moved over to the piano and played his tune, nervously singing the lyrics in a voice that wouldn't win any medals. I'm a typical enthusiast myself and I was prepared from their impassioned build-up to listen to the greatest song in the world, but the rollicking rhythm was so different from anything I'd ever heard that I wouldn't even let him finish it.

"I tell you it's a great song," the little guy insisted.

"I know what I want," I told him heatedly, "and I *don't* want 'Ta-da-ta-da! Ta-da-ta-da!'"

"Well, I have another song," he said, and sang "I Beg Your Pardon, Dear Old Broadway." The moment I heard it I knew it was exactly what we needed to cover the scenery shifting. We gave it to Ethel Levey, and the song writer was overjoyed to get one of his tunes in a Broadway show. It meant that he had arrived.

The song I turned down *was* the greatest song in the world— "Alexander's Ragtime Band"! But "I Beg Your Pardon, Dear Old Broadway" became a hit too. You can't go far wrong on Irving Berlin.

Everything about the Folies Bergère was unheard of in New York, including the prices! It had a champagne bar, a balcony promenade, the first midnight performance in this country, at which an expanding stage slid out over the orchestra pit and put the performers on handshaking intimacy with the first-row patrons. Such now-commonplace service items as glass-topped tables with doilies under the plates, silent flag signals on silver ash trays to call waiters without disturbing performers or other diners, and sealed programs for sale were so novel in 1911 as to be conversation pieces. Even the word *cabaret* was so strange that we felt obliged to specify in advertisements that it was "pronounced cabaray."

Our admission price of $2.50 was half a dollar higher than the Ziegfeld Follies' box-office top, but opening-night seats were in such demand that they were auctioned off at The Lambs' club. Choice orchestra seats went for $25 and $30, while the $20 balcony boxes brought $450 to $700 apiece. New York's elite turned out in full dress, bedecked in the family jewels. Diamond Jim Brady occupied two chairs in the front row. In fact he came night after night to watch one of the chorus beauties, Justine Johnstone, who was only fifteen then, but already as luscious as Marilyn Monroe today. She stood out all the more because she was never quite in step with the other girls. She was later to have her own smart supper club on Forty-fourth Street.

Our patrons were introduced to the novelty of dining to the strains of a concealed gypsy orchestra imported from Europe, and remaining seated for a lavish three-hour show starting with a revue titled *Hell*, by Rennold Wolf, followed by the ballet *Temptations* and closing with a topical revue, *Gabby*, by the brothers Harry B. Smith and Robert Smith. Harry had done the books for all the Ziegfeld Follies. The most prolific librettist of his day, he collaborated on fourteen Victor Herbert operettas, and once had six of his shows on Broadway simultaneously. The *Gabby* score was by Paul Lincke, famous for *The Glow-Worm*, in collaboration with Maurice Levi and Edmond Diet. For the record, the revues were directed by George Marion, with dances and numbers staged by Ned Wayburn and R. H. Burnside.

The final curtain came down at eleven o'clock. As soon as the theatre was cleared, supper patrons were seated and served and the entirely different cabaret show went on from 11:15 to 1 A.M. Among the ten acts were Olga Petrova, The Pender Troupe, and Ina Claire, who made such an impression on Henry Harris with her impersonations that he slated her for a legitimate-stage debut in *The Quaker Girl*, along with Olga Petrova and Elda Furry (who became Hedda Hopper the day after the play closed). Mae West made her first Broadway appearance in the Folies Bergère, so successfully that I subsequently booked her in vaudeville.

The gypsy orchestra shifted their playing to the lobby for the latecomers, and a brilliant piano team in evening clothes took over inside on a grand piano with two keyboards that I had picked up in Europe.

But the first night had its dreadful moments, too. During the show a water pipe in the rear of the theatre broke and flooded the floor, ruining some regal finery. And while I was contemplating the lawsuits that might result from this catastrophe, Harry Pilcer fell and broke his arm as he was starting a dance with Minerva Coverdale down a grand staircase. The show surmounted these mishaps, however, and the audience was so reluctant to bring the memorable night to an end, even after many of them had been there seven hours for dinner, supper, and both shows, that they wouldn't go home. I remember Willie Collier, the actor, and Vincent Bryan, who wrote the music to Gus

Edwards' lyrics for the song hit *Tammany*, taking over the stage and doing an impromptu song-and-dance routine at 4 A.M.

Harris and I felt sure that we would make a fortune from the venture. But the leading New York *World* critic the next morning gave the impression that only a millionaire could afford such luxurious fare as the Folies Bergère offered. Our whole operation was designed for and geared to the tastes and purses of the general public, but the public assumed from reports of that gala first night that it was far too rich for their blood, and never investigated further. Before we could break the myth down, it was too late. Heavy spenders, unaffected by such publicity, filled the place to capacity for a few weeks, until time for their flight from the city's summer heat.

Our overhead was so high that in order to break even we had to keep the theatre in almost continuous operation from noon until early morning with capacity crowds. In a day when theatres weren't air-cooled! We had luncheon matinees on Tuesday, Thursday, and Saturday, with Tea de luxe at the four-o'clock intermission, and Sunday-evening dining concerts to conform with a peculiar law in force at the time. (For years it wasn't legal to wear costumes on the stage on Sunday. The same entertainments could be given as on weekdays, but they had to be called "concerts" and performed in street clothes. Al Jolson gave his Sunday shows at the Winter Garden for many years without costumes or burnt cork.)

I learned from this experience that in show business it is never enough to be artistic. You have to be practical as well.

It seems to me now that the Folies Bergère probably had all the ingredients for a smashing success save one—a little two-by-four square of hardwood. The vogue for ballroom dancing, spearheaded by Vernon and Irene Castle, hadn't begun yet. It was still scandalous to dance in a public place. Only a year or two later that prejudice was swept aside, and then night clubs blossomed like magic, with café society paying much higher tabs for much leaner values than we had offered.

So the Folies Bergère closed. We had spent more than we planned to on the theatre, the extra dressing rooms, and the glittering show itself. Henry Harris and I had to make good on the obligations. I lost everything I had accumulated—about $100,000—salvaging only the framed first dollar taken in at the box-office. But Harris lost much more money than I did, and much more than money.

We renamed the theatre the Fulton. The Folies Bergere "FB" emblem remained dotted through the tilework and French decorative scheme like a lucky symbol, until the house was again rechristened as the Helen Hayes Theatre not so long ago, and it does seem to have been lucky for some memorable first nights I have attended there through the years, including those of *Dracula*, *Waterloo Bridge*, Leonard Sillman's first *New Faces*, *Deep Are the Roots*, and *Arsenic and Old Lace*. And although not enough people would pay $2.50 for the finest entertainment available in 1911 to keep our Folies Bergère alive longer than five months, that same theatre was to house George Axelrod's *Seven Year Itch* for almost three years at a $5.75 top.

But the FB emblem was not a lucky symbol for my loyal, esteemed partner. After the production folded, Henry B. Harris wanted a rest from the strain and worry we had been through, so he took a trip to Europe, and was among the unfortunates who chose to return on the maiden voyage of the *Titanic*.

We Three

The Folies Bergère seemed so successful on the surface it was hard to believe it was a failure. The cast was stunned, and some of the chorus girls cried. After the last performance I made my rounds of regretful good-bys and gloomily started walking up Broadway to the Pasadena Apartments at Sixty-first. I think the name swayed us when we moved in—it was reminiscent of California.

Broadway is a lonely place when you're broke.

I remembered the family's dour estimate of the life I was choosing when we left San Francisco, and Aunt Jenny's warning that I was cutting myself off from California forever. Perhaps I should never have left California. I might now be slowly but steadily working up in some stable business instead of gambling on the unpredictable vagaries of the amusement world. And my little son might be growing up in more security, and where there were lawns and flowers instead of cement and iron and billboards.

In this dejected frame of mind it seemed like some sort of omen when I looked up and was startled to see a California scene with a group of Indians and padres against a colorful mission background. It was a big billboard advertising Mission Coffee.

From habit anything that struck me forcefully became the basis for a vaudeville act. A plot started brewing in my mind around the billboard figures. The beautiful girl in the mission had been found by the Indians, taken to the padres, and brought up by them. The hero would be a surveyor, laying out a railroad line. He would fall in love with the girl and be obliged to tell her that the railroad he worked for was going to destroy the only home she could remember.

I knew right then what I was going to do next. I'd bring the billboard to life in an operetta called *California*. By the time I reached home, my depression was completely gone. The idea kept growing over Sunday, and Monday I went to see Mrs. H. C. DeMille, a play broker of high repute in the Hudson Theatre building, where I had recently had my own offices. Often we had exchanged casual greetings when we met in the halls, and I also acknowledged her son, William, a playwright who had to his credit a number of hits including *Strongheart*, *The Warrens of Virginia*, and *The Woman*. But she also had a younger son, Cecil, who looked at me in a way that made me uncomfortable or ignored me in a way that made me more uncomfortable. The chilly feeling was mutual and we passed each other without speaking for a year.

I told Mrs. DeMille that I would like to engage William to do my operetta. She advised me that William was writing a new play for David Belasco and therefore wasn't available, but Cecil might undertake it. Cecil, it seemed, had written a very short-lived play, *The Royal Mounted*, and collaborated with his brother on *The Genius*, which likewise failed to catch on. He had, moreover, sold *The Return of Peter Grimm* to Belasco, who later rewrote it and attached his own name to it. Cecil also had been an actor, appearing as the elder brother of a child actress named Mary Pickford in William's successful play, *The Warrens of Virginia*.

I had no intention of entrusting my great idea to a lesser luminary than William, and certainly not to an actor who had made a couple of stabs at playwrighting, so I tried to make a strategic withdrawal. But Mrs. DeMille's motherly instinct made a powerful alliance with her business interests, and there was no escape for me without offending her when she insisted I step into a small rear office and meet Cecil.

Cecil and I surveyed each other suspiciously. Much against my better judgment I hemmed and hawed through the story thread of my operetta. But Cecil's eyes were taking on a glint of insight and I could sense his imagination was filling in the gaps, mentally picturing how he would dramatize it. When I finished, he leaned forward and exclaimed, "Say, I like that!"

The minute he said, "I like that," I liked him. And I've never stopped.

Tossing ideas back and forth, we worked ourselves into a lather of inspiration. I agreed to engage him to write and stage the operetta for $100 advance and $25 a week royalty. In my straitened circumstances it was a lot of money, but my mother came to my rescue with her modest savings account.

I secured Robert Hood Bowers to do the score, had a beautiful mission set built, and began rehearsals on the stage of the Longacre Theatre, where I had moved my office: We took *California* out of town for a tryout, and it was a success. We continued our working association on a second operetta and a few other *divertissements* for vaudeville.

My sister was again becoming weary of theatrical activities, although she didn't hate the production end as she had the performing. Still, she frequently voiced a desire to marry a solid, staid businessman and have done with the frantic pace of show business, and her dream seemed about to come true. Bessie had introduced her to a solid, staid businessman named Sam Goldfish, who had started as a glove cutter in her uncle's factory in Gloversville, New York, and became a very successful glove salesman. As an old friend of Bessie's family, he sometimes dropped in to see her on his frequent trips to New York, and then began dropping in even oftener to court Blanche.

But while Blanche was trying to get out of show business, her ardent suitor was trying to get into it. He wasn't keeping his mind on his gloves. He had been transfixed by a two-reel Western picture, *Broncho Billy's Adventures*, early in 1911, and had been nosing around the General Film Company ever since. After they got married, Blanche brought her husband home and installed him in the family circle, just as I had done with my wife. At the dinner table Sam would tell me I should look into the film business.

There were no feature pictures then. The movies consisted of short-reelers made by Vitagraph, Edison, Biograph, and IMP in New York, the Lubin Manufacturing Company of Philadelphia, the Essanay and

Selig companies of Chicago, and a few others. These shorts had one outstanding merit which made them a valuable adjunct to a vaudeville bill. When a theatre played continuous vaudeville, the patrons were apt to sit through several repetitions of the show and keep other customers from getting seats. But astute managers discovered that the average picture of those days would empty a theatre more effectively than a stench bomb, for practically the same reason. Consequently these one- and two-reelers came to be known as "chasers."

When Sam kept urging me to start a picture company, I told him hotly that I would have nothing to do with a business that chased people out of the theatres, even though I might be grateful it did, from the standpoint of a vaudeville producer. One day I became so incensed at his insistence that I said, "Sam, I'm a *showman*. I wonder if you know what a showman is? I'll tell you. A showman is a man who creates entertainment. It may be a side show, a circus, vaudeville, a legitimate play, or opera, but it's something the audience wants to see and will pay to see. I've had years of experience in show business. I've even built a theatre. True, it failed, but it was an artistic triumph. So don't ask me to make pictures—that's the last thing in the world I'd do."

The man I was so condescendingly explaining showmanship to was to become one of the world's great showmen—after he had changed his name to Goldwyn.

I kept on collaborating with Cecil on ideas for new vaudeville acts. We lunched together at the Claridge every day and would meet again in the evening. We used to daydream about exploring the South Seas someday, and started to save money for a yacht by consecrating a box to that worthy cause and dropping small change in it whenever we met. One Saturday night, discovering the yacht fund had swollen to $100, we cruised down to our favorite haunts in Greenwich Village and turned our mythical yacht in on more tangible schooners.

We both loved the outdoors and decided to take a month's vacation in the Maine woods, for which we bought outfits that would have been adequate for an expedition into the wilds of Tibet. A guide took us in a canoe up the west branch of the Penobscot River and then by portage through rough and seldom-penetrated country to Hunt's Camp on Kidney Pond. There he left us on our own, and with sixty-pound packs on our backs we explored what we supposed was virgin country until we found evidence of former habitation. One night we stumbled on to a long-deserted cabin on the shore of a wild lake just as it was beginning to rain. We gloated over the discovery of such opportune shelter and I sat down on the lower of two bunks. It collapsed in a cloud of dust and a couple of displaced bats whirred around.

Our imaginations began whirring around too, and by mutual suggestion we had shortly built up the conviction that someone had been murdered in the cabin. Loath to share the lodgings with ethereal occupants, we took our waterproof double sleeping bag out in the pouring rain, covered our heads with a tent of mosquito netting laced with leather thongs, just in case the rain stopped, and went to sleep. We should have stayed inside with the ghosts. How a bull moose managed to get entangled in the leather thongs without stepping on our faces I'll never know. We suddenly awoke with the animal pawing over us. He snorted and crashed away through the woods in a skirt of Abercrombie & Fitch's best mosquito netting.

These mild adventures weren't enough to satisfy Cecil's high-spirited nature. He had the zest of a Richard Harding Davis. I could see that he was getting restless. Then at lunch one day he said, "Jesse, I'm pulling out. Broadway's all right for you—you're doing well. But I can't live on the royalties I'm getting, my debts are piling up, and I want to chuck the whole thing. Besides, there's a revolution going on in Mexico and I'm going down and get in on it—maybe write about it. That's what I need—a stimulating and colorful change of scene."

I didn't want to lose my best friend. I was groping for some way to divert him from his intention. All I could think of at the moment was Sam's harping topic of conversation, and I grabbed at it. To keep Cecil from doing something foolish alone, I proposed we do something foolish together. I said, "If you want adventure, I've got an even better idea—let's make some movies!"

His eyes gleamed, and before I was over the shock of hearing my own unconsidered suggestion, Cecil put out his hand, grabbed mine, and said, "Let's!"

A portion of the motion-picture industry was built on that one word.

When I saw that I was stuck with it, I began to squirm. I certainly didn't want to be identified with the sort of shabby potboilers that were this country's contribution to films up to that time. In fact I had turned down a proposition from a couple of promoters who wanted me to lend the prestige of my name to a film-shorts company for a consideration of $10,000, telling them my reputation as a high-class vaudeville producer was not on the auction block. But then I had seen a worthy four-reel feature starring Sarah Bernhardt with Lou

Tellegen. It had been produced in France and imported for exhibition by Adolph Zukor, formerly connected with a penny arcade and now starting the Famous Players Film Company.

With no enthusiasm for my own hasty proposal, but with my usual admiration for European examples of entertainment, I said, "Cecil, if we're going to go into this at all, let's for heaven's sake do it in a big way and make a *long* picture like *Queen Elizabeth*."

After lunch we walked down Forty-fourth Street to The Lambs' club, and there destiny took a hand in shaping not our ends but our beginnings, as far as the motion-picture business was concerned. We ran into Dustin Farnum, a matinee idol who had scored a triumph on Broadway in *The Virginian* and shared honors with his brother William and a child actress named Mary Miles Minter in *The Littlest Rebel.*

We asked Farnum if he would like to star in a long picture we wanted to make. He looked around the room and spotted Edwin Milton Royle, author of *The Squaw Man.* That play, which curiously combined London drawing-room settings with Wild West scenery, had been a *tour de force* for William Faversham, and I suspect Farnum may have coveted the role and lost it to his rival. At any rate he said, "You get Royle to sell you *The Squaw Man* and I might agree to join you."

Sounding out Royle, we found him vulnerable to an offer, so I called Sam Goldfish and told him we were in business.

The Jesse L. Lasky Feature Play Company was organized with myself president, Sam general manager, and Cecil director-general. We each held a quarter of the stock and Farnum agreed to accept the other quarter in lieu of salary for his acting stint. We had only $20,000 capital and had agreed to pay $15,000 for the play.

At first we planned to make the picture across the Hudson River at Fort Lee, New Jersey, where a good many one-reel Westerns and other short subjects were being filmed. But I didn't think a two-mile trip would satisfy Cecil's thirst for adventure, so I recklessly tossed in the suggestion that an Indian picture ought to be made in real Indian country—like Flagstaff, Arizona. I remembered seeing some Indians in Flagstaff while traveling with Hermann the Great.

Cecil was delighted with the proposal, as I had anticipated, but Dustin Farnum balked. He said he didn't mind being paid off with stock as long as he could live at home and work across the river, but he insisted on having his $5000 in spot cash before going West. The whole project threatened to collapse—until I talked Bessie's uncle and brother into buying Farnum's stock. If he had hung onto his piece of paper for eight years, he could have sold it for nearly $2,000,000. But Farnum didn't do badly, even so, as the picture put him in the vanguard of early screen heroes, where he maintained a worshipful following for many years.

We hired a cameraman who owned a crank-handled movie camera, and Oscar Apfel, a director with experience on one- and two-reelers, to help Cecil get started. When it was time to leave for Flagstaff, I backed out. I had no great personal faith in the project and I couldn't see myself wasting time in Arizona when I had business to look after in the East. So I said good-by to the rest of them at the train and promised Cecil I'd come out if he needed me.

In the meantime Salesman Sam had learned enough about how pictures were booked to start selling states' rights for our initial production. A print was sold for a flat sum to service a specified territory and could be rerun in its assigned region till it wore out. A small state got only one print, a large state two, and a block like New England, four or five. Sam sold New York state rights for several thousand dollars, New England's for much more, then Pennsylvania, Ohio, and the Pacific coast. Before long we had nearly $60,000 worth of contracts. Sam was a master merchandiser, whether he was pushing a consignment of gloves or a motion picture not yet made by men who had never made one.

While these orders and advance payments were piling up, Cecil seemed to have disappeared. We hadn't heard a word from him for two weeks and we were worried. Finally a telegram arrived—but it wasn't from Flagstaff. It said: "FLAGSTAFF NO GOOD FOR OUR PURPOSE. HAVE PROCEEDED TO CALIFORNIA. WANT AUTHORITY TO RENT BARN IN PLACE CALLED HOLLYWOOD FOR $75 A MONTH. REGARDS TO SAM. CECIL."

Sam hit the ceiling. I insisted that Cecil must know what he was doing, although I really didn't feel too sure of it. When you're president of a company you assume is located in Flagstaff, Arizona, it's very disconcerting to have it turn up in a place you've never even heard of. Sam was all for calling the company back where we could keep an eye on it. We argued for hours. At last we agreed to let them stay and wired Cecil: "AUTHORIZE YOU TO RENT BARN BUT ON MONTH-TO-MONTH BASIS. DON'T MAKE ANY LONG COMMITMENT. REGARDS. JESSE AND SAM."

The reason for that cautious proviso was that we didn't have any definite plans beyond *The Squaw Man.* Sam may have convinced the states' rights buyers of our corporate soundness, but he himself was still hanging onto his job with the glove company, and I still had my fingers crossed.

Cecil had passed up Flagstaff as our shooting locale because the weather was bad when he stepped off the train in Arizona, and he suddenly realized there would be no facilities for processing the film there. But he knew there must be film laboratories in California, because, while no one had yet made a feature picture in the West, a few companies making one-reelers had moved there from the East to take advantage of cheaper land, labor, and materials and to benefit from the milder climate and more dependable sunlight. The latter was a potent economic factor in as much as artificial lighting was still unknown to motion pictures. (Sunlight didn't go out of style even after kliegs came in, because the early carbon-arc lamps had the intensity of an acetylene torch, making temporary blindness an occupational hazard for actors. After a scene the players would poultice their burning orbs with cooling slices of raw potatoes.)

The barn he rented at Selma and Vine streets had excellent accommodations for the cast of our horse opera, save for the *human* actors. Stalls were turned into offices, dressing rooms, and a projection room. One end of the barn was used as a storeroom. In a clearing made among the acres of orange and lemon trees that went with the barn a small wooden platform was built as an open stage. Production started on *The Squaw Man* on December 29, 1913. Before it was finished a few weeks later, Cecil had inveigled me into making a trip to the Coast, contending that my duty as president of the company was to be at my desk, which he had installed in the stall next to his.

I arrived at the old Santa Fe Depot in Los Angeles, called a taxi, and told the driver I wanted to go to Hollywood. He gave me a puzzled look but said, "Get in, boss—we'll find it."

He drove to the Alexandria, then the city's leading hotel, and had a conference with some other taxi drivers, who set his course out of the city over dirt roads, past endless orchards and an occasional farmhouse. We found Hollywood by the lone landmark that antedated even the movies, a sedate rest haven way out in the country, where city dwellers could get away from it all and relax in perfect tranquillity —the Hollywood Hotel—now the bustling site of three modern buildings. The taxi driver suggested that I make inquiries inside the hotel about where I wanted to go.

I told the clerk my name and explained that I was president of the Lasky Feature Play Company. "This is my first trip here and I'm not sure where our studio is located," I added. "Would you please direct me?"

"I'm sorry," said the clerk, "I never heard of it."

"Perhaps I should have told you that the director-general of the company is Cecil B. DeMille," I stated impressively.

"Never heard of him," the clerk said crisply.

Considerably crestfallen, I was starting toward the door when he called me back. "Tell you who might help you," he said. "Drive down this main road till you come to Vine Street. You can't miss it—it's a dirt road with a row of pepper trees right down the middle. Follow the pepper trees for about two blocks till you see an old barn. There's some movie folks working there that might know where your company is."

When I heard "barn," I knew I was on the right track. Sure enough, a sign identified the barn as the Jesse L. Lasky Feature Play Company.

My reception committee was waiting for me at the hitching posts in front of the barn—a dozen horses and a little boy stationed there to direct me inside. He led me to my stall, where I found a fresh bouquet on the desk, and then out the barn through the orange orchard to the stage, which had a clumsy arrangement of canvas diffusers over the top. These worked something like window shades to control the sunlight. It looked like a big raft with a tattered canvas canopy.

After the reluctant and conditional permission Sam and I gave for his rental of the barn Cecil had withheld an accounting of other expenditures, undoubtedly with the admirable motive of keeping our blood pressure down. Among other things he had rented a two-ton Ford truck. It was standing now in front of the stage, with "Jesse L. Lasky Feature Play Company" emblazoned prominently on its side. When he saw me coming, he ran out, grabbed my hand, summoned the company, made a speech of welcome, pushed me against the truck, and signaled the photographer. He knew I would automatically smile for a snapshot, and I think he wanted to send Sam photographic evidence of what would appear to be my happy endorsement of his extravagance in renting the truck.

I guess it was the first picture ever taken of a movie mogul's arrival in Hollywood.

I stayed that night at Cecil's very modest rented house in Cahuenga Canyon, but I don't think I slept much. I had never heard coyotes howling before.

The next morning his wife Constance gave us each a lunch pail which we carried to the studio, and at noon we had our sandwiches with coffee made on a little kerosene stove by the secretary. Her name was Ethel Wales, and she later became well known as a character actress.

Work stopped on the open stage as soon as the sun went behind a cloud. If it was a big cloud, the cast dispersed to dressing rooms or to the lunch wagon across the street, to come rushing back the minute the sun was out again. Picture actors of those days were often referred to as "The Sun Worshipers." It was a ritual for them to go to the window and appraise the weather as soon as they awoke in the morning. On a very cloudy day the cast didn't even show up, knowing there would be no shooting. But we took full advantage of the sunshine when we had it—there were no unions to frown on sixteen-hour days. If it looked like rain, the set was quickly covered with huge tarpaulins to protect the props.

Cold weather brought a special plague of problems. It caused tiny flashes of static electricity inside the cameras which ruined the film. We never knew until a batch had been developed whether it would have to be shot over. On a chilly day a group of drawing-room sophisticates in cutaways and low evening gowns might feature goose pimples, chattering teeth, and congealed breath. The only way we could have heated our bower in the orange grove was with smudge pots, and that would have blocked out the sun. The actors sometimes had to mouth their dialogue while holding back their breath so as not to give the impression that London drawing rooms were even colder than they notably were.

This was in January. By the following July we were making arctic scenes for *The Call of the North* (using salt for snow) at a temperature of 100°, Robert Edeson and the other players cocooned in heavy clothing and parkas, with melting make-up running in rivulets down their faces.

Location trips were very simply arranged. Today a location man goes out weeks in advance to scout and contract for the use of sites, and the company is transported to the selected locations on a coordinated schedule. But in those days, when we wanted to show a country church, say, the whole company set out in search of it. Cecil and I sometimes rode ahead on horseback, with the crew and cast following in two cars. When we found what we wanted, we stopped and shot a scene, then went on to the next setting we needed. No one ever objected to our trespassing or charged us for the use of his property. The scenery was always fresh and stimulating. Now it's all but impossible to find locations near Hollywood that aren't tedious and repetitious to the regular moviegoer. In order to give a modern audience the vicarious thrill of discovery it is necessary to take a company on location to Maine or Oregon or Ireland or Venice, and indeed today's film makers are prospecting the whole world for novel and exotic backgrounds to fill their widened screens.

We reveled in the outdoor life of picture-pioneering and dressed the part in boots, jeans, and lumberjack shirts, not to mention Cecil's pistol. Ten-gallon hats were not a part of the Western outfits we affected, because they would have been awkward while sighting into a camera. Instead, directors wore caps turned backward, and adopted leather leggings for the convenience of location scouting on horseback and as protection against cactus and rattlesnakes in the desert regions. Making a picture was outdoor work on or off location, since interiors were shot on the open stage and sets had no ceilings. But the directors clung to their riding breeches and reversed caps as a badge of their profession long after such garb ceased to serve a useful purpose. Cecil continued to dress for a steeplechase even while putting clotheshorses through their paces in the marble and gold sanctuaries of his famous bathtub scenes many years later.

Some accounts have it that Hollywood became the picture capital because bootleg films could be made there with illegal cameras far from the scrutiny of the highhanded Eastern patent monopoly, with the Mexican border handy for emergencies. I know that spies from the patent companies were circulating in Hollywood when we arrived. We had an approved camera, but, even so, we were afraid of trouble because we were daring to make a six-reel picture which would run sixty minutes. The monopoly discouraged any deviations from the status quo, which called for one- and two-reelers only. They were making easy money with little effort on short pictures and were afraid longer films would ruin the whole business by driving patrons out of the theatres with eyestrain and boredom—or, worse still, the public might get to *like* long pictures and force the film makers to worry about heavier financing and genuine creative talent.

Cecil was apprehensive enough to carry a gun at all times. He was actually shot at on one occasion while carrying the film home at night, which I am sure made him feel that revolutionizing motion pictures wasn't such a bad substitute for a Mexican revolution.

When Oscar Apfel and Cecil finished shooting scenes for *The Squaw Man* and patched them together with the help of the cameraman and a man from the lab that processed the negative and first

D

answer print, I still hadn't seen any of it, since Cecil had wanted me to wait until it was completely assembled.

Everyone connected with the picture, from Dustin Farnum and his leading woman, Winifred Kingston, whom he later married, to the carpenters and secretaries, was invited to the first showing in the barn. It was such a proud occasion that the men put on collars and coats and brought their wives. There were about fifty of us.

Cecil gave a signal, the lights went off, and "JESSE L. LASKY PRESENTS" flashed on the screen. Then the words immediately went into convulsions, dancing and crawling to the top of the screen. "THE SQUAW MAN" followed suit—crawled right up over the edge of the screen, and then magically appeared at the bottom and started working its way up again. "STARRING DUSTIN FARNUM" jiggled and crawled up the screen with the supporting cast. So did the opening scenes of the picture.

Cecil stopped the showing and went into a huddle with the operator. After fifteen or twenty minutes they tried once more, but the images still wouldn't stay put. The invitation preview of Hollywood's first feature film had to be called off and the audience went home.

Cecil was at his wit's end and I was in despair. We brooded and discussed the situation until three or four o'clock in the morning. We had used up all our capital, spent all Sam could collect as advances from states'-rights men, and there remained unpaid bills. And all we had to show for it was a film that wouldn't project. It appeared that the local experts had either botched the processing job through ignorance or that someone working in the lab for interests who didn't want us in business had willfully sabotaged it. In either case we might only make matters worse by taking the film back and giving them further opportunity to cripple it. With so much at stake Cecil decided the only thing to do was to take it to the best laboratory in the country and see whether they could salvage it. The Lubin Manufacturing Company in Philadelphia, founded on optical equipment, had an unassailable reputation both as a leader in commercial film printing and for its own short subjects.

I had to go to San Francisco to straighten out some trouble with one of my vaudeville acts, "Lasky's Redheads," which was playing the Orpheum there, and Cecil and I agreed that I would continue on from there while he would start from Los Angeles with the negative and print, joining me in Chicago for the remainder of the journey.

It was a dismal trip. We sent wires back and forth between the Southern Pacific and Santa Fe trains every day to buck each other up. We didn't dare tell Sam what had happened or that we were on our way East, fearful that he would blow a fuse. Meantime, he was only having apoplexy. With the states'-rights men breathing down his neck he was frantically wiring us in Hollywood for release dates on the picture and getting no replies.

We explained our difficulties to "Pop" Lubin and he turned us over to his top technicians. Cecil went into the lab with them and left me pacing back and forth outside, sweating in an agony of suspense, knowing that if the film couldn't be saved we were ruined in a great big way. How was I going to explain our failure to Dustin Farnum, the staff, my wife's relatives who put up money, all our creditors—and Sam, who had now given up his job with the glove company! It was beginning to have the earmarks of another fiasco like the Folies Bergère. I wished Sam had never mentioned pictures.

After the most harrowing half hour I've ever lived through, Cecil rushed out beaming, threw his arms around me, and hugged me. There was nothing wrong with the negative. We went downtown and got tight.

It had taken Lubin's men only a few minutes to spot the trouble. We had purchased Eastman perforated negative stock, but as an economy measure Cecil had used unperforated positive stock and a hand-operated punch which spaced the holes differently from those on the negative, with the result that the projected frames constantly crawled upward.

We had an accurately perforated print made and took it to New York for an invitational trade showing at the Longacre Theatre on Feburary 17, 1914. As soon as the screening was over we could tell from the reactions of the states'-rights men that our first production was a hit.

The Movie Mill
Begins to Grind

While we pioneered the long film in Hollywood, Adolph Zukor's new company had produced its first feature in New york—*The Prisoner of Zenda*, starring James K. Hackett. The day after our screening I was flattered to find among the congratulatory wires one from the president of Famous Players.

I had never met Zukor but I remembered going into his Penny Arcade on Fourteenth Street ten years earlier, while playing at Tony Pastor's with my sister. The arcade was filled with automatic fortune-tellers, strength testers, and other fascinating gadgets cleverly designed to pick your pocket. But a row of peep-box dispensers of thirty-second dramas was collecting the steadiest stream of coins. It was evident that the proprietor of this copper mine had a bonanza. I learned later that 10,000,000 pennies went through Adolph Zukor's sluiceways that first year.

A year later I sought to enjoy again those thumbnail epics with such fascinating titles as *Old Man's Darling, Beware, My Husband Comes, The Unwritten Law, The Female Highwayman, Gaieties of Divorce,* and *The Great Thaw Trial*. But I was sidetracked at the entrance of the Penny Arcade by an intriguing sight next door. The replica of the end of a railway car jutted out over a sign: "HALE'S TOURS AND SCENES OF THE WORLD. TRAINS EVERY TEN MINUTES." I got in the long ticket line and took a "trip" in a swaying, rattling, scenic observation car riding through the Alps. The phantom Alps weren't Technicolored in those days, but otherwise the illusion was complete, with conductor taking tickets, whistles blowing, and wheels clattering below.

I didn't know that the proprietor of this novelty was the same Adolph Zukor, but it struck me that, if the peep show was a bonanza,

Hale's Tours must be an El Dorado. I was wrong—the novelty wore off in a few weeks, but not before $180,000 had been sunk in the expensive gimmicks in several cities. It is interesting to note that, while this jiggling imitation railroad coach was an unmitigated flop as entertainment over fifty years ago, the device was resurrected or invented all over again, much later, to give movie spectators the feeling of being aboard a train. Process shots of train interiors are still made on a stationary, jouncing coach with changing scenery supplied by a rear-projected film.

So Adolph Zukor had also had his ups and downs in fashioning entertainment to the public fancy, before he created a market in this country for feature pictures by importing the French film *Queen Elizabeth* and then forming with Daniel Frohman a film company dedicated to the principle of "Famous Players in Famous Plays."

I called Zukor to thank him personally for his telegram. He proposed that we meet for lunch. Cecil had gone immediately back to California, but Sam went with me to Delmonico's, where executives of the era were reputed to consummate more deals than they did in their offices.

Zukor was small in stature, but I began to think of him as a titan when he expounded astute theories about the future of the motion-picture business. We found that we had a community of interests, aside from the fact that we were selling our pictures to the same states'-rights men. His vision and quiet dignity still infused me as I walked with Sam to the offices we had taken on Fifth Avenue opposite the Public Library.

"That man is an inspirational force!" I said. "I want to keep in close contact with him."

Sam agreed, and we never failed to have lunch with Zukor whenever I came to New York.

When *The Squaw Man* was presented to the public, we didn't think of it as a pioneering achievement or turning point in screen history. We could already foresee that states'-rights rentals were going to double our investment, and all we could think of was "Let's make some more quick!"

I turned to the plays and the people I knew best. I liked *The Master Mind*, produced at the Harris Theatre with Edmund Breese in the starring role while I was involved in the Folies Bergère. I bought it and *The Only Son*, in which Thomas Ross was still playing, and *Brewster's Millions*, a hit that starred Edward Abeles, adapted from the George Barr McCutcheon best-seller. In each case I signed the

star of the stage play and sent him to California to make the picture
version. I happened to pick plays with male stars, and we made fourteen pictures before we bought one that called for a feminine lead.

I always claimed we made better, if fewer, pictures than Famous
Players in the early days, but I must concede that Zukor knew what
he was doing. All my original stars were top actors on the stage, but
who remembers them today? Zukor often took lesser lights from the
stage but built them into outstanding *screen* names. Among his early
acquisitions were Mary Pickford, Marguerite Clark, John Barrymore,
and Pauline Frederick.

I had seen very little of my family for several months since the
formation of our company, with the continent between us, except for
my hurried trips to New York. But after the first three pictures I
brought Bessie, Jesse, Jr., my mother, and Blanche to California and
installed them in the Hollywood Hotel. The clerk who hadn't been
able to direct me to the studio began to bow when he saw me.

Later Bessie enlisted Cecil in a clever conspiracy to find a home for
us so small that there would be no room for in-laws. Cecil and Constance obligingly moved to larger quarters themselves, giving up the
tiny house in Cahuenga Canyon where I had stayed on my first night
in Hollywood. Since the rent was only $25 a month, I could hardly
complain that I couldn't support two ménages.

Although we had some luxurious houses later, Bessie doesn't speak
of any of them with the nostalgia she reserves for that first home of
our own after five years of marriage. We lived there about a year without my realizing how I had been tricked into shrinking the family
circle. But I distinctly remember it was a tight fit when we had company. We gave a party to welcome a celebrated comic opera star and
his charming young bride, De Wolf and Hedda Hopper, and the
house was so cramped we had to have a porch built on it in order to
have a place to serve dinner! There was a little barn in back, so I kept
a horse and would ride to work down Hollywood Boulevard, carrying
my lunch in a pail. I hitched the horse alongside fifty or sixty others
in front of the studio, where the cowboy extras would feed and water
it.

Cecil, Sam, and I always paid ourselves equal salaries after *The
Squaw Man* was released—at first $250 a week, then $500, and later
$1000, as profits from our pictures rose. So our put-up-lunches were
not to save money, but just to have decent food. Restaurants didn't
exist in the vicinity of the studio, and we didn't patronize the lunch
wagon. There was one drugstore on the whole length of Hollywood

Boulevard, and when a second opened—featuring a *soda fountain*—it seemed a more momentous event than the opening of a Hilton hotel today. You could have bought choice frontage on either Hollywood Boulevard or Vine Street for a few hundred dollars, land that sold ten years later for $1000 a front foot. I sometimes wonder where the center of Hollywood would be today if we hadn't located in that particular barn.

We filmed twenty-one pictures the first year, buying screen rights to plays directly from the authors, not through agents, and paying an average of $5000 for the caliber of Broadway smash that would bring $100,000 to $500,000 today. The company that purchased film rights could remake the same story as often as it deemed profitable, without further payment to the author. Most of our early pictures were remade several years later and there were hundreds of instances in the industry where a story property was milked twice or three times at no extra cost before this unfair practice was arrested at the beginning of the sound era.

Only when the supply of better plays got low, owing to the competitive bidding of Famous Players and other companies, did we have to learn techniques of scenario writing and begin to adapt novels and develop original stories.

Of our next ten pictures after *The Squaw Man*, Oscar Apfel directed eight and Cecil two. Oscar ground them out like sausage, one every three or four weeks. Cecil was much more painstaking, and as his flair for sweeping dramatic spectacle developed, his shooting schedules stretched from five to six to seven and then eight weeks. He was responsible for many innovations in the interest of pictorial realism and would stop at nothing in the attempt to give his pictures "class." This tendency got to be a severe strain on the budget in later years, but in 1914 he managed it for the price of a black velvet backdrop. His brother's play, *The Warrens of Virginia*, became the first picture to show interior night scenes without blazing sunlight streaming into all the doors and windows. Black velvet kept out the midnight sun.

By manipulating sunlight reflectors he was the first director to vary light intensity, when stage directions called for someone to turn down a lamp or knock it over in a struggle.

Then he went further in his experiments with light and shade, striving for artistic composition and pattern. Up until then sharpness of detail was the sole criterion by which motion-picture photography was judged—a scene was highly praised if you could see all the wrinkles in a man's pants. Italian pictures were considered models of perfection because the glaring sun on the Riviera showed up every detail from bloodshot eyes to dirty fingernails. The rest of Hollywood prided itself that its own sunshine made for a close approximation of Italian "quality" in its camera work, but Cecil rejected such a false standard of beauty and achieved some startling and thrilling shadowy effects in one picture by backlighting and sidelighting his actors. As soon as the film reached New York, we had an explosive protest from Sam demanding how in hell we expected him to sell a picture in which the lighting was so lousy that you couldn't even see the characters' faces half the time. (D. W. Griffith had encountered this same sort of objection when he introduced close-ups—he was accused of extravagance in paying the going rate for a complete actor and then photographing only part of him.)

Cecil pondered the telegram a few moments. Then he dismissed it with: "Tell him it's Rembrandt lighting."

I wired Sam that we were the first to use this artistic new technique and we were very proud of it. When he realized the murky shadows were art and not carelessness, he hiked the rental fees for that picture.

While Sam dominated the business and financial end, handling all the selling, distribution, and exploitation, Cecil oversaw production in general. I traveled back and forth, buying plays and engaging stars in the East, building up the personnel in our Hollywood studio, and maneuvering to keep an edge on our competitors. Soon I found myself bidding against Famous Players for nearly every play or star. I scored quite a coup late in 1914, therefore, in buying a block of ten choice plays from David Belasco, the dean of theatrical producers, for $100,000 against 50 per cent of the film profits. This was one of the first percentage deals in the business. We were naïvely assuming that any play would make a good movie, and without reading or having seen all of them I was no more concerned over the adaptability of a job lot of Belasco plays to films than I would have been over whether a dozen Grade A eggs would make good omelets.

Fortunately most of the dramas Belasco produced had an outdoor locale and I couldn't have picked more suitable stories for our purpose if I *had* read them. Nine of them made very successful pictures. The batch included Cecil's play, *The Return of Peter Grimm*. Others were *The Warrens of Virginia*, *The Rose of the Rancho*, *The Governor's Lady*, *The Girl of the Golden West*, *The Woman*, *The Fighting Hope*, *The Case of Becky*, *Sweet Kitty Bellairs*, and *The Darling of the Gods*.

Cecil naturally had first call on the plays we bought and the stars we signed. He picked the juiciest plums from the Belasco buy for himself and unwittingly got hold of the one lemon in the lot. *The Darling of the Gods* had starred Blanche Bates and brought acclaim to George Arliss. Dealing with the conflict between the new and old regimes in the Japanese feudal period, it was a masterpiece on the stage.

Anticipating that we would make a movie to eclipse anything seen before, Cecil imported shipments of Japanese costumes, samurai swords, and art treasures from Japan. Then we began to realize that nineteenth-century Japanese customs were too unfamiliar and the story too complicated to be understandable on the silent screen, and there were insurmountable make-up problems besides. Eyes could be taped to almond shape on the stage, but the art of movie make-up was still so crude that every close-up would show the strips of tape.

So we never filmed the best play at all, and the huge stock of Japanese relics and curios was a memorial to a lost cause. For years afterward Cecil's office looked like a Shinto shrine.

Before the end of our first year we were employing three more directors, George Melford, James Neill, and Fred Thompson. Bessie Barriscale was our first feminine star, but Mabel Van Buren, Edith Taliaferro, and Blanche Sweet were soon assigned to the double row of flimsy dressing rooms for which more orange trees had to make way. H. B. Warner, Theodore Roberts, and Robert Edeson appeared in our first year's crop of pictures and Dustin Farnum was starred in two more.

Extras could be plucked like ripe tomatoes whenever needed, right outside the studio. There were benches under the pepper trees in the middle of Vine Street and they became a gathering place for people who wanted jobs. A director could run halfway across the street and pick up a bit actor, an assistant director, or a prop man. Work was work, and when a fellow got a nod he didn't always know until he got on the set whether he'd be required to chew the scenery or push it around. If he wasn't particular, he worked oftener.

After seeing how audiences took to the long feature states'-rights men were drooling to plunk down money for more of them, sight unseen, to anyone who could make them. D. W. Griffith, William Fox, and Thomas H. Ince lost no time in entering the feature field. It isn't much credit to us that we were successful. So insatiable was the public appetite for this new form of entertainment it seemed impossible to have a failure in those first years. But the public taste is never static and would have passed us by if we hadn't worked sixteen

D'*

hours a day to keep ahead of it, and constantly to improve our product.

We chopped down the remainder of the orange and lemon grove and erected more stages so we could shoot three or four pictures at once. We rented the rest of the acreage from Selma to Sunset and Vine to El Centro, which jumped our rent from $75 to $150 a month.

We had pried a few big names loose from the Eastern stronghold of theatrical talent, but Zukor was closer to the supply. All he had to do was shake the tree. We had to uproot it and transplant it. He was a good picker, too. His choice of glamorous celebrities, especially feminine beauties, made tough competition for our stable of stars— and I do mean stable. We tried to offset his advantage by concentrating on careful preparation, craftsmanship, and all the ingenuity we could muster in production techniques. One morning we might be committed to a policy of irising out every scene and a fadeout after each episode; by afternoon that practice had been superseded by something we thought even better.

We were probably the first studio to employ a technical adviser to improve credibility of screen performances. Cecil directed *The Call of the North*, from Stewart Edward White's novel, *Conjuror's House*, a story of the English and French fur traders and their feuds in the Canadian north woods. Much of the story action took place while these *voyageurs* were ferrying their pelts down the rivers in large canoes to the trading posts. There were no expert canoemen in the area because there were no lakes or rivers in the ranch country surrounding Hollywood. Cowboys were always available for extra work, and we had them playing everything from Indians to English royalty. So Cecil took a score of them to Big Bear Lake, at that time a day's ride over dirt mountain roads impassable in bad weather, and retained the author of the story, himself an explorer and skilled woodsman, to teach them the tricks of canoe-tilting.

At first, whenever we needed a piece of furniture or another prop for a picture, we borrowed it from homes around the studio, and if we couldn't get what we wanted, we revamped the story to make shift with what we had: Then Bill Bowers, who had traveled with several of my vaudeville units as a carpenter-property man, decided to quit "The Trained Nurses" company when it played the Orpheum in Los Angeles, and settle down in California. It occurred to us that we could use Bill at the studio to take charge of obtaining all the odds and ends needed to dress the sets. I think Bill established the principle on which the prop departments function today, namely that a director gets whatever he asks for without argument, no matter how crazy or impossible the request.

I had bought *The Ghost Breaker* and signed its Broadway star, H. B. Warner. Cecil, with his usual insistence on realism, wasn't satisfied to shoot a dungeon scene without what he regarded as proper dungeon atmosphere. He demanded water seeping up through crevices in the rock floor and rats crawling over Warner's prostrate body as he lay helplessly chained to the floor. Bill spent the whole day in a rat-race, but by evening he had made no progress at all. He reported that he had stalked butcher shops, stables, and cellars, and rats seemed to be out of season.

Cecil leveled his eyes on the uncomfortable fellow. "Bill," he said, "you bring two cages of rats tomorrow or don't come back!"

I felt sorry for Bill. I didn't expect to see him again. But when I went on the set the next morning, I found Cecil perfectly happy and H. B. Warner perfectly unhappy, chained in the dungeon with rats swarming over him. But presently I noticed a puzzled look on Cecil's face and I followed his intent scrutiny of the rats. They had stopped scampering and were sitting upright on their haunches licking their bodies. As they preened, more like cats than rats, white spots appeared on their coats. Our ingenious property man, unable to get dungeon-type rats, had obtained some large pet white mice and painted them black. If you think Al Jolson's blackface specialty was new to the silver screen when he made his early talking pictures, you're wrong. We had two dozen blackface performers in *The Ghost Breaker* in 1914.

A minimum number of indoor scenes were used in our first few pictures, and we availed ourselves of ready-made scenery on location as much as feasible. But Cecil and I began to think an art director might be an asset to a picture company, and his mother recommended Wilfred Buckland, who had been responsible for the scenic beauty and superb lighting in Belasco's plays. We brought Buckland to the Coast to head a staff of designers and draftsmen. Some of his settings for early films have never been surpassed artistically. Examples of them are to be found in the Encyclopaedia Britannica. As the first bona fide art director in the industry, and the first to build architectural settings for films, Buckland widened the scope of pictures tremendously by throwing off the scenic limitations of the stage.

We were so proud of this advance that we exploited the patchwork nature of motion pictures by plastering billboards with announcements of "DUSTIN FARNUM IN THE VIRGINIAN—5 PARTS 400 SCENES." The five parts were quite distinguishable, since the projectionist had to change each reel while the audience fidgeted, but I don't know why we thought it necessary to boast about that or about the dramatic continuity having been chopped into four hundred pieces. It was a seller's market, however, and our ballyhoo didn't have to be very smart. This was before the "colossal" school of press-agentry, and our thirteenth production, *Ready Money*, was blurbed in display sheets as "highly interesting," a rather lukewarm recommendation from its sponsors, by present standards, but sufficient to fill the theatres with patrons and our own pockets with ready money.

Wilfred Buckland ushered in an era of artistic expression in the movies, and—quite unexpectedly—in my own home as well. Bessie became good friends with Wilfred's wife, Veda, and, on a trip with her to the artists' colony in Carmel, was inspired to take up painting as a substitute for the music she had given up to please my mother when she married me.

She threw herself into this new endeavor with such feverish intensity that I had Wilfred design a studio for her over the garage of the home we had built at Hillside and La Brea. She was always in it, when I came home from work, and she usually had several canvases going at once. I'd stand in the doorway, eager to tell her about some new star I'd signed that day or a choice play we were negotiating for. But she wasn't interested. It was always, "Oh, Jesse—come see the new flower painting I've started!" Or, "How do you think this landscape is going?"

Once fanned into flame, the fire of self-expression burned within her day and night. At the same time she was constantly seeking a spiritual way of life. She read voluminously on philosophies and religions. She has never really felt at home in the Hollywood social whirl, and has held herself aloof from it as much as possible. Many times I would go to a public dinner, a theatrical first night, or a picture premiere alone while Bessie went to a lecture. We lived in separate worlds. But if I had forced her to live in mine, I would have lost her, and that would have been a tragedy for me.

My mother was just as much opposed to Bessie's painting as she had been to her music, but as she was no longer living with us, there wasn't much she could do about it except grumble. I'm afraid she could never quite forgive my wife for not spoiling me as she herself had done. Blanche was more understanding and, with the tensions of living together removed, came to admire Bessie's courage and character, and in time to feel that my wife was her best friend. The day was also to come when my mother would be inordinately proud of her daughter-in-law's accomplishments, and would brag to all her friends when Bessie had an exhibition in Paris or an art museum purchased one of her paintings.

Bessie had to be dragged away from her easel when it was time for her to leave for the Good Samaritan Hospital for the birth of our second son, Bill. A year later she had to take off her painter's smock again, long enough for our daughter Betty's arrival. With three children and a full-blown career she still found time to make a passionate hobby of gardening and flower culture. But she never found time for Hollywood.

As long as we confined our operations to the filming of plays, the director could improvise necessary changes in translating stage dialogue to silent screen action and descriptive and spoken subtitles. But producing motion pictures without employing writers has severe limitations, and Cecil recommended that we make overtures to a playwright of the first rank—William C. DeMille.

Even though William had been dead set against his younger brother's embarking on our foolhardy venture in the first place, and though I hadn't been able to get him to write my operetta, *California*, we had better luck getting him to write *in* California. He came to Hollywood in 1914, agreeing to stay no longer than three months. He remained forty-one years until his death in 1955. William DeMille's impact on the picture business was immediate and far-reaching. He organized for us the first story department in Hollywood. Under his direction we gathered a few local writers, enticed Robert MacAlarney and Hector Turnbull from their respective posts as city editor and dramatic critic of the New York *Herald Tribune*, and started a class in photoplay construction. William taught the neophytes to tell their stories in action, to hold written and spoken titles down to a minimum. The ultimate to strive for, he impressed on them, was a dramatic story that could be told in pure action, without any titles at all. "*Show* the man falling downstairs!" he'd storm. "Don't tell about it in a title!"

He soon proved too good a writer to waste on writing, so after the scenario department was organized and functioning smoothly, we made him a director. Turnbull took William's place as story head and, later, Sam's place as my brother-in-law.

We instituted the first research department in a film studio after a certain historical picture included a plot sequence which hinged on Blanche Sweet being saved from death by an alarm clock. A deluge of letters pointed out that Miss Sweet must be living on borrowed time as well as a borrowed invention that didn't make its appearance until many years later than the era our picture depicted. Ever since then it has been a policy of all studios to strive for authentic detail by starting research as soon as the subject matter of a picture is decided on.

Looking back now, I believe America's domination of the international film market can be traced to the intervention of the First World War in 1914. Europe really had the jump on us with such quality movie entertainment as Bernhardt's *Camille* and *Queen Elizabeth* from France, and the magnificent Italian productions of *Cabiria* and the eight-reel spectacle *Quo Vadis*. England already had a successful color process, Kinemacolor. These countries might have seized a far greater portion of the world trade had not the war stopped their movie activities just when they were getting well under way. Our industry was slower starting but expanded by leaps and bounds during the European setback, and by the end of the war we were so far ahead technically and had such a grip on foreign audiences that our gross revenues put us in an impregnable, commanding position. We were able to outbid any other country for their own geniuses. And by concentrating so much of the top acting, directing, and writing talent of the world in Hollywood we could continue to make pictures that the whole world clamored to see.

Although the war strengthened our world distribution, it threatened the Lasky Company with the loss of its director-general. Adventurer that he was, Cecil would have joined up as a plane pilot if he could have. He started taking flying lessons even before the war, and in a reckless moment over drinks I said, "Cecil, we've been through a lot of adventures together, and I want to have my first plane ride when you make your first solo flight."

A couple of months later he called me from his flying field in Santa Monica (he was so obsessed with this new interest that he had bought the field) and said, "Jesse, I'm ready to solo. Be here right after lunch."

Without a highball glass in my hand it didn't seem like such a good idea. Neither did lunch. I had lost my appetite. But I didn't see how I could get out of my rash proposal.

I drove to the field in my white Packard Special, which Cecil always referred to as the "Corona-Corona" because of its extra-long wheel base. Rex Ingram had designed it for me after Ralph De Palma's racing car, and it had speed at the expense of power in the forward gears. It could climb hills only by backing up them, a rather inconvenient and humiliating procedure, but then sports cars aren't supposed to be practical.

It was a very windy day, which I complacently figured was going to save my skin.

"Too bad this lousy weather has interfered with your plans, Cecil," I greeted him. "I was really looking forward to soloing with you, but it can't be helped."

"It's perfect flying weather," Cecil assured me. "Much easier for a beginner to take off into a strong wind. Put on this leather jacket, helmet, and goggles."

There were two places in the flimsy little biplane. I sat in the forward one, gripping the sides of the cockpit as though I were trying to hold the thin fabric together. To my amazement we took off without ground-looping, and I was just getting fairly well adjusted to the idea of still being alive when Cecil shouted something to me. I looked back and he kept shouting, but you couldn't hear a thing over the roar of the motor, and the goggles gave him a terrified expression. I thought we must be in trouble. I shouted that I couldn't hear him. Suddenly the motor cut out and so did my heart. All I knew about flying was that when the motor conks out you're a dead pigeon. I began reading big black headlines all over the sky. But Cecil had just shut off the motor for a moment to warn me that he was going to demonstrate some fancy turns. He needn't have bothered. My stomach was already demonstrating fancy turns without benefit of the pilot.

I couldn't bring myself to go up in a plane again for years.

Cecil was thirty-four years old and I was thirty-five. Since we were both over draft age and had dependents, we didn't see service. But Cecil captained a home-guard unit made up of studio personnel and, I have no doubt, prayed for an invasion. Our director-general drilled his "army" with real Springfield rifles, up and down Vine Street with as much relish as though he were showing General Pershing how to do a scene. The drilling was accompanied by a brass band composed of prop men, carpenters, grips, and actors from our lot, led by Tully Marshall, who knew that I was an old-time cornet player like himself. When I arrived on one of my trips from New York, Tully asked me to show up unannounced for a band rehearsal. He told the boys he had a new member for the band, an employee who blew a mean cornet. I stepped out, to their astonishment, and blew my head off— for about half a march. Then my lip gave out from lack of practice. But I got an ovation anyway.

The Flickers Become Respectable

We stepped up our production to thirty-six releases in the second year. Up to this time feature length fluctuated between four and five reels, but five became standard during 1915 despite the clamor of states'-rights men that pictures were getting too long.

That was a red-letter year in motion-picture history, but not because of anything we did. It was the year that D. W. Griffith's twelve-reel epic of Civil War days, *The Birth of a Nation*, began to roll up a record gross that has been estimated at an unauthenticated $30,000,-000, a figure surpassed only by the even longer saga of the Civil War period, *Gone with the Wind*.

Too long indeed!

Griffith liked to mold and shape raw material. Moreover, he wouldn't permit his genius to be encumbered by commercial considerations and hampered by contractual obligations, so he didn't capitalize as he could have on the players he lifted from obscurity to stardom. Consequently, when Cecil and I had been impressed with the performance of Blanche Sweet in Griffith's four-reel feature *Judith of Bethulia*, we called on her at her home one evening, learned that she had no contract with Griffith, and persuaded her to sign with us. She at once became one of our most important stars and made seven pictures for us in 1915.

We had another larcenous inspiration when we attended the opening of *The Clansman* (later retitled *The Birth of a Nation*) at Clune's Auditorium in Los Angeles on February 8, 1915. A young man who played a bit part as a blacksmith had a perfect physique, large, expressive eyes, and flawless features. He was about six feet tall and weighed in the neighborhood of 180 pounds. Seeing him was just like finding a 180-pound diamond, for within a year we would be reaping gratifying profits from eight pictures featuring his brawn and irresistible appeal, and the tonnage of his fan mail would be making our distaff stars jealous. We signed him and kept him under contract to the day of his tragic death eight years later at the height of unprecedented popularity.

Son of the playwright Hal Reid, Wallace Reid had inherited his father's gift for storytelling, had a keen sense of humor, a good singing voice, played the saxophone and piano, and was altogether the most magnetic, charming, personable, handsome young man I've ever met. And the most co-operative.

In the meantime the supply of available plays was dwindling and their prices mounting. I therefore dangled an experimental offer of $250 for original stories before our staff writers, who had heretofore only adapted material from outside sources. Modest as the inducement was, it tapped such a valuable supply of story material that we were never again wholly dependent on Broadway playwrights. Jeanie MacPherson rose to the bait and delivered a splendid original which she called, possibly in honor of our new policy, *The Golden Chance*. Hector Turnbull also qualified for the bonus with a story he titled *The Cheat*, with perhaps some sly innuendo about the inequity of paying $10,000 or more for a stage play and appraising equally serviceable original stories at $250. But to this day stories written directly for the screen are usually bought for a fraction of the sums paid for screen rights to novels and plays. The reason lies in the disparity of exploitation values—the public has never heard of the original story, but a picture made from a book or play of considerable reputation has the advantage of a ready-made audience.

The Golden Chance seemed made to order for Wallace Reid, and, as our golden chance to establish a bright new star in our banner, it called for the best production values we could give it, which meant that it automatically requisitioned Cecil DeMille's services as director.

It was a plaintive axiom among other directors during this period that "The best you can get on the Lasky lot is leftovers." But I rated Cecil's ability as a director-producer-showman so far ahead of the rest that I shouldered the burden of complaints while I kept on slipping him the choice stories and stars.

Hector's story was about a young wife who misappropriates charity funds, loses them on the stock market, lures a wealthy Japanese neighbor into having an affair with her so that she can borrow money from him to cover her defection, and then brushes him off. The discarded lover, a buyer and handler of expensive knickknacks, brands his trademark on her shoulder (close-up of sizzling flesh), is arrested, and a large-scale riot takes place at his trial. Leave the kiddies at home!

This startling story line had the makings of such a sensational hit that I didn't want to entrust its interpretation to a secondary director, that is to say, anyone but Cecil DeMille, already deeply involved with the writing and preparation of *The Golden Chance*. There was a tendency in the industry to consider picture-making as piecework passed from one artisan to the next. But it was always my policy, for the sake of consistent over-all perspective, to use a director as supervising architect of every phase of a production, from writing to cutting, rather than have him serve merely as foreman on the rough construction job. So Cecil had the Reid picture about ready for shooting and *The Cheat* also had to go before the cameras without delay. Neither could be postponed for contractual reasons, the details of which I've forgotten.

Rather than give up either of these choice assignments Cecil undertook to direct them both at the same time. He would start with one crew and cast at nine in the morning and shoot until five. After dinner he slept until eleven and worked the second picture crew from midnight to eight in the morning. After breakfast he started again with the day crew and cast. Both pictures were completed on schedule and were resounding successes. I think that's the only time in Hollywood history that a director has doubled for himself.

The Cheat made a star of Sessue Hayakawa and put Fannie Ward on the pinnacle of screen recognition. It was *later* dramatized as a stage play, reversing the usual procedure for the first time. A grand opera was also fashioned from its pungent elements, first presented at the Metropolitan, and it saw two more movie versions in later years. It was a $250 phenomenon.

A big success on Broadway was Edgar Selwyn's *The Arab*. Having been friendly with Edgar from the time I rented space in the Selwyn offices in New York, I had an inside track in obtaining the play and its star-author-manager for picture production. By this time our press-book blurbs reflected a more feverish appreciation of our own efforts than "highly interesting." *The Arab* was touted as "the most spectacular production ever made by the Lasky Company," a phrase that did yeoman service from that day on. I don't know why we claimed merely a regional championship for our current effort. Modesty, I suppose. In the course of this "most spectacular" saga of sand the heroine was saved from what the press-book terms—I blush to admit—"a fate worse than death."

I'll never forget Cecil's disgusted expression when he made the first test of Edgar in his princely costume, congealed with fear as he mounted a horse *for the first time in his life!* The Arab had been so glib on the stage about his unexcelled horsemanship that such a predicament had never occurred to me when I signed his contract. (History repeated itself, however, when Bill Boyd was given his first Hopalong Cassidy role and had to have a double do the riding.) In desperation Cecil hired a cowboy of about the same build as Selwyn, had a duplicate costume made, and took all the rough riding in long shots with the substitute sheik. This was the first time we had ever used a double and it must have been one of the first instances in the industry.

Edgar still had to sit the horse for close-ups, and he was one of the unhappiest mortals you can imagine. Not only was he frightened and embarrassed—he got so saddlesore he could hardly move. "When this Spanish Inquisition is over," he said, "no one will ever talk me into having anything to do with flickers again." But later he had an illustrious career as a picture producer, forming the Goldwyn Pictures Corporation with Sam Goldfish by combining syllables of their names, and spending the later years of his life as a producer at Metro-Goldwyn-Mayer, which still bears half his name.

Our studio was becoming a mecca for visiting celebrities, and we turned their sight-seeing curiosity to advantage by using them as extras in any crowd scenes we happened to be shooting while they were there. They had the fun of "acting" in movies and we had the fun of getting famous supers for free. Irvin Cobb, then America's ace humorist, visited Hollywood and the Lasky lot, and I took him on *The Arab* set. Within ten minutes we had him in front of the camera as an extra in a street scene. He later turned actor and played several feature roles, but I don't claim to have discovered his histrionic ability. All I claim is that I saved our company $5.00 overhead, the cost of an extra's hire, by inviting him to watch the proceedings from in front of the camera instead of behind it.

Although it was a lark for non-professionals to show their faces in a movie, the top legitimate stars were still loath to tarnish their reputations and court the suspicion that they were slipping by lending their talents to the vulgar medium. They liked the money—$5000 for less than a month's work—and the trip to California, but they insisted that the whole regrettable affair be kept as secret as possible. Some of our first stars, who shall be nameless here, in accordance with their wishes, insisted on a "no publicity" clause in their contracts. So although feature pictures were established in 1914, they didn't become respectable until late in 1915.

To bring attention to our offerings and help overcome prejudice against films in general, we had hired Harry Reichenbach to handle publicity for *The Squaw Man* and subsequent pictures. He had already shown a flair that was to make him the undisputed king of sensational hoaxes, by sparking the crusade that made *September Morn* the most famous painting of the day. He simply hired a crowd of ragamuffins to ogle a reproduction of the nude in a Fifth Avenue art-store window, and then phoned the New York Society for Suppression of Vice that the picture was corrupting youth. During the ensuing battle of the press the picture was exhibited on a nationwide tour and made a fortune for its promoters. We thought that, if Reichenbach could breathe that much life into a still picture, he should certainly be very valuable in exploiting moving pictures. But the frustrating task of trying to publicize our pictures without being allowed to mention the names of their noteworthy stars almost drove Reichenbach crazy. It was like writing up one of Mrs. Cornelius Vanderbilt's society balls and omitting the name of the hostess.

This impasse had to be broken some way, and the problem was much on my mind when Morris Gest, son-in-law of David Belasco and a well-known impresario himself, asked me at luncheon to go along with him to a matinee of *Madame Butterfly*. Geraldine Farrar was making her farewell appearance of the season at the Metropolitan Opera House under Gest's management.

There were no seats left, and we stood in the rear.

Farrar was currently the greatest dramatic soprano in grand opera and a fine actress. I have never seen such adulation as when the final curtain came down. She had a devoted following of young student fans as ardently demonstrative as Frank Sinatra's bobby-soxers in later years. Her idol-worshipers were called "Gerry-flappers." I got a sudden idea and told Gest I wanted to meet her.

Backstage I came quickly to the point. "Miss Farrar," I said, "I don't know whether you have ever seen a motion picture, but my company makes them, and I'd like to persuade you to do the story of Carmen for us. (I knew it was her favorite role.) We have no trouble securing famous plays and engaging their stars," I continued, "but they're always afraid acting in a movie will hurt their stage prestige. I could see by the ovation you got today that your prestige is such that whatever you do, your public will accept it as right."

"You think I could turn the tide?" she asked cordially, intrigued by the compliment.

"I'm sure other stars would follow your lead," I said, "and I can see that you'd photograph beautifully. If you consent, I'm prepared to offer you—in addition to whatever salary we agree on—a number of other inducements . . ." I ad-libbed as many as I could think of—our best director, an orchestra on the set to play music whenever she liked, a private railroad car to take her and her family to Hollywood, a house completely furnished and staffed with servants for her stay, a car and chauffeur at her complete disposal, a private dressing room for her comfort at the studio, which I promised to have built right next to the stage and equipped with a grand piano for her practicing. . . .

Perhaps Geraldine Farrar's decision to accept my offer was influenced by the fact that she had recently overtaxed her voice to the point of despairing she might ever sing again, and the chance to give her throat a rest in silent pictures couldn't have come at a more opportune time. Be that as it may, she proved the most charming, gracious actress I ever brought to Hollywood, and was completely devoid of temperament, contrary to the tradition of prima donnas. If the script called for her to be in mud up to her waist, or with clothing, skin, and hair fire-proofed and cotton saturated with ammonia in her nostrils and mouth for burning-at-the-stake scenes, she didn't demur for an instant.

The Farrar expedition to the wilds of Hollywood was heralded in banner headlines across the continent. Accompanying her in the private car were her parents (her father was Sid Farrar, a famous National League baseball player), her personal press agent, and her manager, Morris Gest, with his wife, Reina. Our New York publicity men saw them off with great fanfare, while I rushed ahead to the Coast to make sure the diva would be ushered in like a visiting queen. The Santa Fe platform and depot were carpeted from her private car to the waiting limousine. School children lined both sides of her path, strewing it with roses. The mayor and other dignitaries formed a welcoming committee and a reception was to be held in Hollywood.

Since she was the first personality in motion-picture history to receive what has since become known as "the full treatment," every detail of it was front-page news.

I rode with Miss Farrar to the two-story house we had rented for her stay. Every room was banked with flowers. I introduced her to the maid, cook, and butler we had provided. As I started back to the studio, I mentioned that DeMille was looking forward to meeting her the next day, after she was rested from her long trip, as he was anxious to talk over her role in *Carmen*.

"Give me a few minutes to change," she said with a smile, "and I'll go with you now."

I think perhaps she couldn't wait until the next day to view her bungalow dressing room, a luxury bestowed on most stars now but unheard of then. Built next to the open-air stage, as I had promised, it contained a tastefully furnished living room, dressing room, and bathroom. I left her in Cecil's office, deeply engrossed with him over wardrobe details.

The next morning as soon as I came in the studio, Cecil said, "I want to show you something you'll never forget." He led me out through the orchard toward the stage. Work had come to a dead standstill. Everyone on our payroll—the cast, carpenters, grips, cowboys, and office staff—was standing bareheaded in a transfixed circle around Miss Farrar's bungalow. The door was open and she was at the grand piano joyously singing an aria from *Madame Butterfly*. The radio had not yet been invented, and those people—many of whom had never before heard an opera singer—were hearing the greatest.

Although she was dignified in billing as *Miss* Geraldine Farrar (stage artists of the first rank were accorded a "Miss" or "Mr." to distinguish them from those who were primarily film actors like Mary Pickford and Wallace Reid), she was "Gerry" to all of us after a brief acquaintance.

Carmen turned out to be the biggest money-maker we had up to that time. And it took the curse off movie work for stage personalities. Reichenbach was no longer pledged to secrecy about what famous actors from the theatre had been seen in a Lasky picture. He could come right out and name them in bold type. In fact matinee idols of Broadway began to look to Hollywood with envious eyes and to demand "the full treatment" with plenty of interviews and newspaper build-up when they entrained for a studio commitment.

After *Carmen*, Farrar worked straight through two more pictures, *Temptation* and *Maria Rosa*. In the latter we teamed her with Lou Tellegen, who had created his same role on the stage and before that had been Sarah Bernhardt's leading man on the stage and in her picture *Queen Elizabeth*. He looked like a Greek god and fascinated the singer from the moment I introduced them. Some months later in New York she invited Bessie and me to an intimate dinner at which she announced their engagement.

A year or so later she interspersed her concert engagements with three more movies. Cecil directed all six of the pictures she made for us. One of them, I note by the list of one thousand pictures made under my supervision between 1913 and 1932, was called *The Woman God Forgot*. I'm afraid I've also forgotten the woman God forgot, but I clearly recall Gerry as Joan of Arc in *Joan the Woman*.

It was more pretentious than anything we had attempted before, and with that picture Cecil started breathing hard on D. W. Griffith's heels as a purveyor of spectacles. He henceforth gave up all attempt to oversee the rest of the studio output as director-general and concentrated on his own pictures, with his shooting time and production costs mounting in an upward spiral. I had to run interference for him with the New York office on the matter of his budgets, at the same time assuming supervision of the other directors and trying tactfully to dissipate their discontent over the favoritism shown DeMille in the allocation of stories and stars.

Cecil, whose attentiveness to authentic detail had led him to use solid-built sets when painted backdrops were usual, had a suit of armor built for Gerry, but by no means jerry-built. It was fabricated to the star's measurements with all the care and expert craftsmanship that went into the fifteenth-century models, and it fit her like a sardine can fits its contents. So much so that when she put it on it clamped the leg muscles in position and she couldn't move. Another suit had to be made, not quite so form-fitting, so she could change positions. I had reason to be thankful for Cecil's insistence on perfection in feminine hardware thirty years later, when I needed a suit of armor for Valli in the Joan of Arc sequence of *The Miracle of the Bells*. Suits of armor tailored for women just don't exist, even in museums. After combing the country I called up Cecil and borrowed the tin riding habit. He collects curios that have served their purpose in his pictures, and he still had it.

The Joan of Arc theme has long been a pitfall for motion-picture producers who think of it as one of the most dramatic and heart-rending stories of all time. It admittedly is, but it has decidedly questionable appeal as escape entertainment. The Geraldine Farrar version was an outstanding production for its time but only passably profitable, even though she had demonstrated exceptional pulling power in several previous pictures. *The Miracle of the Bells* received some extraordinary critical acclaim but was not a financial success, and Walter Wanger's *Joan of Arc* almost bankrupted him, although it was one of the most magnificently appointed productions anybody ever achieved, and won three Academy Awards. It's a peculiar commentary on human nature that the general run of people have an aversion to seeing tragedy in fictional form on the screen, while the genuine article has a morbid fascination for them. I noticed when I was on the board of directors of an automobile race track in what is now Beverly Hills that attendance always boomed far beyond normal the week after a fatal accident. However, the tragic ending is not as unpopular with movie patrons today as it used to be, so perhaps Otto Preminger's picture version of Shaw's *St. Joan* will break the Joan of Arc jinx.

I can still see Geraldine Farrar and John Drew leading an old-fashioned grand march in the ballroom at the Hollywood Hotel, at the first big Hollywood party I have any recollection of. It was given for John Drew when he played an engagement at the Mason Opera House in downtown Los Angeles in 1915, and was attended by the cream of stage and screen celebrities in the West. It was a tame white-tie-and-tails affair, but it started quite a ball rolling. Some fabulous shindigs have been thrown by the movie colony in the wake of that social ice-breaker.

The Power and
the Glory

Sam and I continued to lunch with Adolph Zukor at Delmonico's every time I was in New York, and when I was on the West Coast, Sam kept in touch with him over problems that affected both our companies. Zukor was very farsighted about the picture industry and we were always grateful for his advice. At least I was. Sam frequently clashed with him on matters of policy. But the three of us had a feeling of being partners in a common cause, although our companies were admitted rivals. When Marguerite Clark was a magic name at the box-office, her contract with Famous Players ran out and I tried to lure her away from them by offering her more money—about $5000 a week, as I recall. Zukor topped my bid by a thousand or two and kept her, but then, to show there were no hard feelings, loaned her to us for a picture, *The Goose Girl*, which was one of the most successful of our early productions.

We watched each other's pictures avidly, and if one or the other company introduced a new idea or improvement in technique, the other was so quick to take it up that the originator didn't have time to exploit it before he was imitated. The situation was similar to that of automobile makers all coming out with the same changes at the same time. But Famous Players always bested us in one regard. Whenever they depicted high society on the screen, their elegantly gowned beauties made our dress extras look positively frumpy. Dress extras made only $5.00 a day and had to furnish their own wardrobes. A girl can't build up much of a wardrobe on an occasional $5.00 pay check, so our dress extras were usually qualified seamstresses or other young women clever enough with a needle to make $2.50 worth of material and a Butterick pattern look like a $25 frock.

It always puzzled me how Famous Players could give their pictures a semblance of a style show without spending thousands of dollars on wardrobe. I learned many years later when Al Kaufman became my assistant that, when he had been head of production at Famous Players in New York, he did his casting of dress extras from a little black book containing a list of women friends of Wall Street millionaires. The $5.00 a day meant nothing to those gorgeous hussies—they just liked to flaunt their Paris finery before a camera.

We continued distributing our pictures through the states'-rights men until 1915. Then one of them, W. W. Hodkinson of San Francisco, called all the others together in a meeting with the producers in New York—there were about twenty men present—and proposed that the states'-rights men band together in a distributing company in which they would each own stock. Hodkinson himself suggested that the new releasing association be called "Paramount Pictures." I didn't like the name at all. I didn't think it suggested film artistry. It sounded more like a brand of cheese or woolen mittens. But the first organization to distribute pictures nationally was formed under that name, Hodkinson was made president, and I lived to see Paramount swallow up my own name.

The combine would only agree to pay us $35,000 in advance on each picture against 65 per cent of the gross revenue. Now that they had what amounted to a trust, they could dictate terms to us. With production costs rising, plays costing more, and stars and directors making increased salary demands it became practically impossible to finance ourselves on the meager Paramount advances. Famous Players and the Lasky Company both felt the squeeze badly but couldn't move Hodkinson to more lenient terms.

Zukor could see a battle ahead, and revealed his concern even when he was trying to relax. He was learning golf, and at about the twelfth hole would remark, "Well, I guess we're 65 per cent around the course." One day he called Sam and me and proposed that we merge our two companies under the joint banner of "Famous Players-Lasky." Pooling our resources would make us the most powerful force in the industry and enable us to get the kind of bank financing we both needed to produce more ambitious pictures. Famous Players was making more pictures than we were at the time, and their assets were considerably greater than ours. Mary Pickford's contract alone was a property of inestimable value, even at her current salary of $10,000 a week plus bonuses which brought her income close to $700,000 a year. However, Zukor was satisfied to split the stock fifty-fifty between both companies in order to make the proposition attractive to us.

So we combined. Adolph Zukor became president, I was named vice-president in charge of production, Sam was elected chairman of the board, Cecil retained his title of director-general, and Arthur Friend, a young attorney I had met during my courtship at Long Lake, and who had organized the corporate structure of the Lasky Company for us, was made secretary.

We rented another floor over the one we already occupied at 485 Fifth Avenue and the Famous Players staff moved in. We expanded to several floors there before putting up our own building.

Famous Players-Lasky was the backbone of the distributing organization, supplying 80 per cent of the Paramount product. But Paramount also released the pictures of several smaller companies. Two of these, caught in the same desperate plight as we had been, now merged with us—the Oliver Morosco Photoplay Company and Hobart Bosworth's Pallas Pictures, the latter managed by Frank Garbutt, who shortly assumed a post as our vice-president in charge of finances.

I took charge of the studios and production of all four companies, relieving Zukor to devote his genius to the financial end and later to building a world-wide network of film exchanges and theatres. Our strengthened position made it possible for him to borrow all the working capital we needed from the Irving Trust Company. With Wall Street backing motion pictures entered the realm of big business.

Our pictures had been customarily introduced on the screen with the words "Jesse L. Lasky presents—" followed by the star's name, the title of the picture, and the rest of the cast. Few directors and no scenario writers were given screen credit in those days. Famous Players followed the same practice, starting the main titles with "Adolph Zukor presents—" After the merger it was decided to continue the same way, Zukor presenting all the pictures made in the East, while my name would appear on the Coast product.

My first significant duty in the new setup was to see that our most important asset wasn't sitting around twiddling her thumbs. I made an error of judgment in hastily assigning Hector Turnbull to do an original for Mary Pickford based on the lyrics of the song "Less than the Dust." America's Sweetheart was miscast as a half-caste, and *Less than the Dust* was probably the lowest-grossing and least-popular picture she ever made. It might have ruined a lesser star.

Thus I started the association with Zukor on a blunder that would be hard to top—but Sam managed to top it! He came in while I was conferring with Mary Pickford during preparation of the story and blurted out, "Jesse, don't let Zukor butt in on this picture. He's okay as an executive, but we've always made better movies than Famous Players, so see that you keep the production reins in your hands!"

Mary, naturally feeling more loyalty to the man who had made her the favorite actress of the screen than to the new and untried custodians of her career, reported the remarks to Zukor.

The next day at lunch Zukor was unusually quiet. "Mr. Lasky," he finally said, "I'm sorry to tell you this, but Famous Players-Lasky is not large enough to hold Mr. Goldfish and myself. You brought him into the company and therefore I don't want to ask him to leave. But you'll have to choose between Mr. Goldfish and me. I'm going to the country for the weekend, and I'll await your decision there."

I've never had a harder decision to make, and I had to make it alone, since Cecil was in Hollywood. I hardly closed my eyes for the next forty-eight hours. I had tremendous respect for Zukor's courage and qualities of leadership. I felt sure that with him at the helm our company had a glorious future. But Sam was my sister's husband, and while he lacked Zukor's experience, he also was a brilliant strategist. He was the one who had goaded me into the picture business in the first place. He had helped plan and build this organization, which had now grown beyond the point where it concerned only ourselves. We now had many stockholders, and their best interests had to be considered—which pointed to Zukor's guidance of the company, unhampered by internal dissension. I had to admit to myself, whatever obligation I felt toward him, that Sam was not geared to take a back seat for anyone. He was and still is the kind of dynamic personality that functions best alone, with all the power in his own hands.

I sent word to Zukor that I had made my decision, and he returned to the city. I told him I wanted him to continue as president. He suggested at once that we should do everything possible to soften the blow for Sam.

Calling our associates together, we estimated the value of Sam's share of the stock, which had not yet been listed on the exchange, and borrowed from our bankers to buy him out for about $900,000. He then formed the Goldwyn Pictures Corporation with Edgar Selwyn. That alliance also had rough going, and before it merged into Metro-Goldwyn-Mayer, Sam had again champed the bit and broken out of double harness. Not until he had his own head did he find his proper stride. Since then the whole industry has recognized him as a true champion.

I continued to commute between the coasts and to lunch with Zukor every day I spent in New York. Over the years our lunches shifted from Delmonico's to Sherry's to the Astor, then the Ritz, as each in turn became the fashionable spot for executives to doodle the backs of menus with million-dollar deals. Yet we never called each other by our first names until almost forty years later.

These luncheon dates meant far more to me than the pleasure of being in the company of a kindred spirit. I sought Zukor's judgment and advice on every important move we made in the production end. He kept a finger on the pulse of our business and his keen financial analyses determined the upper limits of the budgets we could safely allot to our pictures. He was always ready to do battle for bigger and better pictures.

One day he said, "Mr. Lasky, we are being throttled, strangled to death! I have fought with Hodkinson to increase the cash advances and the percentages of the gross for our pictures. The man has ice in his veins. He won't see that unless we get more money we can't make pictures of better quality and attract the best talent in the field. It has come to this—we've got to get control of Paramount or we'll be forced out of business. But don't worry—we're not going out of business!"

Zukor quietly bought up the shares of several Paramount stockholders, including Hiram Abrams, who had been one of the New England states'-rights men, and then maneuvered Abrams into the presidency before Hodkinson, conducting what he thought was a rou-

tine election of officers, realized that he was unseated. With control
of the company in our hands from that moment we acquired the rest
of its stock and Paramount became a subsidiary distributing company
owned 100 per cent by Famous Players-Lasky, Inc. Nevertheless we
retained the name Paramount for its trademark value, and used the
slogan "If It's a Paramount Picture It's the Best Show in Town."

Not long after this coup Zukor sent word that he wanted me to
plan a group of features with higher budgets than ever before. Whatever they earned would now be ours to spend for increasingly better
pictures. This enabled us to go forward with confidence that we could
remain in the vanguard of the fast-growing industry, which by this
time included Carl Laemmle's Universal Film Manufacturing Company, the Fox Film Corporation, Metro, and Triangle, which released
the productions of D. W. Griffith, Thomas Ince, and Mack Sennett.

I quickly wiped out the memory of *Less than the Dust* and recovered
Mary Pickford's prestige by sending her to the Coast with orders for
her pictures to be done on a don't-spare-the-brains-or-cash basis, and
Zukor shortly set up another subsidiary company, Artcraft Pictures, to
handle them and other high-budget films which couldn't be released
at our regular block-booking rates. Cecil directed two of Mary's pro-
ductions, *A Romance of the Redwoods* and *The Little American*.
Then on a happy hunch I delivered her into the hands of Marshall
Neilan, a young director who had first worked for us as an actor in an
Edgar Selwyn play, *The Country Boy*. He was responsible for some of
Mary's best-remembered and most typical successes at the height of her
popularity—*Rebecca of Sunnybrook Farm, The Little Princess, Stella
Maris, Amarilly of Clothes-line Alley,* and *M'liss*. William Desmond
Taylor also handled a number of her pictures. Simultaneously we were
starring Mary's brother, Jack Pickford, in such stories as *Freckles* and
Tom Sawyer.

Having the two acknowledged queens of Hollywood, Mary Pickford
and Marguerite Clark, on one lot made for some tempestuous times.
The same kind of parts suited both to a T, and no matter what prized
story property was bought for one star, the other coveted it. Mary was
making $10,000 a week and 50 per cent of the profits from her pic-
tures when she decided to abdicate her shared throne and set up a
monarchy of her own.

Marguerite had the field to herself on the Lasky lot until she married Harry Williams, a young Social Registerite of New Orleans. Williams told me that his wife might continue her screen career, but that
he would not permit her, ever again, to kiss a leading man. This was

the kiss of death in reverse for Marguerite Clark's popularity. We starred her in two or three more pictures, respecting Williams' injunction, but it was no use. Every film in those days adhered to the unwritten law of a saccharine clinch at the end. Marguerite's fans expected this as their due and simply couldn't accept their idol as a frigid heroine. Without wasting any time or more dimes at the box-office they got themselves other idols.

Before long we were able to build up our premium rental line, Artcraft, by absorbing the three giants of the Triangle Company, along with their top stars, Douglas Fairbanks, William S. Hart, and Charles Ray, and their ace writing team, John Emerson and Anita Loos. We developed another brand labeled Realart, using it for pictures in a lower budget and lower rental bracket, to build promising personalities like Bebe Daniels, Vivian Martin, and May McAvoy until they were starring material for the Class A Paramount productions. With this expansion I found myself with a schedule of 104 pictures in 1917, including 52 standard Paramount issues, 18 Artcrafts, and 34 Realarts. The bulk of them were made at the Vine Street studio, but we also used the Morosco Studio in Los Angeles and the Famous Players Studio on Fifty-sixth Street in New York, a former riding academy that, like the original Lasky Barn, had been converted from horseflesh to ham.

We tried to outdo our competitors, not only by collecting the biggest names of stage and screen, but also by presenting a certain number of offbeat attractions, glorifying personalities whose names were household words because of achievements in other phases of show business. We made three or four pictures with Julian Eltinge, the celebrated female impersonator, for no particular reason but that he could put Mae Murray, Gloria Swanson, and all the rest of our glamour stars to shame with the way he modeled women's clothes. When he made an entrance at a Hollywood party, wearing a wig and a Lady Duff Gordon evening gown, neither men nor women could take their eyes off him. It was considered daring to present him at the beginning of each picture *as a man*, since he had never played such a role in his stage appearances!

We later starred Harry Houdini in a couple of thrillers. He did his best acting handcuffed and locked in a trunk at the bottom of a river. Incidentally, his fantastic escapes from such involved confinement would have been easy to fake with trick photography—but he insisted on being dumped in the river shackled, locked, and roped exactly as he was for his incredible public exhibitions.

The idea of building a *silent* picture around the world's greatest singer, Enrico Caruso, was in the same "freak" category, but I didn't think of it that way then. Encouraged by the success of Geraldine Farrar's films and my own penchant for renowned musicians, I thought the whole world would flock to a Caruso picture just to see what he looked like, even though they couldn't hear him sing.

I remembered when Blanche and I were getting sporadic vaudeville bookings for our own musical act during our first year in New York, we had been attracted by posters advertising the American debut of Caruso at the Metropolitan Opera House in *Rigoletto*. We had never seen an opera, although I had taken some voice lessons as well as cornet and piano, and, with my usual excessive enthusiasm for anything I embarked on, had wanted for a time to be an opera singer myself.

We had naïvely thought that we could walk up and buy tickets the night of the opening. We were lucky to get standing room at the back of the top gallery, among Caruso's music-loving Italian compatriots. The critics didn't call him the greatest voice of the century until later, but his reception and the bravos in the gallery had been terrific.

From our eyrie he had looked microscopic, and Blanche had wanted to see him life-size, so we had joined a huge crowd at the stage door waiting for his exit. Some of them hadn't even been able to get in the building to hear him sing. (This scene we incorporated in *The Great Caruso* almost half a century later, of the tenor giving a "vocal autograph" to appease fans that besieged him as he entered his car.)

And so when I read one day in 1917 that Joseph Schenck and his partner Julius Steger planned to make a picture with Caruso, I was mortified at not having had the inspiration myself but hastened to make up for this oversight by negotiating with Schenck to buy his eight-week contract with Caruso for $40,000. He was happy to make a sizable profit on a picture he hadn't even started. It seemed good economy for me to charge this investment off to two pictures rather than one, so we prepared and filmed two original stories. The first was based on a popular Gus Edwards song, "My Cousin Caruso," current when Caruso was at the height of his glory, and concerned a barber who brightened his humdrum life by spinning colorful tales of an improbable cousin, said to be a great opera singer, but whom everyone considered purely a figment of the imagination until he showed up and vindicated the boastful barber. Caruso played both parts, the first dual role we ever had to contend with, and the director and cameraman had to improvise some hanky-panky to show Caruso as the barber patting Caruso as the cousin on the back. We were really getting three performances out of him for the price of one—I thought I was playing it pretty smart.

I was on the set frequently during the shooting of the two pictures, and we became good friends. He was an irrepressible practical joker, and you never knew what to expect of him next, but you could always expect to laugh. Some of his fanciful tricks were crude and not very funny, but we got in the habit of laughing expectantly, as a television studio audience does today when a comedian lifts an eyebrow. He also had a brilliant flair for caricature, and was almost always drawing your picture while he talked to you. I still treasure an impudent sketch he did of me the first time we met.

One day about two weeks after we finished shooting the pair of pictures at the Fifty-sixth Street studio and were in the midst of another production, Caruso barged through the crowded set, with a flower in his buttonhole and a tall young lady on his arm, and his handsome secretary, Bruno Zirato, in tow.

"Lasky," he called across the stage, "I'm married!"

I reacted automatically with a hearty laugh at his little joke. It was just like him to abduct a girl from a Fifth Avenue shop in order to fool us for a few minutes. "Very funny!" I commented.

"No, no—I'm really married!" he cried. "Congratulate!"

"I congratulate you on your sense of humor," I said. "Who'd be crazy enough to marry you?" I laughed some more with the smug satisfaction of seeing through his playful ruse and not being taken in by it.

The lovely girl looked bewildered and embarrassed. Caruso was almost apoplectic as he drew from his breast pocket a marriage license and held it before my eyes. It was my turn to be embarrassed. I whispered quickly to a prop man and in a matter of seconds he had produced from a nearby set a bouquet of American Beauties that exactly matched the shade of my face. I handed them to the new bride and she was charmingly gracious about the whole thing as we conducted them to their car.

When one of our important pictures was given a general simultaneous release, Zukor and I customarily waited for the reports on the first day's business that came into the sales department from all over the country as anxiously as we would have watched race results or election returns on which we had made a huge wager. As the first reports on *My Cousin* came in, it was evident that it was going to spoil our unbroken five-year record of no failures (although *Less than the Dust* had come too close for comfort). The public was smarter than I was, and, realizing they'd be cheated of Caruso's glorious voice, they saved their money. *My Cousin* was such a fiasco at the box-office that we had to refund rental money to many complaining exhibitors. Zukor also ordered all booking contracts for the second picture canceled and we never released it at all—the first time we ever shelved a completed film. I can't even remember the name of it, and please don't remind me!

Our production schedule for that year again called for 104 features, a goal set by the solicitous desire to spare exhibitors who changed bills twice a week from the inconvenience of booking anything but Paramount pictures. The product was sold to exhibitors in blocks, at a fixed price, sight unseen before it was made. This was mass production with a vengeance, and need I mention that, if we had been fabricating aircraft, some of them would have been a menace to life and limb.

Making pictures at such a merry pace, I wasn't able to assign writers to the stories and stories to the directors, along with my other duties and necessary traveling. So I had brought in Frank Woods, an expert in silent screen-play construction who had worked with D. W. Griffith, to take charge of this phase of studio operation. But the responsibilities got too heavy for him to handle alone, so we created a new kind of executive to oversee writing and production of individual pictures, I dubbed them "supervisors" and delegated Hector Turnbull to ride herd on them.

The word "supervisor" has long since passed out of existence in the Hollywood hierarchy and "producer" is now substituted to designate the link between management and production. Those categories are combined in an independent producer such as Sam Goldwyn, who is a company unto himself. But Pandro Berman, for instance, is one of several producers at M-G-M, all of whom are responsible to the production head of the studio. Some production heads confine themselves to supervising producers. Others occasionally engage in production themselves.

Among our early supervisors were Tom Geraghty, Lucien Hubbard, E. Lloyd Sheldon, Ralph Block, Walter Woods, Julian Johnson, William Le Baron, Howard Hawks, Waldemar Young, and Louis "Buddy" Lighton. For some time they didn't even get screen credit, but they were the first members of a profession now represented by the Screen Producers Guild of 180 members.

Soon Turnbull was more than swamped, and as Frank Woods was also overworked and nearing retirement age anyway, I had to look around for still another ringmaster to keep things moving at a furious clip.

Joseph Dannenberg, editor of the Eastern trade paper *The Film*

E.

Daily, suggested Ben Schulberg, who had been in the publicity department of Famous Players before the merger and was now producing low-budget independent pictures starring his promising young discovery, Clara Bow. I conferred with Schulberg and offered him the post. As an inducement to expedite his acceptance I magnanimously agreed to take the Clara Bow contract off his hands for a consideration of $25,000. This was the equivalent of volunteering to relieve him of a million dollars, but neither of us realized the sensational popularity Clara Bow was shortly to enjoy and he gladly accepted.

With Schulberg overseeing half the pictures and Turnbull the other half there was inevitable rivalry between the two and conflicts over the selection of stories, directors, stars, writers, and supervisors available on the lot. But the assembly line did move faster under this divided authority. Production also continued at the Famous Players Studio in New York under Hugh Ford, assisted by Albert Kaufman. The output of pictures from the West Coast was stepped up so drastically, however, that "Jesse L. Lasky Presents—" appeared at the top of the screen about five times as often as "Adolph Zukor Presents—." I thought I detected a slightly reproachful look in the eyes of my luncheon companion. In the interests of better digestion I suggested a change of policy, and from then on all our pictures, whether made in the East or on the Coast, were "presented" by Adolph Zukor and Jesse L. Lasky in tandem.

Hunting Big Game with
Pen and Dotted Line

In the twenties we expanded until we got too big for our britches. While I was turning out a continuous flow of pictures like a frozen-custard machine, Sidney Kent was selling them like hot cakes, and Adolph Zukor was collecting theatre chains like postage stamps, a collection that eventually numbered almost 2000 houses, first under the able direction of Harold Franklin and later managed by Sam Katz.

Not content with dominating the market in this country, Zukor established film exchanges in foreign countries, built showcase theatres in London and Paris and film studios in England, France, Germany, and in India, of all places. The foreign market was extremely important, and I often consulted Emil Shauer, who was in charge of our distribution overseas and had a vast knowledge of that field, in trying to choose subjects that would be as well received abroad as at home.

Some of these ventures were not outstandingly successful, to be charitable about it. The studio in Poona, outside Bombay, was so hot that the film practically melted in the cameras, but it was the forerunner of a booming picture industry in India today.

Our UFA studios in Berlin were a flop financially, but out of it we salvaged Ernst Lubitsch, Pola Negri, and Emil Jannings, transplanting them to Hollywood. Not bad salvaging! They helped us hold our foreign audiences and Lubitsch was later production head of Paramount for a time.

I remember a banquet at the Hotel Adlon, after I had arranged for Pola to make pictures for us in America. I was seated between the beautiful Polish actress and the mayor of Berlin, neither of whom spoke English. Anxious to stifle any qualms she might have about leaving Europe, where she was already a reigning favorite, I told her through an interpreter that with her personality she was sure to conquer America. We both smiled excessively over that, but she appeared puzzled. After churning it over in her mind for some time she turned to me and said, "*Was ist das Personality?*"

"*Ach, das Personality!*" I exclaimed, with an expansive gesture, looking around helplessly for the interpreter. He had vanished. And for the rest of the evening I was busily occupied trying to explain in sign language the meaning of something I can't adequately explain even with words!

Pola did, of course, leave the indelible mark of her tempestuous individuality on Hollywood in many fine pictures, one of the best-remembered of which was *Hotel Imperial*, directed by Greta Garbo's discoverer, Mauritz Stiller.

The building of the Islington studio in London and the first de luxe American-type movie palaces in England and France—the Carlton and Plaza theatres in London and the Paramount in Paris—was supervised by Zukor's brother-in-law, Al Kaufman. One of France's leading architects and a pioneer in the "moderne" movement was engaged to create the Paramount. It was the last word in extreme "moderne" design—also the first word, since there was no other theatre anywhere of such radically advanced simple line and form.

The Vaudeville, an ancient, hallowed legitimate theatre which had seen the greatest triumphs of the French idol Réjane, and whose smart first-night audiences traditionally set the Paris fashions for the season, was torn down to make way for the upstart American movie house. This desecration of sacred ground by foreigners so incensed a clot of sentimental Frenchmen that they dug around in legal archives and exhumed a law dating from Napoleon's time which provided that the façade of every structure on the Boulevard des Capucines must conform to Empire style. So we had to restore the monumental Empire-period façade that had just been scrapped. We could have saved thousands of dollars by leaving the original one standing, and it would probably have lasted three hundred years longer than the new one will, considering the solid way those old edifices were put up. This whimsical union of tradition with progress gave Paris the most futuristic theatre in the world—with an 1810 false front.

I don't know how we managed to do it without a divining rod, but we picked a location for the Islington studios where heavy fog would collect even when all the rest of London was bright with sunshine. As a consequence the inexplicable breezes that caressed the fabric of the heroine's evening gown in drawing-room scenes of our English pictures were caused by huge fans installed to blow the fog away. And some of the artistic soft-focus photography admired by critics in this country was simply fog that eluded the fans. The maddening fog may also have added to the ghostly effects in George Fitzmaurice's *Three Live Ghosts*, which had a London setting. Incidentally, our $15-a-week prop man there was a young fellow named Alfred Hitchcock.

I sent over top directors and writers and casts, and in spite of the difficulties we made some really good pictures such as *The Bonnie Briar Bush*, shot entirely in Scotland. But world travel had not yet become a middle-class sport, and movie fans of that "Buy America" era were apathetic or even hostile to our efforts to show authentic Continental backgrounds. We had anticipated the present trend by too many years, and had to close the Islington studios after a good college try.

No other company of those times could afford to make such premature and costly experiments. Our position as the foremost motion-picture company was not even remotely threatened. We had an efficient production organization with a dazzling roster of stars and directors, an exceptional sales department, the largest circuit of showcases for our product that anyone has ever had, before or since, and no financial worries. Was there anything more we could possibly want or need? Yes, there most certainly was.

The responsibility of putting two new films before the cameras every week began to haunt me. Good film ideas can't be plucked like bananas—they have to be mined like diamonds. While we had organized a competent staff of readers in the New York office to cover all the available material—new plays, books, magazine stories, and originals—it was touch-and-go to meet our release dates. At times high-salaried contract stars and production facilities were idle because of lack of a suitable story. Overhead mounted while we fell behind in our schedule.

As early as 1919, I had told Zukor on one of my New York trips that we were using up ideas as fast as they could be developed or adapted. "We've got to break the bottleneck in the story department," I said. "We can't rely any longer on simply sifting what comes to us spontaneously. We must begin actively to stimulate the creative literary processes. We've got to increase the supply of top-quality screen material and control some of the sources for our own protection.

"The most successful playwrights don't average one play a year," I pointed out, "and then we have to compete with other picture companies for the screen rights. If we could contract with top playwrights and novelists to write directly for the screen, they could probably turn out several stories in the time they now devote to one, and we would have exclusive rights to them. Another possibility would be to finance, or buy out, a big legitimate Broadway producing organization, one with a good backlog of produced and unproduced plays.

Zukor saw my point without argument. "Maybe we ought to try both," he reflected.

At our first luncheon on my next trip to New York he remarked casually, "I bought the Charles Frohman company for you."

My fork and jaw dropped. I recalled the humiliating rebuffs I had suffered at the hands of Alf Hayman when I wanted an audience with Mr. Frohman about producing Sir James Barrie's *The Twelve Pound Look* in vaudeville. Hayman had not only kept me from seeing Frohman, but conveyed the impression that I ought to be flogged for my presumption. A year later Ethel Barrymore had played *The Twelve Pound Look* in vaudeville at her own insistence, and continued to do so, between her appearances on the legitimate stage, for over twenty-five years.

"You are now Charles Frohman, Inc., Mr. Lasky," Zukor pronounced, enjoying my astonishment. "You wanted plays. Well, you can wallow in plays—German, Hungarian, French. You also have four theatres in New York, Chicago, and Boston in which to grow *new* plays for us."

"That's fine," I said when I found my voice. "Just what we need. But I can't run a theatrical empire and the studio too."

"It doesn't come under distribution or exploitation," Zukor said calmly. "It's production—and you're head of production. I've made an appointment for you to see Alf Hayman, who's been general manager of the company since Frohman went down on the *Lusitania*. He will take his orders from you."

Hayman had a strained expression when he faced me in my large office the next day, but neither of us referred to our previous encounters, when the tables had been turned. Nervously he briefed me on the whereabouts of stars I had watched in rapture as a boy in the gallery— stars it was now my privilege to move about like chessmen. Did I want to bring Otis Skinner into New York from Chicago? What was my pleasure in regard to the tryout of Ethel Barrymore's new play? No suitable vehicle had been found for Maude Adams. Would I consider a revival? William Gillette's *Sherlock Holmes* had about run its course at the New Amsterdam. Did I wish to put it on the road?

The first thing I wanted to put on the road was Alf Hayman. It didn't take a Sherlock Holmes to know he had also run his course. I could have overlooked my own personal feelings, had he been well liked by the Frohman company stars and not been hampered by the same revulsion for the motion-picture medium as he had shown toward vaudeville. I was still casting around for someone to replace him when Bessie and I spent a weekend at Holbrook Blinn's country place. Among the dinner guests were Blinn's neighbors, Major Edward Bowes with his gifted wife, Margaret Illington, and a young Dartmouth graduate, Walter Wanger. Wanger was bright, suave, and keenly conversant with the legitimate theatre. He had already produced an arty play, *'Ception Shoals*, starring Alla Nazimova. We were delighted to give him a lift back to town in my new Stutz Bearcat, since he had no car.

Before we dropped him off, I had decided he might have the qualifications to run the Frohman company, and asked him to meet me the next day. He did and I spent the whole morning delving into his background. He spoke French and Italian, and knew London like a book. But I didn't ask all the questions. With a consuming interest he probed the particulars of my liaison work between the West Coast studio and the Eastern business office, a function that had kept me bedded on Pullmans eighty nights the previous year.

I explained that it was a full-time job to buy plays, keep stars and directors happy, give personal attention to important productions, and collaborate in over-all business policies, and that I couldn't spread myself any thinner. I had to have an executive for the Frohman company of the utmost capability and self-sufficiency. Wanger seemed an ideal choice for the assignment, and he was thrilled with the prospect, but even more intrigued with my problems as a studio executive.

"Walter," I said after he had repeatedly veered our discussion from the Frohman company to movie-making, "I don't think I'll entrust this post to you after all. Let me think it over."

When he came back for my answer, I told him I had made up my mind that he was too good for a job with a limited future. "If I make you general manager of the Frohman company, you will have reached the top rung of a short ladder before you start," I remarked. "But in the picture business you could keep on climbing. In short, I'd like to make you my right-hand assistant."

Walter Wanger amply justified my faith in him. He worked with me for five years, then I made him general manager of Famous Players-Lasky production on both coasts. Still later, as head of his own company, he produced such outstanding pictures as *Stagecoach*, *Queen Christina*, *Gabriel*, *The Long Voyage Home*, *Over the White House*, and *Canyon Passage*.

I could hardly wait to "wallow" in the extensive library of foreign dramas we had acquired, and hired Benjamin Glazer to translate and adapt some of these treasures. But I still lacked a general manager for the play company.

Then, while dining in the Plaza, I saw my friend Edgar Selwyn sitting with a stout young man in English-tailored clothes. He introduced his companion as Gilbert Miller, son of the beloved Frohman star, Henry Miller, and himself a well-known manager of three London theatres, whose latest success on both sides of the Atlantic was a musical production of *Monsieur Beaucaire*. I made his acquaintance and very shortly he was placed in charge of our Charles Frohman company under an arrangement which gave him a free hand to produce any play he thought worth doing. He continued in this capacity for thirteen years, collecting 50 per cent of the profits, which amounted to $800,000 in one year.

We understandably urged him at the outset to favor dramas and comedies that ostensibly had picture value, but he believed the venture would be more successful if he didn't allow Hollywood considerations to interfere with his selection or staging of plays. I didn't attempt to dictate his policy in this regard, and I couldn't know it would boomerang to the embarrassment of the parent company a few years later when he produced a dramatic tour de force by one of France's most illustrious playwrights, Édouard Bourdet, translated and adapted by Arthur Hornblow, Jr. Although *The Captive* had no picture potential whatever, Gilbert Miller gave it a brilliant production with Helen Menken in the lead. The drama critics did handsprings over its artistic merits, but because of its Lesbian theme the play was raided by the police. A censorship jury quickly exonerated it from the charge of lasciviousness, but the newspapers saw an opportunity to scream "MOVIE MILLIONS POLLUTING THE STAGE!" They carefully ignored the fact that we "polluted" the stage that same season with Holbrook Blinn in Molnár's *The Play's the Thing*, Ethel Barrymore in *The Constant Wife*, and Jeanne Eagels in *Her Cardboard Lover*, but kept up a barrage of undercover sniping until we removed the telltale evidence of our alliance from all advertising and playbills.

Famous Players-Lasky continued to finance the Frohman company plays, but they were henceforth presented under Gilbert Miller's name alone. The tumult and shouting died as the public was allowed to forget our connection with the unfortunate play and such hits as *Journey's End*, *Scarlet Sister Mary*, *The Good Fairy*, *The Animal Kingdom*, *There's Always Juliet*, and *The Late Christopher Bean*.

Gilbert and his wife became cherished friends of ours and were often with us on our travels in Europe. Gilbert and I would look over the current crop of European plays together and scout for actors and authors. He was personally acquainted with most of the leading Continental dramatists.

During one of these trips we left our wives in Paris and took a train to Berlin on a Saturday night. In order to have pocket money we prevailed on the dining-car steward to change a $50 bill into German currency. It was shortly after World War I and inflation was at its height. The rate of exchange fluctuated from day to day, and on that day it was about a million marks to the dollar. The man returned with bales of paper marks. We had to empty a small suitcase and use it for a wallet. Gilbert carried it everywhere we went, and even after a weekend of sight-seeing, night-club hopping, and staying in Berlin's world-famed hotel, the Adlon, we had an abundance of marks left over from that converted $50 bill!

The whole trip had the aspect of a comic opera. We started back to Paris after completing our business in Berlin, and were in our berths when the train stopped for customs inspection at Kehl on the French border. Gilbert showed his passport. I searched for mine and couldn't find it. Then I realized with dismay that I must have dropped it when I had got off the train that afternoon to buy some lead soldiers for Jesse, Jr. He was ten years old and loved to stage military maneuvers with the toy soldiers I brought him from all the countries I visited.

After a heated conversation with the customs officers, of which I didn't understand a word, Gilbert whispered, "I've used every argument I could think of. I even told them you're the most important man in America, but it makes no difference—you can't cross the border without your passport."

We had to dress hastily, throw our things in our bags, and vacate our comfortable compartment. We stood on the platform, looking longingly and dejectedly after the train as it pulled out. It was past midnight, and we had to rouse a sleeping porter at The Golden Star Inn to get a room. Early the next morning Gilbert awakened me and said he'd go over to Strasbourg on the French side, enlist the aid of the American consul, and be back by the time I'd had a leisurely breakfast.

I didn't know what I was ordering when I jabbed my finger at the menu as though I were playing "pin the tail on the donkey," but it turned out to be edible and sufficient. I got up to pay the bill with the same empty gesture with which I had reached for my passport. Gilbert, accustomed to paying the bills for both of us because I didn't understand the language, had all my money with him.

The waiter eyed me suspiciously. I tried to explain my predicament, but of course he couldn't understand. I went to the desk, followed closely by the waiter, and made signs to the clerk that I wanted my restaurant bill charged to my room number.

"*Wie ist Ihr Name?*" he asked.

I replied, "Lasky—Jesse Lasky," but to him my name was mud. The sleepy porter hadn't bothered to register us. I had not only been trapped in Germany, I was a prisoner in the inn until I could pay for my breakfast. The desk clerk called the manager and they discussed the situation with guttural explosions, excited arm-waving, and baleful scowls in my direction. To forestall possible banishment to the kitchen to wash dishes, I went back to my table, ordered more coffee, and drank it nervously. Every time the waiter began to hover menacingly, I ordered more coffee. I was uncomfortably at high tide by the time Gilbert got back. He had had to wait for the consulate to open, and then wait some more while the consul went out for his morning constitutional. A German-American clerk started to apologize for the delay

E*

and then recognized Gilbert, having formerly been a bartender at Schultz's saloon at Forty-fourth and Broadway, where he had served us both many times. As soon as the consul returned, the clerk oiled the diplomatic wheels so well that the consul perked up, said he'd like to meet me, and signed a pass for my entry into France.

The French customs officers looked at the letter and opened my bags to discover the regiments of German lead soldiers, which seemed to them highly irregular until it was explained that they were to be used for mock battles and our purpose in coming to France was to purchase the captors of the German toy soldiers.

We reported dutifully to the consul, who welcomed us effusively and outlined a schedule for our entertainment that stupefied us. He was determined to make amends for our embarrassment with an elaborate program of conviviality.

"You will rest this morning after your severe ordeal," the consul advised us. "Then this afternoon you will be my guests at a fine beer garden, and tonight—the opera. Unfortunately there isn't time to arrange a dinner for tonight, but tomorrow I will assemble all the town dignitaries for a dinner in your honor."

Gilbert and I looked at each other in alarm. All we wanted to do was get back to our wives in Paris. "We're overwhelmed by your graciousness, sir," Gilbert said, "but before accepting your hospitality, we feel it incumbent upon us to appear at our best. Would you be kind enough to send us to a barber?"

The consul suggested we leave our luggage in his office, but Gilbert insisted we needed it. So a man was sent with us to the barbershop and I was in the chair with my face lathered, as unsuspecting of the plot underfoot as the consul himself, when Gilbert finally persuaded the attendant not to wait. Then, snatching the barber's apron off me, he wiped my face and yanked me out of the shop and into a taxi. We made for the railroad station, but had to wait an hour for the Paris train, hiding behind newspapers and then sneaking aboard like a couple of criminals.

It was base ingratitude, I admit, but being ensnared in the toils of our rescuer seemed worse than our original plight.

When we had settled in the dining car, some delectable Rhine salmon took our minds off our misadventures, and the menu said we could have second helpings if we wished. When the waitress asked Gilbert "*Voulez-vous encore du saumon?*" he replied, "*Oui,*" and was served another portion of the ambrosia. The waitress then turned to me and inquired, "*Vous avez eu une suffisance, n'est-ce pas?*"

I assented with a fervent *"Oui!"* and drooled in anticipation, but to no avail. Gilbert, the scoundrel, kept a straight face and enjoyed my perplexity for hours, finally explaining that his *"Oui"* had meant that he wanted more salmon, but my *"Oui"* meant I'd had enough.

In Budapest we celebrated my fortieth birthday with a theatre party at the Vigszinhaz. Even though I couldn't understand what was being said, I enjoyed it because the vigorous charm of one performer transcended language barriers. I talked to him backstage through an interpreter and told him that he'd be an assured success in America if he'd learn English. He took me at my word, learned English, came to America months later, and we put the name of Paul Lukas on a contract.

The *wagon-lit* was sold out from Budapest to Venice, but Gilbert Miller pulled some political strings and got an official embassy car and driver for the trip. Wherever we stopped a crowd gathered around, impressed by the United States seal on the car. Gilbert would stand up, address the spectators, and then bow obsequiously to me. "I've told them you're the Ambassador to Hungary," he'd say under his breath, "and they expect you to make a speech."

I kept a smiling face toward the crowd as I told Gilbert what I thought of his practical jokes. He "interpreted" my remarks in terms of appropriate flattery to the townspeople, judging from the way they cheered me.

I remember passing some public baths in the town of Ráczkeve which were proudly advertised as "Completely renovated in 1748"! They were built by the Turks around A.D. 1500.

We came back from that trip considerably richer in literary sources. Gilbert Miller had acquired Ibáñez's *Blood and Sand* and Molnár's *The Swan*, both of which he produced successfully on Broadway before we made picture versions. I had talked to Robert Hichens, E. Phillips Oppenheim, and H. G. Wells without inducing them to channel a portion of their talents to pictures—but negotiations with Henry Arthur Jones, Edward Knoblock, Arnold Bennett, Sir Gilbert Parker, W. Somerset Maugham, and Elinor Glyn were more fruitful.

Our storage bins of screen material also contained some very choice Barrie plays. I had purchased them in a block of ten on a previous trip under the same terms as those by which I acquired the Belasco plays earlier—$100,000 against half the profits.

Of the Barrie plays, which included *Peter Pan, A Kiss for Cinderella, What Every Woman Knows, Sentimental Tommy, Alice-Sit-by-the-Fire,* and *The Admirable Crichton,* the first to be filmed was *Crichton.*

Cecil immediately utilized it as a vehicle for Gloria Swanson, whom he was already building into the screen's first real glamour queen through such pictures as *Old Wives for New, Don't Change Your Husband,* and *For Better, for Worse.*

After *The Admirable Crichton* was completed, but before its release, the publicity and sales departments made strong objections to the title. They said that the public so rarely encountered the word "admirable" they would confuse it with "admiral" and stay away from theatres showing it, under the impression it was a sea picture. For some unaccountable reason sea pictures weren't very popular at that particular time. I informed Cecil of this snag.

"I'll give them a title they'll like," he said with some vexation, and, after pondering it overnight, announced with a trace of sarcasm, "We'll call it *Male and Female.* I guess the sales department and the public will understand *that!*"

Needless to say, the sales department was delighted with the switch, and the picture went out under the more provocative title. I was making another trip to London on the same boat that carried the first overseas print. Our general manager for England, J. C. Graham, was relieved to see me, and I understood why when he reminded me that our contract with Barrie contained a clause that obliged us to show him the film adaptations of his plays before they could be released in Great Britain. Mr. Graham passed the hot potato to me. An appointment was made to run the picture for Sir James in a private projection room. The two of us went in and sat down, and I was screwing up my courage to signal the operator to start when the immortal writer said, "I'm looking forward to seeing *The Admirable Crichton.*"

I shuddered. I wanted to burrow down into the protective upholstery of my loge, but I knew I had to break the news before he had the shock of seeing it on the screen.

"Sir James, it's a . . . that is . . . I mean a fine picture," I stammered. "It wasn't my idea, but you see, sir, the American idiom isn't exactly the King's English, and our director, Cecil DeMille, is a very determined and sometimes difficult man and . . . well . . . he decided to call your *Admirable Crichton* . . . he decided to call it . . . *Male and Female.*"

There was a dead silence and I waited for the heavens to fall. Then Sir James's hand shot out so quickly it gave me a start. But, instead of striking me, he grasped my hand and said, "Capital. I wish I'd thought of it myself."

I had no thought of running a matrimonial agency, but after my sister Blanche divorced Sam Goldwyn, my business dealings for the studio brought both of them together with their second mates. Blanche married Hector Turnbull, whom I brought West as one of our first writers, and Goldwyn married Frances Howard, a new, young actress whose sensitive performance in *The Best People* so impressed me on opening night at the Lyceum Theatre that I signed her at once to play the princess in *The Swan*, the role recently recreated by Grace Kelly. And just as Grace Kelly did, while her screen portrayal in *The Swan* was delighting audiences everywhere, Frances Howard renounced her brilliant career in favor of her real-life romance. If Grace's life pattern continues to parallel that of her predecessor in *The Swan*, she is destined to play an indispensable role in her husband's success and happiness.

Elinor Glyn had written a titillating English novel that caused an international sensation before I got into the picture business. *Three Weeks* was the *Forever Amber* of its day. Another company owned the picture rights. But I concocted a title *The Great Moment*, which I thought had the Glynish feeling of *Three Weeks*, only more so, and persuaded Madame Glyn to come to America and fashion a slinky story for Gloria Swanson to go with the title. One of her stipulations was that she must approve the choice of leading man.

Madame Glyn was as adept as Salvador Dali at drawing attention to herself. From the moment she stepped off the *Mauretania* in New York and proceeded to a press reception at the apartment we had arranged for her to live in, she was "good copy." The good copy needed illustrating, so I offered to take her to the photographer's myself directly from the reception.

As we were leaving the apartment, she snatched up a leopard-skin rug, thinking it might come in handy as a pertinent prop for the portraits, since the *pièce de résistance* of her torrid best-seller had taken place on a leopard skin. I was helping her into my car when she decided she'd rather walk, and bestowed the leopard skin on me with a queenly flourish.

My promenade down Fifth Avenue with the garish rug on one arm and the garish Glyn on the other was like a nightmare. Everyone turned and gawked, but the flashy leopard pelt on my arm couldn't begin to compete for attention with Madame Glyn's flamboyant taste in clothes and her flaming red hair.

New York didn't stimulate her productive faculties, and she didn't make much progress on her scenario until we transplanted her extrovert temperament to the more conducive atmosphere of Hollywood. In due time the scenario was finished and the cast picked, but Madame Glyn wouldn't approve our choice for male lead. The director, Sam Wood, reported to me with a persecuted mien that he had trotted out every other available leading man on the lot for her inspection and she wouldn't go for any of them.

"She says they don't have 'It,' whatever she means by that," he added.

I went to her office and explained that delay in starting the picture would cost the studio thousands of dollars and we would have to decide on a leading man at once. But she was implacable. She wouldn't let the picture start until we gave her a man endowed with It. She couldn't tell us what It was, because there didn't seem to be any other word to cover It, so she had given It that designation herself. But she assured me that a person either had It or he didn't, and all the actors we had submitted thus far didn't.

As evidence that she genuinely desired a solution to the unfortunate impasse and wasn't just being capricious, she offered the lead in the picture to several lads who took her fancy as she roamed the lot and the streets of Hollywood. They might be carpenters or cabdrivers—it made no difference to her that they weren't actors so long as they had the elusive It. It seemed quite unreasonable to her that we refused to consider any of these God-given vessels of It. We eventually compromised by pulling Milton Sills off another picture he had been scheduled to make, when Madame Glyn met him at a party and announced ecstatically that he harbored the indefinable quality.

She was equally fastidious about the actress entrusted with the portrayal of her heroine, but since she couldn't do anything about replacing Gloria Swanson, having been hired to tailor her own talents to the star's needs, she attempted to refurbish Gloria's literary taste, deportment, speech, and choice of clothes. Happily, there was nothing in her contract that gave her dominion in these matters, and Swanson survived.

Elinor Glyn's bizarre behavior and comments attracted plenty of attention in Hollywood, as they were very possibly calculated to do. One of the stories that went the rounds concerned her meeting with Charlie Chaplin.

"Dear, dear, so this is Charlie Chaplin!" she said, acknowledging the introduction. "Do you know you don't look nearly so funny as I thought you would?"

Chaplin surveyed her critically and responded, "Neither do you."

Elinor Glyn's quest for *It* became the talk of the studio, then spread through Hollywood and soon the whole country adopted her catchword for what was later known as sex appeal. The *It* vogue reached such proportions that Ben Schulberg suggested that we cash in on it with a picture entitled simply *It*. The publicity department made a big fuss about our paying Elinor Glyn "$50,000 for one word." They weren't far wrong, because our top writing team, Buddy Lighton and his wife, Hope Loring, should get full credit for the screen play of Clara Bow's biggest hit. From then on Clara was referred to as "The *It* Girl."

Although Glyn's whims were often on the farcical side, they made good publicity for her pictures, and one of these whims curiously contributed to my mother's comfort. When the green-eyed novelist invaded Hollywood, she let it be known that she couldn't possibly live anywhere but in the penthouse of the Ambassador Hotel. But as she wanted to eat her cake and bake it, too, we prevailed on the management to install a kitchenette in the penthouse—the only one in the hotel. When the authoress returned to Europe, I took over the apartment with its unique home-cooking facilities for my mother. With her diet cook she lived out the rest of her life there.

A Great Lover

Drops into Our Laps

Typical of the picture business is the unremitting state of hostility between the production center on the West Coast and the administrative offices in New York. The viewpoint of the businessman cannot be completely reconciled with that of the artist. East is East and West is West, etc. The East complains that costs are too high, shooting schedules too long, titles hard to exploit, stills unimaginative, and everything else without exception hopelessly bungled. The West righteously resents all this niggling interference with the creative processes and constantly demands more financial leeway for the competitive struggle to make pictures bigger and better than those of rival companies.

Sometimes, if the West squawked loudly enough, the East blessed an effort with crossed fingers, loosening the purse strings more than usual. But too often this indulgence resulted in *longer* rather than *better* pictures, which caused the exhibitors untold pain, since long pictures cut down the audience turnover in their theatres and decreased the theoretical maximum revenue. Then the home-office boys and the Wall Street watchdogs would scream in outraged betrayal. I had to bear the brunt of much unappreciated advice about cutting costs and running the studio on a rational basis like any other business.

Particularly when a general business slump threatens, the banking interests involved in studio production get edgy about the enormous sums poured into what seems to them intangibles or extravagances. During one of these periodic storm and stress periods our bankers, Kuhn, Loeb & Company, recommended that we engage an efficiency expert endorsed by them and give him power to make drastic reductions in overhead wherever he saw fit.

Our pictures were showing good profits at the time, and neither Mr. Zukor nor myself relished the idéa of dissecting the goose that was laying golden eggs. But Kuhn, Loeb's money talked in a compelling voice, and we ruefully consented to have investigator Harris De Haven Connick installed in our hair.

One of the first economic ratholes Mr. Connick plugged up was the insidious practice of using too many words in telegrams. Disagreements over scenes, ideas, cuts, titles, and other details of pictures in work occasioned daily telegraphic exchanges. The phone couldn't be used for quick communication because it took hours to place a long-distance call. (The first transcontinental' phone call from a picture studio, arranged by appointment with the telephone company a day in advance, was such a sensational publicity stunt that it got a full turnout of press reporters and photographers to preserve the historic occasion for posterity. About all Mr. Zukor said was "Hello, is that you?" and all I said was "Yes. Is that you? . . . How's the weather there? . . . It's fine here, too.")

We were in the habit of writing our telegrams in the form of letters, with the salutation "Dear So-and-So" and closing with "Regards" before the signature, an affectation probably stemming from the same exuberance that makes show people call each other "Darling" and "Sweetheart." Gushing communications were inimical to Mr. Connick's business sense and engineering training. A little close figuring told him that three superfluous words shaved from thousands of telegrams would mean a saving of countless pennies. He thereupon issued an edict that no more *regards* were to be bandied carelessly between the two coasts. We dutifully acceded and the resulting holocaust nearly wrecked the studio. Without the softening effect of the accustomed "Regards" routine criticisms and friendly suggestions took on the sting of a slap in the face. After a month of regardless telegrams sensitive feelings on both coasts were in such turmoil that we took to bootlegging the forbidden word, and to this day I have never sent another telegram without including "Regards."

Another of his ideas for holding down picture costs was to limit the expenditure for any story property to $10,000. He evidently didn't realize that one story can be worth more than another, and that by spending twice as much for an uncommonly good one you are likely to reap four times the profit that you will on a run-of-the-mill feature.

Mr. Connick was a capable man in his own field, industrial engineering. He had been in charge of the construction and operation of the Panama-Pacific International Exposition. He had also been the construction engineer on numerous sewer projects in the West. But very few pictures, I'm proud to say, could profitably use a sewer connoisseur as a technical adviser.

Zukor issued an ultimatum that, if the efficiency expert stayed, he would go—and Connick was banished, his tenure having lasted but a few months. But while he was still on the studio payroll (we also suffered the indignity of subsidizing the indignities we suffered), I flagrantly violated his edict regarding story purchases.

Jeane Cohen, my secretary in that period, plagued me to read a novel, *The Sheik*, that had left her quivering. I think Walter Wanger gave it to her to get a woman's reaction, and possibly to avoid reading it himself. Jeane was always insisting that I read something she had liked, and I shied at such suggestions like a skittish horse. Reading potential picture material was the function of the full-time $25-a-week readers who would dextrously compress the gist of a four-hundred-page book into a two-page synopsis. I'm sure producers today are on more intimate terms with the literary properties they acquire, but I purchased many a book knowing no more about it than what was in these capsule reports.

I was often too busy even to read outlines and would call in the reader who covered a particular story to ad-lib an outline of the outline. This system reached an irreducible minimum of effort on one occasion when Jeane was characteristically bubbling over with a story she wanted to tell me, and I, in no mood to be bothered with it, recklessly said, "Jeane, I'll buy the story only on condition that you don't tell it to me!" This was a fairly safe gamble since everything committed to celluloid automatically made money. (The economy drive had been instituted, not because we weren't making money, but because the bankers wanted us to make more money.) The pig in a poke proved so popular with film audiences that I later purchased other stories by the same author; not, however, with the same brash disregard of their content. I peeked at the synopses first.

So when Jeane begged me to read Edith M. Hull's *The Sheik* before it had been synopsized, I reluctantly compromised with her. "Get one of the girls in the story department to tell it to me," I said. She rushed to the story department with the book and had Julia Herne drop her work and read it then and there. Trained to skim a book very quickly, Julia came in my office shortly and did such a good job of describing the story and acting out some of the sizzling scenes that I could appreciate at once its fascinating appeal from the feminine viewpoint. I bought Julia a railroad ticket and sent her out to Hollywood on the next train to tell the story to George Melford, feeling that the romantic melodrama was right up his alley. He agreed that we should buy it.

The author had set a price of $12,500 on film rights to her book. But I bought it anyway, in defiance of the $10,000 limit Connick had set, and then, to my embarrassment, didn't know what to do with it. I belatedly realized that none of our stars would be convincing as a passionate desert savage. Wallace Reid was too much the good-natured, big-brother type, Rod La Rocque too suave and sophisticated, Thomas Meighan too wholesome and casual. Jack Holt was two-fisted and a good rider, but the role didn't suit him, either, or anyone else we had under contract. We had to lay the story aside and I forgot about it in the press of other things.

A few months later I attended the opening night of *The Four Horsemen of the Apocalypse* at the Lyric Theatre. That picture thrilled me as *The Birth of a Nation* had. Everything about it was magnificent. Rex Ingram's direction of his first important picture was outstanding, June Mathis's script was superb, the camera work incomparable, and, to top it all, an unknown young Italian actor discovered by June Mathis gave one of the best silent-screen performances I have ever seen. As the tango-dancing gaucho of the Argentine, Rudolph Valentino's every movement had the lithe grace of a panther. The picture was lavishly produced at a cost that would have given a man like Connick apoplexy. But it did fabulous business for the Metro company, which was headed by lovable, careless, prodigal Richard Rowland. I read the unstinting praise of the movie reviewers the next morning, enviously wishing that Valentino could have been my find.

Several weeks later my secretary announced that Rudolph Valentino was in the outer office and would like to see me. I had him shown in at once, and had scarcely finished telling him how much I admired his work as the lonely, disillusioned Julio when he asked me if I would happen to have a part for him.

At first I couldn't believe he was serious. Metro had made the picture of the year and developed one of the greatest box-office draws of all time in Rudolph Valentino, but they didn't realize it and hadn't bothered to take an option on his future services.

It was incredible, and such a thing couldn't happen today, when all the high-powered agents in town would swoop down on a player of Valentino's promise as soon as he hit the screen in a juicy part. But agents didn't have a viselike grip on the industry then. Moreover, Rudy had quarreled with Rex Ingram during the filming and thus had already created an impression of being a bit difficult. This shouldn't have affected Dick Rowland's astute business sense, but he was so involved in a pending deal to sell Metro to Marcus Loew that he was blind to the biggest asset he had.

Rudy had waited around about a month after the release of *Four Horsemen*, then, when it became apparent that Metro's interest in him was very lukewarm, he went out looking for a job. Since we were the biggest studio in town, he approached us first and, needless to say, I didn't let him go any farther. He walked out of my office with a five-year contract.

I hired June Mathis as script writer for our new star. I issued orders to institute a search for story material suitable for a Latin hero, and my secretary, as she took the dictation, cried impetuously, "But Mr. Lasky—you already have the best possible story for him!"

Sure enough, I had overlooked *The Sheik*. Then it occurred to me that we owned still another property that might have been tailor-made for Valentino, a literary prescription for smoldering passion, gorgeous costumes, and the splendid poise that was Rudy's hallmark. This was Vicente Blasco-Ibáñez's bullfighting saga, *Blood and Sand*, which

Gilbert Miller had bought in Spain and recently staged for our Frohman company, starring Otis Skinner.

Valentino is a legend as the most perfect lover the screen has ever known, but he was not the most popular star on the lot even during his comparatively short reign. Diffident and reserved, he was always on his dignity and not inclined to mix with studio personnel. I was never on very intimate terms with him and he had few close friends. For several years he set the pattern of heartthrobs for the nation's women. He inspired a fanatic devotion among his following that survived his death and has been equaled only by the posthumous adulation accorded James Dean. And yet he was not the idol he could have been. He was badly mismanaged, and there wasn't much we could do about it.

He had more sheer animal magnetism than any actor before or since. *The Sheik* and *Blood and Sand* placed Valentino on a pinnacle of adoration before he knew the *a b c's* of screen acting. He became a far more accomplished actor later on, but women didn't attend his pictures to see him act. They went to swoon.

After a first marriage went on the rocks Rudy fell desperately in love with Winifred Hudnut, stepdaughter of Richard Hudnut, the cosmetic manufacturer. An exotic designer and art director, she was known professionally as Natacha Rambova. Rudy trustingly put all his business affairs in her hands when he married her, and we started having trouble with him from that moment. If we wanted to see him, we had to make an appointment with Natacha Rambova.

Our ideas about furthering Rudy's career constantly clashed with his wife's, but she wasn't one to arbitrate. She commanded. When she insisted on his doing perfumed parts like Booth Tarkington's *Monsieur Beaucaire*, in powdered wigs and silk stockings, we had to take him on her terms to have him at all. She designed his costumes herself, and, to give her due credit, they were magnificent. But we hadn't bargained for a dilettante foil for Rambova costumes. The role of a prince who disguised himself as a barber would have been better suited to a Julian Eltinge. Bob Hope in recent years clowned his way through this same flimsy tale, milking abundant laughs from its unconscious humor. It just wasn't the kind of story to show Valentino's prodigious sex appeal to advantage, and box-office comparisons with his early pictures showed that the patrons were disappointed.

We wanted to build him in earthy plots on the order of those which Cecil had used so effectively to enhance Gloria Swanson's essential glamour. But his wife held out for classic stories or esoteric themes.

We reached a stalemate, he refused to make pictures and left the screen for two years, then we arbitrated his contract and parted company.

Valentino made other pictures after leaving us—one in particular, *The Son of the Sheik*, has been revived many times since. But, contrary to popular belief, when he died of peritonitis following an operation at the age of thirty-one, his star was on the wane. He never even approached the potential we knew he had for breaking hearts and box-office records. I do think, however, that if he had lived until talking pictures were introduced, he might have suffered the same bitter experience as Jack Gilbert, who was displaced in the film firmament when his public heard him speak for the first time. Valentino also had a rather high-pitched voice which seemed somehow unsuited to his physique.

We were chagrined to lose him, of course—he was a prize property, even though his wife obstructed us from exploiting to the full his box-office appeal. In a pettish frame of mind I determined to prove we could do very well without him. My pique was aggravated by knowing that we had spawned a vogue for Latin lovers only to be left empty-handed while our competitors capitalized on our creation with Ramon Novarro, Gilbert Roland, and Valentino himself. (The catchy name of Gilbert Roland was synthesized from equal parts of "Jack Gilbert" and "Ruth Roland" and applied to an eager lad named Luis Alonso, whose bosses used to threaten to take their name back when he had the temerity to disagree with them.)

"If it's the last thing I do," I swore, "I'll find a Latin actor of his type and we'll develop another Valentino, just as great." I put our talent scouts on the alert, and sent out publicity indicating that we were in the market for a successor to Rudy. The studio was deluged with Mexican and Italian aspirants, none of them fit to shine Valentino's shoes. I was beginning to wish I had taken defeat gracefully instead of making such a fuss about it. Manufacturing a Valentino—even with the aid of vast studio facilities for talent screening, coaching, make-up, and publicity—wasn't so easy, as Eddie Small found out when he spent nine years trying to cast his screen biography of Valentino.

One night in 1924 Bessie and I were dining with Margaret Miller and some other friends at the Ambassador Hotel, watching the amateur dancing contest, which, as a concession to the current craze for such exhibitions, was a Friday-night feature at the Cocoanut Grove. The women were captivated by one dancer in particular, a handsome young man with a Latin look, identified by the number 19 on his back. They chattered about his charm and rooted for his victory all through the contest. The other women in the room evidently experienced the same fluttery feminine feelings, for when the prize winners were decided by applause, No. 19 and his partner got a deafening ovation.

Partly to give the ladies at my table a thrill and partly with the thought that a nation of women might be susceptible to the same thrill I asked the waiter to tell "No. 19" that we would like to meet him. Learning that his name was Jack Crane and that he wouldn't be averse to a picture offer, I asked him to see me at the studio the next day.

He was waiting for me when I arrived, and I noted that he exuded the same personal charm early in the morning in the intimacy of a business office as he did in the flush of competitive excitement before a large audience. It was a real part of him. It went where he went. That's all I needed to know.

"Jack," I said, "we've lost Valentino, and we'd like to replace him. You're the right type, but Jack Crane is no name for a Latin lover. We'd have to change it."

"I don't care what you call me," he smiled, "if only you call me."

"Help yourself to a cigar," I said, and as I motioned to a box of Ricardo cigars on my desk, my eyes fastened on the label. "And you may as well help yourself to a name at the same time," I added. " 'Ricardo' will do as well as any." I started combing the alphabet for a surname to go with it. "Ricardo A . . . A . . . nothing there . . . Ricardo B . . . Balboa . . . Booth . . . nothing there. Ricardo C . . . C . . . Cortez . . . that sounds like it. How about it?"

"Suits me," he assented.

"It certainly does," I said. "It suits you to a T."

Ricardo Cortez made a name for himself, stage name though it was, as the kind of person—in contrast to Valentino—with whom it was a joy to work. He had a long and successful career but he didn't replace the star of stars. Nor did anyone else. The throne remained forever empty.

I won't deny that it flattered my ego to wield a power that could give an obscure but struggling and deserving young person a new name and a new life gilded with the trappings of wealth and fame. As a boy I was always fascinated by stories of knighthood, when commoners were transformed into landed nobles by a tap on the shoulder. The Cinderella plot has never become hackneyed for me.

We had an energetic talent scout in the East who prospected in night clubs, shows, and other likely places and brought any promising finds to me personally at one of my two New York offices. The Fifty-sixth Street studio had been outgrown and abandoned, but in 1919, Zukor had built the Famous Players-Lasky studio in Astoria so that we could continue to utilize the cream of Broadway talent that couldn't or wouldn't go West, and when I was in the East I divided my time between the home office and the Astoria studio.

The talent scout discovered an adorable thirteen-year-old youngster named Augusta Appel, who was appearing with Gus Edwards in a vaudeville revue. I gave her a contract as soon as he brought her to my attention, appropriated a name from a snatch of poetry that kept running through my head, and sent her to Hollywood to start her movie career. She became Lila Lee.

Another time the scout turned up with a modest, shy, inexperienced and naïve apparition of loveliness. To this day I've never seen a more dazzling beauty than Lucille Langhanke was at sixteen.

Wasting no time, I said, "Miss Langhanke, we're going to give you a contract, but we'll need your parents' consent, and it will be necessary to change your name. I think you'd find the name of Lucille Langhanke something of a handicap if you achieve the success I believe you will."

As usual when I needed a name or an idea, I had no trouble plucking one out of the air. George M. Cohan's song "Mary's a Grand Old Name" was current at the time and I figured Cohan was pretty smart —if he endorsed "Mary" as a grand old name, it was good enough for me, or, rather, for Miss Langhanke. Then I had an impulse to contrast the simplest name in the world with one that reeked grandeur—like Waldorf or Vanderbilt. But I hadn't settled on one when I told Louella Parsons about my new, half-named discovery.

"How about Astor?" Louella suggested.

The girl's father, a Brooklyn music teacher, objected vigorously to the rechristening. But I still think Mary Astor is a better name than Lucille Langhanke.

In later years my good friend and insurance broker, Artie Stebbins, asked permission to bring a girl by the name of Jane Peters to my office. I had already heard of her—it seemed as though all the men I knew were trying to meet and date her, with good reason. She had personality, gaiety, a matchless face and figure, a wonderful sense of humor and gift for comedy. I confess I had no inkling of what a favorite she would become but I did think she was worth signing up. I asked her if she would mind changing her name. For some reason I thought "Jane Peters" was too prosaic for a girl so lavishly endowed with verve and beauty. She told me the name of Lombard was an old family heirloom, and her voice was so musical it made me think of Christmas carols. The first time she wrote "Carole Lombard" was on the starring contract I offered her.

Someone suggested an extraordinary bundle of talent in the person of Will Rogers, then starring in The Ziegfeld Follies. We corraled him for a picture called *One Glorious Day*, and he made a number of silent movies after that, but his capacity for drawling, trenchant humor, while it delighted his co-workers on the set, couldn't be appreciated in films until the advent of sound.

Asked whether he liked pictures as well as the stage, he answered, "Oh, sure. Why, up to the time I went into pictures I had never annoyed more than one audience at a time. This is the only business in the world where you can sit out front and applaud yourself."

Will Rogers became a legend, and his favorite saying, "I never met a man I didn't like," worked in reverse. I never met a man who didn't like Will Rogers.

When It Rains

It Pours

It is generally conceded by movie historians that the closest approach to an art form the films have yet achieved germinated in the Mack Sennett custard-pie laboratory and came to full flower in the silent slapstick masterpieces of Charlie Chaplin, Harold Lloyd, Buster Keaton, Harry Langdon, and our Paramount comedians, Fatty Arbuckle, and Raymond Griffith. Sound enhanced every other type of picture, but it was the death knell of pantomime comedy. The classic hilarious comedies of "the good old days" belong exclusively to the past generation. Movie fans of today have nothing that can touch

Safety Last, The Gold Rush, Steamboat Bill, Jr., and *Tramp, Tramp, Tramp.* The masters themselves—Chaplin, Lloyd, Keaton, and Langdon—were never able to duplicate their former successes after the screen found its voice.

Fatty Arbuckle's career came to an inglorious end before the sound era. Arbuckle's two-reel comedies were produced by Joseph Schenck and released through Famous Players-Lasky, but they did so well we wanted all three hundred pounds of him for ourselves. When his contract was up for renewal, we outbid Schenck, and proceeded to launch him in feature-length comedies. He made at least a dozen for us, all of them high-grossing hits. Arbuckle was conscientious, hard-working, intelligent, always agreeable and anxious to please. He would invent priceless comedy routines and also had a well-developed directorial sense.

Automatic salary jumps at option time had stepped his pay up to something like $7500 a week in the last year of his contract, and as other production costs were also rising, his pictures became fairly expensive to produce. We were anxious to save money by some tactic in order not to have our New York office on our necks with the perennial complaints of extravagance. I recalled the time I had taken over Caruso's eight-week contract from Schenck and made his high salary do double duty by rushing through two pictures instead of one. It would have been a master stroke of economy if the first picture hadn't flopped so badly we couldn't release the second one at all. I thought we wouldn't be taking such a chance on Arbuckle, whose drawing power at the box-office was firmly established. So I schemed with Ben Schulberg to go even further—and make *three* Arbuckle pictures in a row, without a day lost between them. The fat comedian was passed from the first director right to the second, with still another director impatient to call, "Camera!"

It would be hard to imagine more strenuous work than making those old-fashioned lightning-paced comedies. I don't know of another star who would have submitted to such extortionate demands on his energy. But Fatty Arbuckle wasn't one to grumble. There were no temperamental displays in his repertoire. He went through the triple assignment like a whirling dervish, in his top form. They were the funniest pictures he ever made. We were sure they would reap a fortune. Schulberg and I congratulated ourselves on pulling a fast one that would save the company untold overhead. Three Arbuckle pictures in the vault at one time was like a cache of gold.

Fatty was understandably worn out after this marathon, and came

in my office to say that he was motoring up to San Francisco to relax
for a few days. He told me to be sure and let him know if I got up
that way and we'd get together. Undoubtedly if I had been there at
the same time, I would have been one of the guests at the ill-fated
party he gave in his suite at the St. Francis Hotel.

A girl died following the party that night, there were allusions to
intimacies, and Arbuckle was indicted on a charge of manslaughter.
Two sensational trials ended in hung juries. Not until a third trial
was he acquitted, the jury returning in less than a minute with a state-
ment that they felt a great injustice had been done the defendant and
he should be completely exonerated. All of us who knew him felt
that he was a victim of circumstances and not guilty of a crime.
But the unfortunate affair occurred at a time when churches, women's
clubs, and reformers already had blood in their eyes over Hollywood's
alleged sinfulness and the moral laxness depicted in some films. A hundred censorship bills had been introduced in thirty-seven states that
year.

Right on the heels of this tragedy, one of my favorite directors, William Desmond Taylor, was found murdered an hour and a half after
he had a conference with me about the Mary Miles Minter picture
he was preparing and had left my office for his home, where the mur-
derer was possibly waiting for him.

The implications of the case were even more sordid than the
Arbuckle scandal, and all the more shocking because Taylor was considered a model of propriety. He was a handsome Englishman of such
quiet dignity and quality that we used him as Exhibit A when we
wanted to show off Hollywood's culture and refinement. In the early
days society held itself aloof from picture people except when they
needed celebrities and entertainers for charity affairs. William De-
Mille, whose breeding and background were impeccable, had been
refused admittance to the Los Angeles Country Club because of his
association with the movies. We tried in subtle ways to overcome this
prejudice. Bessie and I had cherished friends in Pasadena—which was
then the social hub of Southern California—and when we entertained
for them, we usually managed to score a point for Hollywood's prestige by inviting William Desmond Taylor and seating him next to a
society leader. He invariably made a favorable impression.

The murder was never solved, but the newspapers had a muckrak-
ing orgy for months, casting suspicion on everybody including the
butler (actually a valet-chauffeur who disappeared and was never
heard from again), in the stereotyped manner of the most preposter-

ous fictional mystery thrillers. The lurid headlines are said to have sold more newspapers than the entry of the United States into the war. And to the same extent that the newspaper business profited the cause of motion pictures was hurt.

There had been ominous rumblings of public opinion even before the Arbuckle and Taylor cases blew the lid off. Some "quickie" opportunists had hitched onto a postwar trend which manifested itself in a sudden rash of bawdy books, plays, and songs, and were making movies that violated good taste and decency. One town in Massachusetts retaliated by banning all motion pictures. More and more pressure groups were demanding federal censorship and regulation of films. Litigation and dissension within the industry itself also put it in a bad light. The nation's box-offices were beginning to reflect our loss of good-will.

I believe it was Lewis J. Selznick who suggested that the leaders of the industry offer Will Hays, then Postmaster General under President Harding, a position in charge of marshaling our forces and fighting adverse legislation as well as damaging propaganda, and also impressing workers in the industry with their ethical responsibilities. Such astute strategy was typical of the president of Selznick Pictures (not to be confused with the later Selznick Company, Inc., headed by his brilliant son, David O. Selznick). Lew had become a picture pioneer in the first place by the craziest—and most inspired—hoax anyone ever perpetrated. He had called on P. A. Powers at Universal to peddle some diamonds at a time when the company was divided into two hostile factions, with Powers and Carl Laemmle battling for control. Selznick quickly perceived that, if he appointed himself general manager under cover of the confusion, each side would assume that he had been hired by the enemy. He accordingly had the appropriate letterheads printed and also put himself in charge of all purchases and expenditures, which greatly facilitated getting his name on the payroll. He actually lasted long enough in this precarious position to learn something about making pictures and to whet his appetite for more of the same.

Selznick's plan for keeping the industry's skirts clean had the unanimous approval of the presidents of Famous Players-Lasky and Realart, Fox, Goldwyn, Metro, Robinson-Cole, Triangle, Universal, and United Artists at an emergency meeting I attended in New York. Hays shortly resigned from the Cabinet to become arbiter of the motion-picture industry and chieftain of its new trade association, now known as the Motion Picture Association of America. Zukor was on the original board of directors and I accompanied him to the meetings whenever I was in town. Because I was more closely identified with Hollywood than the other company heads, and was shortly leaving for the Coast, it was suggested that I precede and act as good-will ambassador for our new good-will ambassador. The newspapers had hinted that he was coming out to spearhead a crackdown and cleanup, and there was considerable resentment in the studios to the prospect of submitting to a "czar."

It was with considerable trepidation, therefore, that I arranged an invitational dinner at the Ambassador Hotel to present "General" Hays to some eight hundred of the industry's leading executives, directors, writers, actors, and other key men. If he were to accomplish his purpose, it was essential that he command their confidence and co-operation. Two previous attempts at self-regulation by the industry had failed—in 1915 and 1921. Before introducing Hays I made an impassioned plea for every man's support of Hays and our contemplated campaign for the betterment of motion pictures. Other speakers hammered the necessity of putting our house in order before somebody else did it for us.

The next day about two thousand studio personnel who couldn't be invited to the banquet were assembled in the Hollywood Bowl. Again I introduced Will Hays and explained his function. Later we took him to visit all the studios and discussed further the plans proposed by the New York executives to institute a code governing film subject matter to be controlled by the Hays office. To our great relief Hays inspired the respect of everyone, and the entire industry backed his measures of reform, thereby stemming a tide of wrath that could have crippled the motion-picture business had it been allowed to go on. The term "czar," incidentally, was an undeserved misnomer coined by the press. Will Hays was a kindly adviser and gentle counselor, even a politician, if need be, but not in any sense a dictator. Neither was he a figurehead at $100,000 a year, as some believe. In fact the men who hired him decided that they weren't paying him enough for what he accomplished, and extended his three-year contract by another ten years, with a salary raise to $150,000.

The first bit of advice Hays gave us cost our company over a million dollars, wiping out a good share of our profits for that year. He strongly urged us not to release the three Arbuckle pictures in the face of inflamed public sentiment. "His present notoriety might make the pictures even more profitable than they would ordinarily be," he told us, "but if you play them, you'll be playing into the hands of your enemies, besides doing the industry irreparable harm."

The decision was up to Zukor. He didn't waver over it. The three comedies were never shown.

Twice I had tried to reduce overhead by squeezing two and three pictures into the production time of one—and both times the films had to be shelved at a total loss. Caruso and Arbuckle taught me it isn't wise to bet on parlays.

Will Hays hadn't been long in office when a third scandal broke over Hollywood, involving the symbol of clean-cut American youth and idol of a nation, Wallace Reid.

If anyone had asked me in the summer of 1921 to name the greatest individual assets Famous Players-Lasky had, Wallace Reid, Fatty Arbuckle, and William Desmond Taylor would certainly have been on the list. All of them would also have been high on a list of my favorite personal friends. I wouldn't have believed that the company could weather the loss of such a fantastically valuable trio, especially under circumstances that stigmatized Hollywood in general and our studio in particular.

Wallace Reid was the easiest actor to cast and work with in the whole of my experience. He had a terrific vogue in automobile-racing pictures—the audiences couldn't get enough of him behind a steering wheel. We virtually turned these road-racing items out on an assembly line and every one was a money-maker. But that didn't type Wally. He was believable in almost any role we gave him. However, he wasn't believable as a heavyweight fighter in *The World's Champion*, taken from a Broadway play. He was rapidly losing weight and couldn't stand on his feet for more than a short time. He made a valiant struggle to get through his scenes, but it was obvious that something was wrong. Then Zukor wrote me that the whole country was teeming with a rumor that Wallace Reid was taking dope, and that if it was true we were sitting on a powder keg. Will Hays called me long-distance and told me I would have to do something about it.

I sent for Reid. As fond as I was of him, it was very difficult for me to say what I had to. I told him about the rumor, which had now fanned into a whirlwind of gossip, and that as head of production I was being held responsible for his actions.

"It isn't true!" he said, looking me squarely in the eye. "And don't you believe it!"

Perhaps it wasn't true at that moment. His loss of weight and un-natural fatigue during the shooting of the picture were symptoms that might have accompanied a desperate attempt to "kick" the narcotic habit.

"I want to believe you, Wally," I told him, "but the only way the rumors can be stopped is by absolute proof that they're false. Would you mind if I got a doctor to examine you?"

"Why should I?" he said. "Go as far as you like."

Our studio manager, Charles Eyton, borrowed a young railroad physician from the Southern Pacific. I told the doctor what we suspected and that we wanted him to live with Wallace for a time, never letting him out of his sight, and then bring us the facts, whatever they were. He was agreeable. I called in Wally again and told him our plan to spike the rumors, if there was nothing to them, by assigning the doctor to keep him under constant observation. No one need know that he wasn't just a pal, accompanying him wherever he went.

Wally assented readily without a shadow of annoyance. He was the perfect image of a man with nothing to hide. The doctor stayed with him two weeks, then reported back to me. "To the best of my knowledge, Mr. Lasky," he said, "Wallace Reid is not using narcotics. I've eaten my meals with him, slept in the same room with him, followed him to the bathroom, played golf with him, searched his belongings. He's co-operated wonderfully. I don't know anyone else I could live with like Siamese twins for two weeks without wanting to murder, but he is unquestionably the nicest chap I've ever known."

I breathed a premature sigh of relief and notified Hays and Zukor that there was nothing to worry about—the doctor had given Wally a clean bill of health.

A few weeks later Reid was taken to the Banksia Place Sanitarium, his health so undermined that he never recovered. Will Hays and I visited him there just before he died in 1923, only thirty years old.

There was no question of the doctor's integrity. Either he fell under the spell of the magnetic personality that exerted its effect on the whole country, and unwittingly slackened his surveillance with the conviction that it wasn't necessary, or else Wally was fighting a battle alone to salvage his reputation at any cost, and actually kicked his habit by his own will-power—too late. It was established later that he did not contract the addiction as a thrill seeker. It started from being given narcotic injections to relieve distracting headaches that resulted from a head injury in a train wreck.

Cruzing over

the Santa Fe Trail

We had made 360 features in nine years since *The Squaw Man* and there wasn't an epic in the lot of them. Of course if I relied on our exploitation brochures of the period to reinforce my memory I could readily believe that each and every one of these masterpieces put *The Birth of a Nation* to shame. A maudlin little number with Agnes Ayres and Jack Holt was casually referred to as "the greatest of all dramas." *Find the Woman*, worshipfully touted as "the greatest mystery ever screened," is still such a great mystery that I seriously doubt if you can find the woman—*or* the man—who could tell you who was in it or what it was about. Exhibitors were solemnly warned: "Picture theatres that miss Charles Ray in *The Egg Crate Wallop* will have an aching void that no other picture can ever fill." Several thousand picture theatres have an "aching void" today, but I wouldn't attribute it to not having played *The Egg Crate Wallop*.

Despite these sales blurbs my memory tells me that these three particular pictures and the other 357 didn't live up to the effusive promises of the press books. We were the most successful picture company on the face of the globe, our product improved from year to year, and we kept well ahead of our competitors, but I knew in my heart that we had never produced a history-making, cinematic milestone—and the guilty knowledge was always a source of extreme annoyance and personal embarrassment to me. The seven-year-old challenge of *The Birth of a Nation* still stood, a silent reproach that, with all our facilities and the pool of creative talent we commanded, we couldn't, or at any rate hadn't, done anything that overwhelmed picture patrons the way Griffith's masterpiece had. The fact that Griffith himself never again matched his first triumph was small consolation.

The way our first superspecial road-show attraction grew out of a cheap, run-of-the-mill program filler is one of those incredible, irrational accidents that make show business so unpredictable that no rules, no yardsticks can be applied to it. I suppose it started with the highly colored tales my grandfather told me in my early boyhood about his crossing the plains in a covered wagon in 1848, to settle in Sacramento, where my father was born. The skirmishes with Indians, the crushing hardships endured by the pioneers were branded forever on my imagination even before Edison invented his peep-show Kinetoscope.

I had to do so much commuting between my offices in New York and Hollywood that I felt like a transient in both places. Sometimes when I arrived on the Coast, waiting telegrams would demand my presence in New York for a conference, and when I got back there, some trouble would pop on the Coast that called for immediate personal attention. The only office I had that gave me a feeling of permanence and security for more than a few hours was a drawing room on the California Limited. Whenever I left New York, Jeane Cohen, the bright, shrewd secretary who had finagled me into buying *The Sheik* and later casting Valentino in the lead, would load me up with scripts, synopses, and business papers to read on the train. After changing from the Twentieth Century to the Santa Fe in Chicago, the three-day stretch without interruptions enabled me to do some of my best thinking and planning while crossing the prairies of Kansas into New Mexico and Arizona.

As I departed on one of these trips, Jeane handed me a copy of Emerson Hough's novel about the westward trek of the pioneers, *The Covered Wagon.* "What's the idea of giving me this book, Jeane?" I chided. "I can't waste time reading a story we've already bought."

"Please read it," she insisted, "so you'll appreciate it. You only read a synopsis when you authorized its purchase and no synopsis could do it justice."

"I've got more important things to do," I objected, slightly nettled. But I picked up the book somewhere over the plains of Kansas and became so absorbed in the struggles and adventures of the pioneers determined to reach the West or die in the attempt that for the whole day I became again a child at my grandfather's knee, listening to the most exciting tales a boy ever heard. And every time I glanced out the train window at the rolling prairies, the mountains, the desert, I saw the vast panorama of sky and earth forming a backdrop for those heroic souls whose first wagon train actually took much of the same route three quarters of a century before—a procession that united the West with the East, a migration but for which I myself would not have been born in my beloved California. Superimposing the past on the present by reading about that trek while actually retracing it myself, as I looked out the window of a speeding luxury train at the same scenery my grandfather had viewed from a lumbering Conestoga, was an emotional, almost mystical experience.

It was routine when I arrived at the Coast studio for Schulberg and Turnbull to give me a schedule of the new pictures in preparation, with tentative casts, directorial assignments, and estimated budgets. I would make changes I thought necessary and send it to Zukor, who would submit it to the sales department and other executives and return it with their criticisms and consensus of opinion and his own suggestions. I then gave it back to Schulberg and Turnbull, who jointly carried out the program.

I noted with dismay that *The Covered Wagon* was entrusted to George Melford, a director who could always be relied on to bring in a picture on time and within his budget, but I couldn't help feeling that his artistry was suspect, because he wore a large elk's tooth as a watch charm! I was even more alarmed to learn that Mary Miles Minter, a disciple of the brittle, china-doll school of acting, was to be given the role of Molly Wingate, the hardy, pioneer heroine. *The Covered Wagon* was not the ideal vehicle for Mary Miles Minter. A Rolls-Royce was more her style. The picture was budgeted at $110,000, a normal expenditure for a Western.

"Boys," I said, "I want this picture taken off the list."

"I'm glad you're going to shelve it," Schulberg admitted with evident relief. "It's been a headache. Minter is sulking because she doesn't want to play in a Western and two directors turned it down flat. Melford only agreed because he takes anything that comes along."

"I'll talk to them," I said. "And I'm not taking it off the list permanently. It's going to be the greatest show we've ever made but not the way it's set up now."

Schulberg was flabbergasted.

I sent for Melford.

"George," I said, "why do you let them shove things like this *Covered Wagon* on you? You're too good-natured. With all the experience you've had, you shouldn't have to direct Westerns. That's for unknowns who haven't proved themselves."

Melford beamed. "This kind of assignment doesn't bother me," he

F

confided. "I can knock them off with my left hand. But to tell the truth, I *would* like a story I could get my teeth into."

"I'll personally see to it that you get a fine drawing-room play, and you can forget *The Covered Wagon*," I promised.

"I wish you were here on the Coast all the time," he sighed.

Next I called in Mary Miles Minter. Although she was the wrong type to play a rugged pioneer woman, she was a very popular star and had to be handled with considerable tact. "Mary," I said, "I see they've cast you for *The Covered Wagon*, and I don't like it. You're at the stage where every picture you appear in is important. You'd be wasted in a horse opera—gingham dresses and no make-up. You should be showcased in Paris gowns, moving in an atmosphere of society and sophistication."

"You mean I don't have to play in *The Covered Wagon?*" she asked incredulously.

"You don't have to play it," I assured her.

She leaned over and kissed me in bubbling gratitude and rushed out of my office to spread the good news.

I had knocked the props out from under the picture. Now I could reconstruct it as I wanted. Who could direct with an authentic primitive feeling and vigorous touch the sweeping scenes of cattle fording the river, the wagon train winding endlessly through unpopulated spaces, the Indian fights, the buffalo hunt? I remembered that James Cruze, a young character actor who had recently been made a director, was supposed to have Indian blood. If so, he was closer by inheritance to the pioneer days than any of our other directors and should have had a natural instinct or affinity for the courageous drama of the barren plains. To this day I don't know whether he really had some Indian forebears—I never checked on it—but hearsay to that effect was what prompted me to call him in for a conference. I gave him the Emerson Hough book, and he read it overnight.

I can still see him as he barged into my office the next morning wearing riding breeches, brown shirt, and his cap on backward in the approved directorial style. He had such explosive enthusiasm and inspired imagination for the spectacle aspects of the story that I put it in his hands with full confidence. He had ridden all over Nevada and was mentally earmarking perfect locations for the dramatic high spots. He even knew where the necessary buffalo were to be had. To play the main character, Will Bannion, he suggested J. Warren Kerrigan, a matinee idol who had slipped almost into oblivion for no apparent reason.

Lois Wilson, a wholesome young actress we all liked but who had never had a real opportunity to show her worth, was decided on for the heroine. Ernest Torrence was cast as Jackson, the tough, hard-bitten old plains trader who joined the caravan and figured prominently in the overland journey, and Tully Marshall as the immortal guide and pathfinder, Jim Bridger.

The new conception demanded that everything be done on a lavish scale. We couldn't cut corners. We began to throw money around like confetti. All the ranches within a hundred miles of our location in the Snake Valley of Nevada were combed to find four hundred wagons, which were rented and transformed into covered wagons by the prop department. We hired horses and all the oxen we could find. We made financial arrangements to use the buffalo herd and the necessary locations. I asked the estimating department for a revised estimate on the basis of our expanded plans. They quoted, with some misgivings, the figure of $500,000. That would be equivalent to $5,000,000 today.

A few days after I sent my quarterly budget East, Zukor phoned. "Mr. Lasky," he said in his quiet way, "we've gone over your proposed pictures for the next quarter and we all agree the list is very good. But there seems to be a typographical error on your budget for a Western called *The Covered Wagon*. It says $500,000. Isn't the decimal point in the wrong place?"

"No," I said, "it will cost half a million dollars to make *The Covered Wagon*."

There was a ponderous silence. "But Mr. Lasky," he protested unemotionally, "don't you realize Westerns are dead? Even Bill Hart's *Three Word Brand*, which we released three months ago, will hardly break even. The top boys in distribution think you've lost your mind or that you're out of touch with the changing times for wanting to make another Western at all."

"Mr. Zukor," I said anxiously, "they don't understand—but you will. This picture is more than a Western. It's an epic."

"An epic?"

"E-P-I-C," I elucidated, trembling in my boots for the money we'd already spent without authorization, preparing for an elaborate production.

There was a long pause. Then the still-calm voice came over the wire. "An epic, eh? Well, that's different. You go ahead and I'll take care of the sales department." That was all the argument needed to convince the champion of bigger and better pictures. If Adolph Zukor hadn't been in the driver's seat, *The Covered Wagon* would no doubt have stopped dead in its tracks right there. When the carnage was over in the sales department, he wired me: "BUDGET APPROVED. REGARDS AND GOOD LUCK."

The company of 127, a large technical staff, a thousand locally hired extras, and 750 Indians worked for eight weeks in a 500-tent camp 85 miles from a railroad. Then they moved to Antelope Island in the Great Salt Lake for the buffalo hunt.

When I saw the completed picture in the projection room, I wasn't satisfied with the way the story ended near Fort Bridger, before the wagon train split. So I had it rewritten to show both the California and Oregon contingents continuing to their goals, and had the company reassembled and the wagon train rebuilt in Sonora, California, for the necessary snow scenes.

Actually I went over the original and revised budgets combined. *The Covered Wagon* cost $782,000, but it was one of the largest money-makers in silent-film history. We recovered our full investment from two theatres alone—the Criterion and Grauman's. It played the Criterion to standing room on a two-a-day schedule at $1.50 for fifty-nine weeks, breaking the world record of forty-four weeks for *The Birth of a Nation* nine years before. It could have run on for three years, but there was such a clamor for its release to other New York theatres that the first run was ended while still doing capacity business.

Robert Sherwood, at that time a leading dramatic critic, called it "the one great American epic that the screen has produced."

It pioneered a new type of extravagant, spectacular Western; it inaugurated a policy in our company of one tremendous road-show attraction every year which could be booked like a stage play with reserved seats at more than twice the usual admission prices; it gave J. Warren Kerrigan a new lease on his professional life, and made stars of Lois Wilson, Ernest Torrence, and Tully Marshall, and lifted Cruze to the ranks of screen immortals.

I'd like to think the destiny that wove magic around the greatest picture Famous Players-Lasky ever made was compounded of less capricious and gossamer stuff than my grandfather's telling me lies that I believed in my childish innocence, my secretary handing me "something to read on the train," George Melford wearing an elk's tooth, and a rampant rumor that Jimmie Cruze was part Indian. But I've been too long in this unfathomable business to expect to find rhyme or reason in it.

Thou Shalt Not

Spend Wantonly

Neither George Melford nor Mary Miles Minter ever chided me for sweet-talking them out of the picture that made cinematic history. They couldn't very well, since I had persuaded them that it was their own choice. Anyway they were kept happy with other pictures. Keeping everyone on the lot in a frame of mind conducive to superior productive activity was another of my more or less official duties.

Our epics were few and far between, but for years Famous Players-Lasky had a higher batting average of hits than any other company, and it was no accident. Old-timers will tell you that the atmosphere of camaraderie and mutual co-operation in the early days of the old Lasky lot was never surpassed then or since.

We worked hard and played hard. If a picture was behind schedule, the whole company pitched in with the spirit of a fighting football team and stayed on the job until eight, nine, ten, or eleven o'clock, stopping only for cold suppers brought out to the set.

On Saturday nights we dined and danced at the Alexandria in Los Angeles, The Ship Cafe or Nat Goodwin's on the Santa Monica Pier—or Levy's famous downtown restaurant, and a little later at the Montmartre on Hollywood Boulevard. Our social sorties were informal and more for fun than display, as the syndicated columnists of those days paid little attention to who was seen where with whom.

It was an era of wonderful nonsense. Gloria Swanson once sent word to a friend sailing for Europe that she couldn't be on hand to wish her *bon voyage* in person but that she would send something to the ship for her to read on the way over. The poor victim of Gloria's whimsey found her stateroom packed solid to the ceiling with newspapers. Sid Grauman was the greatest hoaxer of the period. He had become famous for his incomparable prologues, staged first for us when we built the Million Dollar and Metropolitan (Paramount) theatres in Los Angeles, and later at his own Egyptian and Chinese theatres. At a meeting of theatre managers to discuss closing the theatres on account of an influenza epidemic he arrived in a hearse. Another time he led a guest speaker at an important function to a darkened room and introduced him. The man didn't discover until he had finished his speech that the room was full of wax dummies. The real meeting was taking place in another part of the hotel.

In the palmy days of Hollywood stars rose faster and were more colorful than conservative. But the tendency today is toward simplicity. The overstressed and overstrained phase has passed. No longer does a top film name feel obliged to wear two Rolls-Royces to live up to the public's ideas of glamour. War and taxes made glittering extravagance unfashionable, unpatriotic, and, what's more to the point, impossible.

We enjoyed the confidence of our stars and directors, who, I'm proud to say, showed a do-or-die loyalty to their organization that seems antiquated in today's scheme of things. They might stop in my office at any time for advice or just to chat. With the one exception I've already mentioned—Valentino—you didn't have to make an appointment to talk to them in the presence of their lawyers or agents or business managers. Once while I was dictating the door opened suddenly and a woman's slipper landed in my lap, followed by Tallulah Bankhead. She threw her arms around me and gushed, "Darling, it's been such a wonderful day. Clive Brook is the *perfect* leading man. What an actor!"

I doubt if even Tallulah could feel that joyful and unrestrained in a picture studio today.

I even enjoyed the excitement of a high-strung star's tantrums. Wanger tells a story of Gloria Swanson storming into my New York office, a blistering cyclone of wrath over real or imagined wrongs done her at the Coast studio, and accusing me in steam-heated four-letter words of being the Machiavellian instigator of all her woes. I don't remember the incident, but Walter says I heard her out and then in pretended awe of her self-control, I said, "Gee, Gloria, if they'd done that to me, I'd have been *angry*."

She had no sooner blazed her way out of the office and I had marveled in sheer admiration, "What a temperament! Isn't she magnificent?" than a new young actor with gracious manner and perfect breeding came in to express appreciation for our having signed him. As he left, Walter says I turned to him and remarked, "That lad will never get anywhere. No fire!"

I suppose movie-making couldn't have remained an adventure forever. It had to become just another giant industry. But I never get over being thankful to have been a part of that glamorous Cinderella era of Hollywood's history.

As an example of a player's loyalty I'll cite an instance that also illustrated the range of diplomacy a studio head had to use in handling a consignment of human explosives. It had to cover all situations, from maneuvering one player out of a choice role to maneuvering another into a bad one, while leaving both with the conviction they were getting the best possible treatment.

I arrived on one of my Hollywood trips to learn that Clive Brook, the same engaging and gifted English actor who had Tallulah Bankhead throwing her shoes in the air, had refused to play a part assigned him. The production was ready to start and Schulberg was about to have a stroke. He had pleaded with Clive and threatened suspension, all to no avail. He begged me to use my authority to make the actor live up to his contract.

I thought I'd have a look at the script before summoning Clive. I didn't have to read far to know why he objected to it. The characterization was inconsistent and vague. Now I was in a quandary. How can an actor turn in a creditable performance if he doesn't believe in what he's doing? I didn't blame him for balking, but as responsible head of production it was up to me to iron out the difficulty in some way.

He came in determined to battle it out.

"Clive," I said, "I'm ashamed to look you in the face. I've just read the script. How they expect you to put up with this claptrap is beyond me. It's without a doubt the weakest leading role I've ever read. I appreciate your position—you don't have to explain it to me. But sit down and listen to the other side of the story.

"The studio pays you $182,000 a year. It must see that you make five pictures a year to protect that investment. They didn't give you this inferior story deliberately. The story department chose the best they could find without throwing us off schedule. It doesn't come up to our usual standard and we'd like to chuck it out, but we can't. The sales department has already booked it. The release date is set and must be met. If we can't deliver it—with Clive Brook as the star— exhibitor contracts will have to be canceled and it will cost the company a lot of money. I agree with you that it's a poor excuse for a story and an insipid role for you—it can't possibly do you any good. But the company desperately needs the picture."

The stubborn set of his chin had softened and Clive shrugged philosophically. "When do I start?" he asked with the stoic smile that ingratiated him with a whole generation of moviegoers.

In gratitude for Clive Brook's co-operation in this ticklish situation I saw to it that his next role was one of the best he'd ever had, that of Heliotrope Harry in *Forgotten Faces*, from a Richard Washburn Child story about a man who broke out of jail to see his daughter married.

The purse-string holders hadn't yet recovered from my audacity in tapping the till for three quarters of a million to make our first epic, when Cecil—never to be outdone by anyone else, in or out of Famous Players-Lasky—began pouring money into his newest effort, *The Ten Commandments*, with boundless energy. It looked to the business office like an "open-end investment" that was dissipating a huge chunk of company capital for doubtful returns, to say the least. They pointed out that heretofore the public had shown a decided preference for religion in churches rather than in movies.

I couldn't much blame our New York executives. They had objected strenuously when Cecil estimated his budget at one million, then, when his expenditures topped a million by the time he was little more than halfway through, a roar of agony reverberated clear across the continent. They demanded that I bring him down to earth from Mount Sinai.

I had to remind New York that Cecil's position as director-general made him a law unto himself. There was nothing I could do, and because I had caught some of Cecil's contagious courage and enthusiasm for his controversial venture, there was nothing I wanted to do. But one evening at dinner I did let him know that the bosses felt we had already sunk in the picture more than we could ever recover, and wanted me to clamp down on his spending.

Cecil's eyes blazed. "What do they want me to do," he snapped, "stop now and release it as The Five Commandments?" He stomped out in a rage, and I wished I had kept to myself the knowledge of the sales department's mounting alarm over his lavish disbursements.

A couple of days later he entered my office grimly with his attorney, Neil McCarthy. "We've raised some money," McCarthy said, "and you can notify your New York crowd we're prepared to buy the negative Cecil has shot thus far for a million dollars."

I called the New York office and told them of the McCarthy-DeMille offer, adding that I had seen enough of the picture to know that it was going to be magnificent, and that if we sold out to them now in order to recoup our investment, we would lose a fortune in potential income and be the laughingstock of the industry. I was sufficiently eloquent that *The Ten Commandments* remained under the same management, but during the rest of the shooting the wrath of God didn't match the wrath of DeMille.

There is one person who consistently outdoes DeMille in the spectacular proportion of his productions. That person is—DeMille. This rapidly expanding trait got to be more than our Eastern office could stomach, despite the fact that *The Ten Commandments* was tremendously successful and that Cecil's prodigious expenditures invariably paid very handsome dividends. Rental terms had to be jacked up to meet the strain, which gave the sales department trouble, besides which the conservative elements didn't favor risking such sums on a single picture.

I was informed that Cecil was going to get the ax unless he allowed his contract to be altered to give the company more control over his pictures. I told him what was brewing, but I knew him well enough to know what the end would be. Sid Kent came to the Coast to try to effect a workable compromise, but Cecil was still boiling over the controversy of *The Ten Commandments*, and would submit to no interference on his pictures. If he couldn't choose his subjects, and produce and direct them as he saw fit for our company, he would get out and produce them independently. His contract was not renewed and he left the employ of Famous Players-Lasky in 1924.

Sam and Cecil and I had started the company. Sam had been forced out; now Cecil was going. Would my turn also come?

During the filming of *The Ten Commandments* I took my twelve-year-old son on the set where Theodore Roberts as Moses was given God's words in letters of fire with an assist from a special-effects technician named Roy Pomeroy. As I tried to explain the significance of the Ten Commandments to Jesse, Jr., I couldn't know that thirty years later he would be interpreting the same subject to an audience of millions. Cecil DeMille recently got around to a pet idea he had nursed for years. He made a new *Ten Commandments*, using authentic Old World settings, at a cost of more than $1,000,000 per commandment. And a collaborator on the screen play for this latest DeMillion-dollar spectacle was Jesse Lasky, Jr. It's a Cecil B. DeMille production, released by Paramount. What a sense of satisfaction and ultimate

F*

vindication it must give him to have *Paramount working for DeMille* on a $13,500,000 version of the same picture that got him in hot water when he dared to spend $1,000,000 before completing it.

In dropping our ace director at the height of his earning capacity for the company the men who held the financial reins were merely following their established policy of trying to run the business according to proven procedures, without breaking any new ground. DeMille was always breaking new ground. His instinct for anticipating popular trends and tastes was like a divining rod.

Maybe we did press a little too hard in rebellion against the "status quo" thinking of the business office. I'll concede that we gilded an already gaudy lily when we insisted on showing some scenes of *The Ten Commandments* in color, before an American laboratory color process for motion pictures had been perfected. Every print was painstakingly painted by hand, frame by frame. The tinted objects jumped around on the screen like a cat on a hot tin roof.

Herbert Kalmus came to me shortly after this and told me that he had a method for photographing natural color. Always a pushover for new ideas, I ordered it used at once in a picture with vistas of scenery to take full advantage of the chromatic effects. Zane Grey's *Wanderer of the Wasteland* was the first full-length Technicolor feature sponsored by a major studio, and it gave the new process an enormous boost in its bid for popularity with movie makers and the public. I particularly remember the dramatic use we made of color in one scene where the hero, tracking down the wounded villain, who has concealed himself in a gold-mine stamp mill, notices a trickle of muddy water flowing from the mill sluiceway slowly turning red—and is thus led to the hide-out of his quarry.

Two of our cinematic landmarks of the twenties were directed by Herbert Brenon—*Peter Pan* and *Beau Geste*. Both pictures have since been remade and to my mind fall short of Brenon's inspired prototypes. *Peter Pan* was one of the group of ten James M. Barrie plays I had acquired several years before. It never occurred to us to cast a boy in the leading role. Nina Boucicault, Pauline Chase, and Cecilia Loftus had become renowned in the title role in London productions, and Maude Adams had had one of her greatest successes in it in America, so we followed the unbroken stage tradition and looked for a petite actress who could convincingly disguise her sex. We had decided on a pert kid named Mary Brian, when along came another unknown, even better suited to the part. Betty Bronson was given the lead and Mary Brian shifted to the role of "Wendy."

Perhaps because I was nervous about the pitfalls of bringing a children's classic to the screen and also anxious about Brenon's sensitive moods, I dropped a casual suggestion to my secretary as I left for Europe on one of my perennial talent-and-author forays. I asked her to write Herbert a letter once in a while, just so he wouldn't get to feeling like a forgotten man, cut off from the world in the isolated California spot where the company was going to be on location for a long time. Jeane good-naturedly obliged, passing on studio chitchat which in one letter included the chance remark "All the men around here are buying Paramount stock."

Brenon never answered these newsy letters, but she kept on writing them, and six months later he came back with his masterpiece completed. He called Jeane and asked her to spend Christmas Eve with him. She must have fluttered a bit as she dressed for dinner with such a celebrated escort.

He squired her to a fashionable restaurant and assailed her with small attentions.

"You were my inspiration, Jeane, writing me those wonderful letters," he intoned, "and besides, you made a lot of money for me."

Jeane looked puzzled and he explained. "You said all the men were buying Paramount stock and I knew you wouldn't say that unless you had a reason, so I read between the lines and it said, 'Herbert, *buy Paramount stock!*' So I bought a thousand shares. After I finished the picture, I found the stock had gone up ten points, so you made $10,000 for me, Jeane, and I want you to help me spend it."

"Oh, Herbert, I couldn't," Jeane demurred coyly, visualizing diamond bracelets up to her elbows.

"Please help me spend it, Jeane," Brenon implored. "My wife wants a mink coat and I'm sure you must know some place where I can get it wholesale!"

Brenon was not so conscientiously thrifty when I sent him with a company to make a Thomas Meighan picture, *The Alaskan*, on location in Northern California. We could have built the sets at the studio and covered them with salt (bleached Corn Flakes weren't used as a substitute for snow until later). But salt and faces sweating from klieg lights couldn't evoke the spell of the Yukon as well as real snow and breath clouds you could cut with a knife. So an Alaskan mining-camp village was erected at Lake Tahoe, and Brenon's whole cast and company moved there to be ready to start the picture the minute a heavy snowfall covered the bare new boards.

It didn't snow for weeks, but nobody complained. Lake Tahoe is a gorgeous setting for an extended vacation. Marvelous food, exhilarating winter sports, and, best of all, nobody could be blamed for not working when they were waiting for it to snow. They were pretty careful not to let any weather reports seep back to the studio. It was a gold-digging operation, all right. Every week shipments of gold bullion or a reasonable facsimile arrived from the accounting department of the studio to grubstake the gold-bricking gold miners.

Finally I heard a rumor that the whole company was having one whale of a time but no film was going through the cameras. I rarely explode, but that time I called studio manager Charles Eyton in my office and blew the roof off. He promised to do something about the situation right away. He did, too. He had several carloads of salt sent from San Francisco to the Nevada border and poured on the roof tops and grounds of our synthetic mining camp. Eaves were meticulously strung with fake icicles. A pall of gloom settled over the company. Their idyl had come to an end. On the morrow they would have to work.

But sometimes in the picture business the best way to lose money is to try and save it. That night it snowed—generously and photogenically. The next morning the whole landscape was tucked in under an eider-down coverlet. There was snow everywhere, as far as the eye could see—except on our expensively duplicated gold-rush town. For there the salt had melted the snow and the water had washed the salt away, leaving a naked, incongruous eyesore thrust up through the white-blanketed countryside as though insolently defying the elements.

There's no business like snow business!

We Feel Our Oats

In the space of ten years motion pictures had grown from a suspect enterprise which respectable actors were loath to associate themselves with, confined to converted stores and cheap little theatres, to a major influence in shaping the fashions, the manners, and the taste of middle-class America, an influence felt throughout the world. Plush and gilt movie palaces had mushroomed over the land and become practically temples of worship, where the masses attended services faithfully at least once a week, not so much to follow the sometimes artistic and moving stories on the screen (because insipid plots often rang up a healthy clatter on the cash register too) as to take lessons in deportment, hairdressing, what to wear, and even modish architecture and interior decoration.

Hollywood's leadership in style and comportment, which persists to a lesser degree even now, grew out of measures we took to keep our pictures from being outdated before they were shown. An outstanding picture might take a year to film and cut, wait several more months for a release date, and be in circulation for a year or longer after that.

If you show on the screen a character who is supposed to be a fashion-plate wearing hats and dresses of two or three years' vintage, it makes your whole effort look ridiculous. We had to find some way of dressing actresses in styles that would be current three years after the pictures were made! Obviously the only way to do that was to set styles ourselves. Instead of merely buying custom gowns from Paris and New York couturiers, we would have to employ directly designers of a caliber to generate trends in the fashion world, and have them create ultranew, ultrasmart gowns, hats, furs, lingerie, and accessories for our stars to wear before the cameras.

After looking over the field Walter Wanger recommended Howard

Greer, who had learned his craft under the greatest of them all, Lucille Duff Gordon. We brought him to Hollywood and he was our fashion arbiter for five years before leaving to launch his own House of Greer, Hollywood's leading custom salon of the thirties. Edith Head, still chief designer of Paramount's wardrobe department, started out of art school as Howard's assistant, and the immensely gifted Travis Banton shortly joined the costuming staff.

If the wardrobes were advanced, the settings for those wardrobes had to be just as exotic and forward-looking. We hired Paul Iribe, a French architect with ideas years ahead of his time, and Paul Chalfin, architect of the incredibly extravagant $15,000,000 James Deering estate, "Viscaya," on Biscayne Bay. Inevitably other companies followed suit. Metro-Goldwyn-Mayer brought in an incomparable art director, Cedric Gibbons, who still masterminds the settings for Culver City's gems.

And so, because celluloid in cans tended to get stale, Hollywood became a world style center in and of itself, rivaling Paris and New York. Coiffures, gloves, and gestures originated for screen purposes were copied all over the world. As Will Hays was fond of saying, trade didn't follow the flag, it followed the movies. People began to ask in stores for a bed with a built-in bookcase or an ingenious kitchen arrangement they had seen in some picture, ideas dreamed up by our staff artists as symbols of gracious living to indicate the social strata of fictional characters or merely to make a scene photograph attractively.

The whole vogue for streamlining that has affected practically everything we touch got its impetus from the movies. So did the phenomenal growth of interior decorating as an art and business.

As over twenty thousand motion-picture houses established a habit almost as strong as eating and sleeping, the larger theatres vied with each other in opulence. They augmented film fare with $25,000 organs, hundred-piece orchestras, uniformed corps of ushers, and elaborate stage "presentations" or prologues. The legitimate theatre suffered a decline which threatened to extinguish it. It was partly a matter of economics—the playgoer saw perhaps $40,000 worth of entertainment for $4.00. In one of the ornate competing Broadway movie houses, he could see a million dollars' worth of entertainment for a quarter or half dollar, an eye-filling spectacle using the equivalent of six hundred baggage cars of scenery and props, sometimes with a cast of thousands, and in addition he was surrounded with enough trappings to make him feel like the Aga Khan for three hours.

It was in this period that Zukor decided to raise our own skyscraper, the Paramount Building, in the heart of Times Square, housing our offices and the most beautiful film palace anywhere. The Paramount Theatre might not rate among the first ten today, but it was certainly the paragon of its time, before the Roxy or the Music Hall was built.

The forty-story building, with eight setbacks topped by the well-known four-sided Paramount clock and a twenty-foot illuminated globe signifying world conquest by the motion picture, dominated Broadway for miles. The marquee and five-story glass arch over the lobby entrance gleamed like a jewel in this setting. Roofing the four-thousand-seat auditorium required the heaviest single lifts in the history of construction—eight trussed girders weighing 144 tons apiece. More than a half million dollars went into Italian-marble trimming for the grand lobby alone. In order to obtain one of the four special colors needed, quarries which had been worked intermittently since the time of Julius Caesar but had been closed for forty years had to be reopened.

The public could luxuriate in the lush appointments and décor of an Elizabethan Room lounge, a College Room, The Chinoiserie, The Venetian Room, Peacock Alley, The Club Room, The Hunting Room, The Music Room, The Colonial Room, or The Empire Room. As an alternative one could go in the auditorium and hear the world's most famous theatre organist, Jesse Crawford, play the world's largest orchestra unit organ.

The picture on the screen was often an anticlimax.

Mayor James J. Walker laid the cornerstone of the building and spoke at the inaugural program, which was a dazzling assemblage of notables. Daniel Frohman and I brought Thomas Edison over from New Jersey to be guest of honor, and as I conducted him to a suite in the Astor across the street from the theatre, I had qualms about the maddening din of Times Square. I apologized for not arranging a quieter if less convenient location for his night's rest. Smiling graciously, he said, "I have the good fortune not to be disturbed by noise." I had momentarily forgotten his deafness.

I remember standing with Zukor, Will Hays, and Edison in the upper foyer on opening night and receiving the congratulations of dignitaries until a late hour. The papers next day devoted whole pages to the event. Paramount already had nearly two thousand theatres in the U.S., Canada, England, and France, but this was the first time any picture company had raised a skyscraper monument to itself. Zukor and I were two happy men as we met for lunch and started for our habitual haunt, a table at the Ritz, which had followed the

Astor as a hangout for film heads and had in turn nearly run its course as THE place to lunch. But this was a very special triumphal occasion and we felt we should celebrate it in some very special and unusual way. Casting around for a more exciting rendezvous than the Ritz, we stopped to ogle a white-coated chef tossing flapjacks in the window of a new Child's restaurant.

"Showmanship," observed Zukor, with a twinkle in his eye. We went in, seated ourselves at a marble-topped table and ordered two stacks. As we devoured them with gusto, I heard some of the clerks and secretaries at adjoining tables comment on the gala opening of the Paramount Theatre and mention that Edison, Zukor, and Lasky had been there in person.

"If it hadn't been for Edison," one of the young men scoffed, "you never would've heard of those other guys."

"Yeah," agreed his companion, "thanks to Edison, those two millionaires are probably dining at the Ritz right now off of gold plates."

I looked at my plate, golden with syrup, and glanced with amusement at Zukor, but he hadn't even heard. He was already dreaming up half a dozen other new and far-flung enterprises.

When I had lived with my mother and sister in Jones Boarding House on Forty-fourth Street years before and booked my vaudeville acts at the United Booking Offices around the corner at 1495 Broadway, I could hardly have dreamed that both buildings would someday be razed to make way for a stately edifice in which I would have a resplendently furnished office suite directly above the spot where our third-floor room in the boardinghouse had been.

Bessie had a field day helping plan that office. She collected and matched old English pieces to achieve the atmosphere of elegance with which she thought I should be surrounded. The oversized antique desk, Queen Anne table, sofas, Gothic tapestries, oriental rugs, library of prized editions, and other doodads cost around $35,000. But Bessie was becoming internationally known as an artist by this time, and I couldn't quibble with her taste. I didn't have the heart to tell her a comfortable office chair and a practical modern desk would have been more suitable for working purposes than those museum pieces which made me feel old before my time.

And so it came to pass that the boy who blew his cornet behind a rosebush in San Jose until he was blue in the face, hoping John Philip Sousa would stroll by and hire him, years later sat in an elegant, uncomfortable chair in his sanctum high above Broadway and hired John Philip Sousa. It happened when Sam Katz, who had been drafted from the Chicago firm of Balaban and Katz to head all our theatre operations, announced at a board of directors meeting that he was inaugurating a new policy at our Paramount Theatre downstairs. The film presentations would henceforth be supplemented with stage attractions, starting off with Sousa's band. I couldn't resist a Horatio Alger flourish. I said, "This isn't my department, Sam, but if we engage Sousa, I want to sign the contract."

And I did.

After his first matinee performance I went downstairs to the theatre and there, in the wings, met Mr. Sousa at long last. I told him how he had unwittingly broken a boy's heart thirty-five years before by not walking down Santa Clara Street after his afternoon concert in San Jose. He smiled when I confided that I had always kept the mouthpiece of my cornet by my bed, now as a sentimental habit, but at first so I wouldn't lose my embouchure (the muscular lip control a cornettist must acquire the hard way through months or years of practice). It had given me a feeling of security, I added, to think that I could always go back to blowing a horn if vaudeville producing or the picture business didn't work out too well.

"Well, since they *have* worked out too well," Mr. Sousa laughed, "you'd better thank me for not walking down Santa Clara Street. If I had, you might be sweating in a band uniform out there on the Paramount stage today."

The Epic That Didn't Epic
But Did Start a Revolution

When a producer manages to bring off an extraordinarily successful picture, he is immediately under pressure from his sales department and the exhibitors to perform the miracle again in the same way. Then envious salesmen of other companies urge their bosses to "do a picture like So-and-So's—you see how the public is eating it up." So all of you try to stir up the same ingredients, the same or similar theme in a comparable locale, and, if you can command or borrow them, the same combination of author, stars, and director. That's how "cycles" are born.

But somehow you never achieve the same spontaneity when you're imitating as when you're creating, and inevitably you don't get the same flattering audience response. Still, you gamble on beating the game *this* time because you're a gambler at heart or you wouldn't be in the picture business.

I couldn't rest on the laurels of *The Covered Wagon* forever and risk having people think it was a fluke. I had to prove to myself and the industry that I could toss off epics of America's stirring past at the drop of a hat. I began shopping around for the elements of a new masterpiece. I was sure I had one within my grasp when Harry Carr, predecessor of the Los Angeles *Times* columnist and dramatic critic Edwin Schallert, came to me bursting with an idea he said was so great it would top *The Covered Wagon* or any other picture ever made. After I'd heard the idea, I thought he was minimizing its possibilities.

The most celebrated naval vessel in American history was the century-and-a-quarter-old frigate *Constitution*, immortalized in Oliver Wendell Holmes's poem, *Old Ironsides*. Congress had just authorized its reconstruction for a barnstorming coastal cruise to allow the school children of the nation to view the glorious relic.

It looked like a natural to tie in with the flood of publicity the project would receive by filming a sea classic about the noble ship. Dramatic high points would be Stephen Decatur's impassioned plea to Congress for ships to halt the depredations of the Barbary pirates ("'Millions for defence, but not one cent for tribute!'"), the refurbishing of our pitiful navy with *Old Ironsides* and her sister ships, the bombardments off Tripoli under Decatur's command, and the decisive battle in the War of 1812, when the gallant vessel sank the British *Guerrière*, raising our navy and out nation to the status of a world power in twenty-five minutes of brilliant fighting.

We hove to with a will to out-epic *The Covered Wagon*, giving James Cruze the directorial reins, naturally. The leading roles went to Charles Farrell, who was yet to capture all feminine hearts with his immortal performance as "Chico" in *Seventh Heaven*, and Esther Ralston, winner of the Miss America beauty contest I had judged at Atlantic City the year before, and whom we had already starred in *The American Venus*. The supporting cast included the 24-carat names of George Bancroft and Wallace Beery. I wangled an extraordinary budget of $1,500,000 and I recall paying Phil Wrigley $100,000 to use his Catalina Island as our base of sea operations. *Old Ironsides* and her sister ships were faithfully reproduced at a cost which I presume exceeded the amount Congress allotted for the originals. A glittering world premiere was arranged to present our triumph at the Rivoli, with Secretary of the Navy Curtis D. Wilbur and a host of admirals in attendance, and a Navy band playing in the lobby.

A week before it was to open, an inventor named Lorenzo del Riccio asked to see me. He had been unable to make an appointment with any of the other executives at Paramount, but I sent out word that I'd give him five minutes to explain what he wanted.

I had never forgotten Henry B. Harris's advice about not turning anyone away without a hearing, after the time I almost missed my chance to audition Ruth St. Denis and launch her on a professional career. Through the years I've made a real effort to keep myself as accessible as humanly possible to people who think they have reason to see me. Only a few times has this open-mind, open-door policy backfired. Once when we were looking for a girl with a perfect figure to play a sculptor's model in *The Naked Truth*, a woman brought a sweet young thing to my office and announced, "Your search is over. My daughter has a perfect body. Show Mr. Lasky, dear!" And before I could utter a word of protest, the girl dropped every stitch she had on. She did *not* get the job. Then there was the waiter at the Carlton Hotel in London who wanted to be a writer and would serve me a manuscript when I was hungry for steak. But at other times being a good listener paid off in spectacular ways.

The five minutes I gave Del Riccio that day really hit the jackpot. During our brief interview seeds were sown that were to revolutionize the whole motion-picture industry a quarter of a century later.

Del Riccio told me he had invented a supplementary projector lens capable of enlarging a screen image to vast proportions, and would like to demonstrate it to me. I sent him over to the Rivoli and phoned the manager to have our chief projectionist make whatever arrangements were needed and to send for me when they were ready to run a test.

They reversed a painted backdrop for a screen to fill the whole proscenium arch and threw the picture on the dirty canvas in normal size. Then all of a sudden as *Old Ironsides* came to the rescue of a merchantman seized by the Tripoli pirates, the picture opened up to more than four times its natural size and the full-rigged ship expanded in all its glory while sailing right into my lap. I've never felt such a dramatic impact from anything in a full lifetime of show business.

I coined the name "Magnascope" on the spot, and eagerly authorized the necessary expenditure for a big screen in order to project the sea-battle sequences in overwhelming magnitude. We recut the picture to make the most of these scenes. Dr. Hugo Riesenfeld, arranger of the musical score and orchestra leader, stepped up the tempo and volume of the music as the picture suddenly grew gigantic before the startled eyes of the first-night audience. There hadn't been time to advertise the big-screen innovation before the premiere, and everyone was so taken by surprise that all stood up and cheered wildly. The New York *Times* broke precedent the next morning by running its review of the picture on the front page.

In striking contrast to *The Covered Wagon,* which no one at the studio wanted to be associated with in its early stages, and for which Zukor had to do battle with the sales department in an effort to justify my budget, everyone took it for granted that *Old Ironsides* would outshine all pictures that had gone before. Hadn't *The Covered Wagon* proved that a picture stressing the hardy, heroic qualities that built our country was sure-fire at the box-office? The theme of *Old Ironsides* seemed so foolproof that we had put through a budget three times as big as the one that caused the squawk at the home office, and this time there wasn't a murmur. We had produced the picture lavishly with infinite care and devotion. Our mature judgment and experience told us we had an epoch-making winner even before its phenomenal premiere and the critical acclaim it received. Every portent augured well for repeating *The Covered Wagon's* success or surpassing it.

Everything, that is, except *good timing.* Had it been shown soon after the First World War, or after the first rumblings of World War II, it might have ridden on a wave of national patriotism to set new records, as did my later picture *Sergeant York.* But in 1926 it was just stale history, apathetically received and soon forgotten. Many a ship of mine has come in through the years, but *Old Ironsides* was not one of them. In show business you can always expect the unexpected.

Even the wide-screen device was ill-timed. It was a quarter of a century too early. We offered Del Riccio $100 a year during the life of the patent for each installation of the Magnascope lens, but on the advice of his own lawyer he sold it to us outright for $25,000. In the following two years we installed it in many of our theatres, but most of them didn't make much use of it. They didn't need to—business was so good in those days that gadgets and gimmicks were superfluous. However, the Magnascope was used again to enhance the dramatic punch of certain scenes in our pictures *Chang, Wings, The Last Waltz*, and Walter Wanger's *Stagecoach*.

Del Riccio told me only the other day that, had his lawyer let him accept our first offer, he would have collected $2,380,000 in royalties. He doesn't have the same lawyer any more.

The week after the premiere of *Old Ironsides* I put Del Riccio on the payroll and arranged to set up a research laboratory for him at the Long Island studio, the first of its kind in the industry. He was to work on anything he thought would improve motion pictures technically. I held the purse strings on appropriations for his experiments, but I had faith that he knew what he was doing, and I don't remember ever turning down his requests for funds, even though I couldn't comprehend the technical explanations of his projects.

I thought then and I still think that the industry as a whole should support a motion-picture research laboratory. And I believe that the fourteen devices that came out of Paramount's little laboratory in the years of its existence from 1926 to 1929 offer ample evidence that such a plan would benefit every studio.

Lorenzo del Riccio has never sought publicity, and I dare say few readers of this book have ever heard his name, but the ramifications of his influence on the picture business today are so imposing that this story should be told. It never has been told until now, and I guarantee that plenty of people in the film industry itself will be astonished to learn the facts.

Del Riccio had brought his projector attachment to Paramount rather than some other company from a perverse sense of loyalty, because he had worked at Famous Players-Lasky before—until he was fired! This was in the period when our operations were expanding so rapidly that it had seemed expedient to cultivate our own hothouse of executive material. A training class was started at the Long Island studio for five promising young men, each picked from a different leading Eastern university. Del Riccio, a graduate of Brown University, was invited to join the group. Not one of them became a motion-picture executive, but all of them made their marks in other ways. William Bullitt was later Ambassador to France, Tom White managed Catalina Island for picture locations, Monty Woolley became an actor and Frank Tuttle a director.

One of the pictures being made at Astoria was *Peter Ibbetson*, and it was beset with the kind of billing dilemma that still plagues picture makers today. In deference to Elsie Ferguson's fame as a leading legitimate actress one of the concessions we made to induce her to sign with us was a clause in her contract stipulating that she was to have star billing, her name above the title of the picture, in first position and larger type than anyone else's.

That was all right until we put her in *Peter Ibbetson* with Wallace Reid, who had attained stardom by popular acclaim and been rewarded with a contract guaranteeing him top billing and the largest type in advertising displays.

When you make a picture with a high-ranking stage star and a reigning screen favorite, you probably shoot the works and assign it to a big-time director. So we gave this one to George Fitzmaurice, who had a contract for his name to appear above the title and in larger type than the stars of his productions.

Two of the three would have to play second fiddle, but none of them would give in. The deadline for the billboard art to go to the lithographers arrived and the matter still wasn't settled. I sent a release form to Bob Kane, the studio manager, who was also in charge of the training class, and told him we had to have it signed by at least two of the principals before the day was over, so that we could okay the twenty-four-sheet posters without the specter of future lawsuits hanging over our heads. He in turn passed the hot potato to the understudy executive who hung around his office, charging him to get the signatures if he had to use jujitsu.

Del Riccio walked up and down the halls composing persuasive entreaties and started to track down Miss Ferguson. Then he thought he'd better tackle Wallace Reid first. But, remembering Reid's physique, he started for Fitzmaurice. Then he decided none of it was any use and went back to the office to think it over. Kane glowered at him but didn't say anything. Finally, just before closing time, Del Riccio got up and slipped into the dark projection room where the rushes were being run, sat down beside Fitzmaurice, and said, "Here, George—sign this thing."

Annoyed at the interruption, the director hastily scribbled his signature while still looking at the screen. He probably thought he was signing a requisition for paper towels.

"Sorry to trouble you, Wally, but this has to have your signature." He couldn't see what he was signing either, and was too preoccupied with the rushes to ask questions.

Del Riccio put the two signatures under his coat and walked out. And that's how Elsie Ferguson got star billing in *Peter Ibbetson*. If she had been sitting in the projection room where Del Riccio could have got her autograph easier than Wallace Reid's, his name would have taken precedence on the film the New York *World* called "the greatest picture the world has yet seen."

The trainee was a little bit unpopular on the Fitzmaurice set after the posters hit the billboards, and even Bob Kane didn't appreciate the stratagem when the storm broke over his own head. Del Riccio was packed off to California to work under studio manager Vic Clarke and keep a supervisory eye on the operations and expenditures of the Victor Fleming, William DeMille, and George Melford companies.

Fiscal spying wasn't much to his taste anyway, and when one day Cecil DeMille yelled at him to get a broom, he decided that the Famous Players-Lasky organization would have to train another executive to get brooms. Instead of getting the broom he walked off the lot and went to Germany and France to study optical engineering. So Clarke fired him—or at any rate he would have if he had seen him again.

Del Riccio brought back the Magnascope lens instead of a broom. He had previously studied photography at the Eastman Laboratories in Rochester, so he came back from Europe with a good knowledge of optics as well as the inner workings of cameras.

I gave him the research laboratory, and Sam Katz, in charge of our Publix Theatres, soon furnished him with a literally gigantic problem.

Katz was a strong believer in presenting a gorgeous stage prologue along with a motion picture. The stage shows at the New York Paramount were very expensive and siphoned off a lot of money that I felt should have gone back into our real business, that of making motion pictures. But Katz put stage entertainment into all the film houses he could and was determined to give the smaller towns live revues too, even if, paradoxically, they had to be on film. In other words, he wanted to distribute to lesser theatres a canned simulation of the extravagant prologues created for the New York Paramount.

Del Riccio's problem was to find a way to squeeze an elongated rectangle, the aperture of the Paramount Theatre stage below the teaser curtain, which was two and a half times as wide as it was high, into the stockier rectangle of a standard 35-mm. motion-picture frame, which was only one and a quarter times as wide as its height, and to unsqueeze it for projection. He did it with an anamorphic lens, a pair of adjustable prisms which distort an image into a desired shape. The device was first used for mural painting in the King of Saxony's palace in Dresden and then patented in England by Paul Rudolph in 1898, but no one had ever thought of putting it on a motion-picture camera.

There were no such lenses in this country that would serve his purpose. But he knew that a professor he had studied under in Paris had made some anamorphic lenses. He sent for Professor Henri Chrétien and had him make a pair of the trick lenses to be attached to a motion-picture camera and projector.

At the same time Del Riccio was working on other projects. He perfected the first really satisfactory 3-D camera and viewing spectacles at the Paramount laboratory. He didn't invent 3-D. There was an old patent, which had only a year to run, on a method using color filters and colored spectacle lenses. It produced a stereoscopic effect, but looking at a moving picture through one red eye and one green eye was visually irritating as well as cockeyed in spectrum values. Commercially the patent wasn't worth even the $1000 we paid for it until Del Riccio combined it with a polarizing patent and achieved clear-view spectacles for use with either Technicolor or black and white film.

Our supercharged optical engineer was also building a camera to use 56-mm. film. This would make it possible to project on a much wider screen in the theatre without any loss of clarity. The picture quality would be better than with the Magnascope, which merely enlarged. With a slight alteration existing projection equipment could accommodate film 56 mm. wide, but no wider. Del Riccio determined that his new frame should have the height-to-width ratio of 1 to 1.85 after going to the Metropolitan Museum of Art and making a statistical survey of what the old masters had found to be the most pleasing proportions for pictorial representation.

The Magnascope fomented a race among all the picture companies to bring out a wider film. Del Riccio no sooner started working on his 56-mm. camera than FBO (later RKO) tried 60 mm., someone else had 63, Warners committed themselves to 65, M-G-M settled on something else and Fox outdid all the others with a 70-mm. process called Grandeur. The confusion was comparable to that in early railroad history when every company used a different-gauge track.

The anamorphic lenses came in handy once when Clara Bow put on a little weight in the middle—of a picture—by squeezing her into narrower dimensions for scenes in which she had to wear a bathing suit. But the plans for filming the Paramount Theatre stage shows fell through, and a research board of which I was not a member decided there was no future in lenses designed for that specific purpose, so Chrétien was dispensed with and allowed to take the lenses he had worked on back to Europe. Del Riccio was instructed to concentrate on his 56-mm. camera instead.

We completed one 56-mm. film but released only the standard 35-mm. version, and abandoned the 56-mm. width for a political reason. Paramount and Warner Brothers had decided to merge. One of the compromises made in preliminary negotiations was to give up our 56-mm. program and adopt the 65-mm. width that Warners favored.

We had wide film ready for the market before anyone else, but we now had to start all over again and design new projectors as well as cameras. Then we couldn't get anyone in this country to make the equipment because Fox had bought into the companies controlling that business. Del Riccio was sent to France and Germany and worked night and day getting cameras and eighteen projectors built for 65-mm. film to be ready to compete with Fox's Grandeur.

In the meantime the merger plans struck a snag. It was agreed that Adolph Zukor was to be president of the new company and Harry Warner vice-president. Harry and Albert Warner insisted that Jack Warner have charge of production but Sidney Kent and Zukor told them there could be no merger unless I headed the studios.

Fox showed several films in Grandeur (the same size as Magnascope) in its larger houses, and the public may have liked them, but it was hard to tell when the theatres were crowded anyway. There wasn't the incentive that there is today for exhibitors to install expensive new equipment to attract business.

I think that, if we had gone ahead with our 56-mm. plans, the widescreen revolution would have taken place in 1926 or 1927 instead of 1952, as it was the only wide film that didn't require new projectors. After delaying eighteen months for the switch-over to 65 mm., sound films and then the depression overtook us, and it was too late. All our 65-mm. cameras and projectors were stored in barrels of grease, and wide film and big screens were forgotten. The research laboratory was closed and Del Riccio left our employ, but that isn't the end of the story.

There was another flurry of interest in wide-screen effects on the part of the industry in 1935; it started when Adolph Zukor ran into Del Riccio on the street, asked him what ever happened to the lenses he made for Sam Katz's stage shows, and suggested testing them for regular feature pictures. Del Riccio obtained the lenses from Chrétien and shot ten reels of tests including scenes of a Ben Blue picture then in work, before the Paramount front office decided to pass up again the anamorphic system.

Del Riccio's time wasn't wasted, though. While on the Paramount lot for the tests he learned that Bing Crosby was planning to cover the finish line of his Del Mar track with a still camera and, in the event of a contested race, throw the photographic decision on the tote board. Del Riccio had long had an idea for a new kind of camera in which the film would move continuously instead of intermittently, but had never built it because, although he knew he could invent the camera, he wasn't sure he could invent a use for it. That is, until he heard about Crosby's plans and realized it would be ideally suited for contested track decisions. He made and patented the well-known photo-finish, or strip, camera, and its infallible eye first appeared at the opening of Del Mar and has since reversed judges' decisions at many a racetrack throughout the entire world.

On July 7, 1946, Howard Hughes crashed while testing an experimental photographic-reconnaissance plane and nearly lost his life. He crashed on top of Del Riccio's house, which was inundated with six hundred gallons of gasoline and burned to the ground with everything in it. Del Riccio thought his lenses were lost in the fire, but they turned up several years later in the shop he used. In December 1952, Paramount wanted to see the lenses again. They still had the tests taken seventeen years before. Then Warners borrowed them and made some tests. Then Columbia borrowed them and made some tests. Then Fox bought Chrétien's lenses, called the process Cinema-Scope, and *The Robe* was the first picture ever made with the lenses fashioned twenty-six years before to fit exactly the 2½-to-1 opening of the Paramount Theatre stage. Today every major studio in Hollywood is using the CinemaScope process—*except Paramount!*

In the summer of 1953, Paramount sold the 65-mm. cameras and projectors to Michael Todd, and the first picture ever made with *that* twenty-four-year-old equipment (which owes its existence strictly to a merger that miscarried) was *Oklahoma*. He called it the Todd-AO (American Optical) process. And appropriately enough, the Rivoli Theatre on Broadway presented the world premiere of *Oklahoma* on the same-size screen it introduced more than a quarter of a century earlier for the Magnascope sequences of *Old Ironsides*.

The twenty-five-year-old 3-D cameras which had never filmed a picture? They were taken out of moth balls in 1953 and used by Pine and Thomas, the wizards of low-budget films known as "The Dollar Bills," to make their Paramount productions *Sangaree, Those Redheads from Seattle,* and *Jivaro.* Paramount also used the disinterred equipment for the Martin and Lewis picture *Money from Home* and two other feature releases.

Even Cinerama, the king-size wide screen of them all, can be credited to Paramount research of the twenties. Fred Waller, who engineered the three-camera, three-projector process, got his big-screen ideas from Magnascope and the other pioneering work in that field that he saw going on around him. He was in charge of our special effects through that period.

What patents there were on the fourteen devices Del Riccio invented or developed in the Paramount laboratory have all run out. Anyone can use them—and they have already done much to bring back the audiences that motion pictures had started to lose to television.

Sic Transit
Gloria Swanson

If I had lived earlier, I think I might have been an explorer. I still have that insatiable curiosity about what's on the other side of the mountain. It started with my early fishing trips with my father and was fed by my pack trip to Maine with Cecil and my annual quest for outdoor adventure in inaccessible country. I went on camping trips with Zane Grey, and pack trips with hired guides in Alaska, in the High Sierras, the Canadian Northwest, and down the Colorado River. I gloried in shooting the rapids of the Balsas River in Mexican jungles where, until then, white men had never penetrated, and I retreated with no dignity whatever from ominously muttering giant savages on Tiburón Island after our supply of beads and baubles gave out.

When duty kept me moored to my various offices, I sometimes got a vicarious thrill of adventure from sending camera expeditions to far places for native life films. After Robert Flaherty made his classic study of Eskimos, *Nanook of the North*, I sent him to the South Seas to record Samoan tribal life in the same way. He spent eighteen months on the project and came back with what the critics called "an epic of race" and "sheer astounding loveliness." I think *Moana* was actually a better picture than *Nanook*, but it lacked the more gripping drama of man's struggle against nature in a rigorous clime and was not a commercial success.

We made another documentary-type masterpiece at about the same time dealing realistically with the true savagery of our own hidden race of primitives in the Great Smoky Mountains of North Carolina. Karl Brown, a young cameraman who had worked with D. W. Griffith, got the idea while filming *The Covered Wagon*, on location in Utah with James Cruze, of doing a picture about the covered wagon that got lost, the pioneers who quit, the derelict settlers who cut themselves off from the outside world and stopped the clock three hundred years ago. It sounded different and a challenge, so we gave Karl his head and he dedicated himself to capturing on film the Neanderthal pattern of existence of these ignorant, indifferent mountain whites, without studio sets and with actors who had never seen a movie and didn't realize they were acting. Handicapped by the cheap-sounding title, *Stark Love*, the picture proved somewhat too stark for the tastes of our audiences, although the critics lauded its uncompromising integrity.

A really remarkable primitive-life documentary film of the period was *Grass*, filmed for $12,000 in Persia by Merian C. Cooper and Ernest B. Schoedsack, a couple of hardy souls who met in the Russo-Polish War. Schoedsack was an ace newsreel cameraman whose beat was the battleground of any current hostilities. Cooper was an intrepid flier whose war record includes sixty medals and being shot down and taken prisoner in both Germany and Russia. Their film was a gripping chronicle of the trek of fifty thousand Bakhtiari tribesmen with their flocks over a treacherous river and a twelve-thousand-foot mountain range—to grass where the sheep could feed. The pair were using it as a lecture film when I happened to see it and arranged for its distribution by Famous Players-Lasky. It was a big hit, running at the Criterion in New York for many months.

When Cooper and Schoedsack came up with an idea for a wild-animal picture featuring an elephant stampede through a native village in the Siamese jungle and such everyday hazards as marauding tigers, they didn't have to belabor its exciting possibilities. I dispatched them forthwith to northern Siam with my blessing and the budget they asked for, which was $60,000. They sent back film as they took it, and *Chang* was roughly assembled at the studio by the time they themselves returned from their fourteen-month sojourn. They had exceeded their budget by $10,000, but I was delighted with the picture and impatient to congratulate them. I expected them to come right to my office as soon as they docked, but instead they disappeared for several days. When they did put in a nervous appearance, they handed me a check for $10,000, mumbling apologies for running over their budget and the delay in raising money to pay back what they "owed" me. They had been ashamed to face me until they could make it good. You would have thought they were confessing to embezzlement.

I laughed with relief and tore up the check. I hadn't restricted their budget to the figure they set themselves before they started out, which was so ridiculously low I would have agreed readily to a much larger sum. I had simply authorized the accounting department to supply them with funds as needed. They were actually working on an *unlimited* expense account but didn't know it. They shared in the profits of *Chang*, which was the most successful travel film anyone had ever made.

I next had the team direct civilized actors, a new experience for them. For *The Four Feathers*, from A. E. W. Mason's book, Cooper and Schoedsack spent a full year shooting spectacular footage in the wilds of Portuguese East Africa and the Sudan, and interlaced these scenes with matching shots made in the studio. It was the first prefab picture to put popular stars in authentic, exotic foreign settings without taking them out of Hollywood. Hundreds of pictures since then have been indebted to this procedure, and the practice became even more commonplace after the perfection of "rear projection," enabling live action to be shot against a moving picture thrown on a background screen.

Schoedsack later filmed *Rango* for us in the Sumatra jungle with a cast of wild monkeys that made our other stars look to their laurels. The team joined forces again for the RKO fantasy-thriller *King Kong*. Cooper rose in the business to become head of RKO Pictures and served in World War II as Claire Chennault's first chief of staff, and later, with General George Kenney's Fifth Air Force, engineered the strikes on Wewak and Hollandia that broke the back of the Japanese air power in the Southwest Pacific.

If I didn't bother my head over Cooper's and Schoedsack's expenditures, I can't say the same for Erich von Stroheim. Accounts of his fabulous extravagances were certainly embroidered by overzealous publicity men, but there's no denying that he did things in the grand manner. Cecil had been wont to give the business office chronic headaches, but at least his disbursements were geared to what his pictures would bring in. Von Stroheim, however, was something of a genius at spending money without regard for possible returns, driven only by his sincere passion for artistic perfection. He was also unfortunate in not being able to trim his stories to an acceptable length. He thought the public would rather see one long picture, with an intermission, than the usual feature-length picture with a comedy and newsreel, but the idea was so revolutionary at that time he never got a chance to demonstrate it.

His acknowledged masterpiece, *Greed*, had run seven and a half hours when the film was first assembled. It had taken nine months to shoot, the director being such a fanatic for realism that he refused to make one scene of it in the studio, working instead in an abysmally dreary house on Polk Street in San Francisco, reported to be the actual house where the brutal murder recreated in the film had taken place years before. It would have been a typical Von Stroheim tactic to rent and use a real murder house, but whether he did or not, at least he made his actors believe they were in the authentic setting—which served his purpose as well—and he made them live in the squalid place to absorb the feel of it. Nor would he compromise for the desert scenes. He worked his cast for weeks in the worst part of Death Valley at temperatures soaring above 100°, using two cars full time to shuttle the sick ones to the nearest town. After months of inner struggle he managed to cut the forty-two reels to twenty-four and vowed he couldn't shave another inch. Metro-Goldwyn-Mayer took it out of his hands at that point and reduced it to ten reels. Even in this shortened, patchwork version with choppy transitions it was a landmark in screen history. But one of the greatest box-office failures of all time.

Despite the number of other intrepid producers who had burned their fingers at the fire of genius Patrick Powers, one of the pioneers of the General Film Company, put Von Stroheim under contract. And with more enthusiasm than I had ever seen poker-faced Pat display, he tipped me off that Von had a wonderful story of the pomp and glory of prewar Vienna, and tried to sell me a package of the story and director.

I turned the project down, reminding Pat that the controversial Austrian was hardly ever in at the final accounting of the pictures he directed (which he usually wrote and appeared in as well). However, when Powers offered to put up half the financing himself and personally keep a strict check on every phase of the production, I felt the risk was worth taking—but I kept my fingers crossed.

Von ran true to form and shot a fearful amount of film in spite of all Powers could do to hold him down. We were both distraught. When he was halfway through the editing, it was apparent that the film would have to have intermissions for dinner—and possibly breakfast.

So again Von Stroheim was absent by request at the final "butchery" of one more of his artistic triumphs, and again he disclaimed credit for the mutilated remains. We hacked it down to four hours, but didn't think it was good enough to road-show in that form as a superspectacle. We simply chopped it in two and released it as two pictures, *The Wedding March* and *The Honeymoon*. And I gave a long-term contract to Von's discovery, the lovely Fay Wray, who made her first appearance as the star of that tandem production. Many first appearances have wound up on the cutting-room floor. I think hers is the only one in Hollywood's history that wound up as a double feature.

It may be harrowing for geniuses to work with money-mad producers, but producers can have moments of despair too.

Gloria Swanson was now our top star. She was making $6500 a week and her pictures bolstered our whole program. To get them, exhibitors were compelled to give playing dates to blocks of weak features that we might otherwise have had trouble selling. The government finally broke up the practice of block-booking, but while it existed, Gloria was worth very much more to us than her own pictures brought in.

It had been Cecil DeMille's idea six years before to take her from Mack Sennett comedies, drape her in the slickest creations the fashion designers could whip up, and put her in provocative social dramas against lavish settings. He—and later directors Sam Wood and Allan Dwan—built her into as important a property as Mary Pickford had been in our early days.

I suppose any woman who has the world at her feet and is treated like an empress long enough will begin to feel like one. I certainly didn't help to keep Gloria's pretty head on her shoulders by deciding on *Madame Sans-Gene*, based on Sardou's classic play of Napoleon and the washerwoman, for her next picture, or by having the inspiration to film it in France.

From the time of her arrival in Paris her every appearance caused a near riot of worshiping fans. She was accorded the display of devotion usually reserved for reigning royalty. Even the French Government conspired to that end by placing at our disposal the palace at Fontainebleau and other historic locations with rich treasures as props for our picture. Then she made her nobility legal by marrying the Marquis Henri de la Falaise de la Coudray, a wonderfully charming fellow who endeared himself to all of us as "Hank." With her new husband Gloria queened it back to America and across the continent in a private railroad car furnished by the studio. It was too good a publicity break to pass up—comparable to the recent Grace Kelly-Prince Rainier nuptials—and we milked the transcontinental trip for all we could, winding it up with a party for our salesmen that has never been eclipsed in my Hollywood experience of elaborate functions, with Gloria enthroned in the midst of it.

As luck would have it, her contract with us was about to expire. I got frantic phone calls first from Sid Kent and then Zukor to sign her up again at any price. But when I called her, she said she wasn't interested in a new contract—at any price. She wouldn't come to the studio, so I hastened to her home on North Crescent Boulevard. I offered her $12,000 a week and then $15,000, to no avail. She had a business adviser, Maurice Cleary, with her, and didn't seem at all the friendly, gay-hearted Gloria I had "done" Paris with after we wrapped up *Madame Sans-Gene*.

I made every concession I could think of that might tempt her. Finally, in desperation, I offered her $300,000 a picture for three pictures a year plus 50 per cent of the profits, her pick of directors, a voice in her stories, and her own wardrobe designer. When she still showed no glimmer of interest, I returned to my office, disheartened. Calling Zukor, I admitted my failure. He listened to the terms I had proposed and, after conferring with Kent, authorized me to raise the ante to a million dollars a year, and half the profits!

A little later I called him back and reported that Gloria had turned down the highest offer ever made to any screen celebrity. Actually I hadn't bothered to make the offer because I knew it wasn't worth wasting even a five-cent phone call on. Nothing could have dissuaded her from forming her own company. Its initial venture was *Queen Kelly*, written and directed by Erich von Stroheim. It was such a monumental fiasco it was never released, and very nearly bankrupted our beloved, misguided movie queen.

Even before Gloria left us in the position that General Motors would be in if Cadillac walked out, I had had an uneasy feeling we were using up our natural resources of star personalities faster than new ones could be developed. For one thing, we put them in more pictures—six or eight a year instead of one or two, as is usual today. Careers became full-blown in a matter of months instead of years. They lost their luster much faster, too, but in those years of fabulous salaries and low taxes a film idol could make a fortune in the short time before his public tired of him, and retire in luxury for the rest of his life. The smart ones did.

The screen's need for new faces, therefore, was as acute then as it is now, if not more so. But where were they to come from? Plenty of attractive, photogenic young people were called to my attention—but they couldn't act. There was the bottleneck, I decided. But acting was something that could be taught. Why depend any longer on chance to bring the happy combination of looks and acting ability to our door? Why not purposefully bring the two together?

Accordingly, I had organized the Paramount School at our Astoria studio, the first of several large-scale efforts I have made in my lifetime to uncover and assist genuine dramatic talent that might otherwise remain forever hidden in out-of-the-way places for lack of a little training and encouragement. It was the first time any studio had undertaken to develop its own young players with an eye to future needs, but now most studios do the same thing in individual instances where an investment in coaching and training seems warranted.

We selected twenty-four talented boys and girls from all over the country, using our scattered film exchanges for the weeding-out process on the basis of photographs, school standing, amateur dramatic activities, etc. We paid their transportation and living expenses in New York during six months of courses in dramatics, make-up, costuming, etiquette, and the various skills such as riding, fencing, dancing, swimming, and automobile driving which were all-important to a player in silent pictures. I remember there was even a Charleston specialist on the faculty.

The graduating exercises were held at a dinner in the Ritz-Carlton Hotel on March 2, 1926, and the sixteen who had made the highest scholastic showing were given diplomas in the form of studio contracts for a year with options. At the banquet we seated the students next to our leading stars and such theatrical luminaries as Lee Shubert, Florenz Ziegfeld, and Charles Dillingham.

A story, *Fascinating Youth*, was written with parts tailored to individual types for the sixteen contract winners, and directed by Sam Wood. It turned out to be a pretty good picture. Two gifted performers emerged from the school and were featured in the film—Charles "Buddy" Rogers from Olathe, Kansas, and Thelma Todd, plucked from the Massachusetts normal school where she had been studying to be a teacher. Josephine Dunn, Jack Luden, and a few others learned enough about the business to hang on for several years in secondary parts. But the results on the whole didn't justify con-

G

tinuing the school. What I had failed to take into consideration was that looks and talent and training aren't enough by themselves. More important than all three is personality—and that's something you can't turn out by factory methods. To be sure, Buddy and Thelma benefited amazingly from the school, but they had personality galore, and untapped dramatic ability as well, before they came to us, or they would never have landed on top.

So the Paramount School didn't become, as I had fondly hoped, the West Point of the film industry. But it didn't cure me of trying to open the door to talented youth over the country who would never have a chance to make the grade in Hollywood without a helping hand.

The Famous Players-Lasky studio in Astoria had a turbulent career. We made some pictures there with New York stage stars, and also shifted West Coast stars to the Long Island studio occasionally to give them a change of environment and the stimulation of New York. Valentino made two of his pictures there.

The Eastern studio enabled us to make a compact with Florenz Ziegfeld to use his Ziegfeld Follies company in a picture called *Glorifying the American Girl*. While the studio was teeming with gorgeous "ponies," as chorus dancers used to be called, and stunning show girls from the Follies, our Wall Street bankers developed a sudden interest in seeing how pictures were made, and our own business executives gave unstintingly of the time they should have spent in their own offices, to act as guides. I know, because it just happened that endless details seemed to require my attention at the studio just then.

The Astoria studio was also a great convenience in screen-testing stage people we contemplated using. Ethel Barrymore watched a test she had made and said, "My God—I look like Elsie Janis imitating me!" We took a test of the dancing team, Fred and Adele Astaire. Someone (it might have been me) said, "Well, she's all right, but what could you do with the bald-headed guy?"

What couldn't we have done with the bald-headed guy! RKO invested in a toupee and made millions from the cover charge. Fred's sister Adele never appeared in pictures at all.

Even though the Astoria studio filled a definite need as an adjunct to our facilities in the West, it was always a headache to the production department. Overhead was higher in the New York area, the studio was limited in size and utility, weather destroyed sets on the back lot time and again, and locations for exteriors were more of a problem than amid the scenic variety of the West. Besides all this it was hard to keep the studio fully active when the West Coast studio had first call on story properties and when, indeed, most stories could be filmed more advantageously in Hollywood. This situation once led to the absurd contretemps of our Astoria producers making one of their finest pictures in the Hollywood studio.

I had only to okay the more important story purchases that Ben Schulberg at the Coast, and Bill Le Baron, now in charge of Astoria, wanted to make for the respective studios. But often, when I was in New York, I had the story department short-circuit very desirable properties directly to my office for a quick decision, so that our competitors wouldn't get the jump on us in the bidding. Thus my able lieutenant, Walter Wanger, read Percival Christopher Wren's best-selling novel about the French Foreign Legion, *Beau Geste*, when it first came out and passed it to me with the highest recommendation. I was also so impressed that we bought it instantly, without even consulting Schulberg. Then, when I sent it to him for his reaction, there was no reaction. We suspected that he resented its purchase without first having been submitted to him for approval. To make matters worse, the sales department insisted that they couldn't sell a picture doubly handicapped by "a French title no one can pronounce" and the absence of a love story.

I wasn't in a tenable position. I had committed a *faux pas* in the estimation of the sales department and the Hollywood studio. If ever the Long Island studio justified its existence in my eyes, it did then by rescuing me from this embarrassing dilemma. I asked Le Baron to read the book everyone else had turned thumbs down on. He was as keen as I was about it. I won't suggest that he liked it because Schulberg didn't, but there was a good deal of rivalry and jealousy between the two studios.

And so I gave the New York studio a story that had to be made in the Imperial Valley sand dunes of California because of its desert locale. The Eastern personnel was sent West, and Schulberg was obliged to furnish studio accommodations for the interlopers and to watch the picture being shot in his own bailiwick under the Astoria banner by Herbert Brenon, now assigned to the Eastern company, and supervised by Julian Johnson, who had been until then our Eastern story editor.

Neil Hamilton, who played the part of Digby Geste, recently reminded me of the climactic scene where the French outpost in Morocco, Fort Zinderneuf, garrisoned by twenty-two Legionnaires, was stormed by a horde of Arab tribesmen who came riding furiously over the dunes from every direction. The scene was so important that a dozen extra cameramen had been brought from Hollywood to photograph it, and Brenon was anxious for them to pick up plenty of action when the besieging Arabs were fired on from the fort. Just before giving the signal to charge, he yelled to the riders, "A ten-dollar bonus to every man who takes a fall!" At the first burst of fire from the piddling Legion guard all the riders, two thousand strong, "dropped dead" in their tracks!

I had obtained a $500,000 budget, but went over it to almost $1,000,-000, and the picture became the road-show sensation of the next season. It made stars of William Powell and Alice Joyce, and enhanced Ronald Colman's reputation very considerably.

When the sales department first saw the finished production, they still thought it would be a flop at the box-office, and continued to think so while it played to standing room at the Criterion at a $2.00 top. "That's just New York," was their skeptical attitude until it began racking up records in other cities. Then they about-faced and demanded that we buy Wren's two sequels, *Beau Sabreur* and *Beau Ideal*, which didn't appeal to us at all because the plots paled by comparison with the first book.

But we did what we could with *Beau Sabreur* and it was such a flop we never even made the third one.

I had done everything I could think of to break up that silly jealousy and intrigue between the East and West studios. I had once made Walter Wanger head of the Long Island studio and then fired him because he had a diabolic knack for fanning the flames. A perfectionist himself, he can be caustic in his criticisms. But he was too valuable to lose, so after he had cooled off in Europe awhile, I brought him back as general manager of all production. At the time of the *Beau Geste* armed truce, he was over both Le Baron, who had replaced him at Long Island, and Schulberg in Hollywood. I had hoped that forcing the two studios to co-operate on the same picture might ease the situation, but it worsened, if anything. The only solution seemed to be to concentrate all production in Hollywood. So for a million dollars we bought a twenty-six-acre site with a nucleus of buildings known as the United Studios, moved from Vine, where we had expanded from the Lasky Barn to the limits of ten acres to "United"—hoping that was an omen of harmony—and closed the Long Island studio.

As a sentimental salute to our beginnings I insisted on taking the original barn along with us and plopping it down in the midst of our new Famous Players-Lasky studio on Marathon Street. I thought it would be well never to lose sight of the modest way we started. The old barn is still there, today used as a gymnasium, in the middle of what is now the Paramount lot. Some facetious signs hang in the ping-pong room—"Absolutely No Gambling Permitted by the Management," and "Please Settle After Each Game." Surely a high-water mark in gambling was the chance we took in that very room on *The Squaw Man.*

But the corpse in Long Island didn't stay dead for long. The Astoria stages came to life again with the advent of sound pictures and were very useful to us until we closed them once more in 1932. Then, during World War II, the Army took them over. My elder son, Jesse, Jr., was stationed there for a time, writing and supervising Army training films.

Abracadabra

Sidney R. Kent was the father of the motion-picture sales convention, a yearly event designed to supercharge our apostles with faith and characterized by the hysterical shouting of a revival meeting. These annual pep rallies unquestionably proved their worth and the custom was quickly adopted by all companies in the field. However, it was a vast annoyance for us in the production department to have to take time off from the actual making of pictures to exhort the sales force to fever pitch with grandiloquent promises and incendiary teasers about the product they could expect in the twelve-month season starting in September.

We were confident that the mill would keep grinding and that the salesmen would have the required number of celluloid reels to deliver to their customers a year or two years hence, but we were often pretty fuzzy in our own minds about what would be on those reels. Nevertheless, without even the benefit of a crystal ball, we had to convince the salesmen that every story had been carefully blueprinted and that every effort would be an epic, so they would be keyed up to go out on the road and give their all. This was one of the evils of block-booking, when pictures were sold in job lots before they were filmed, and often before they were even conceived. Now, of course, they are made and previewed before theatres contract to show them.

It took a genius to merchandise up to $50,000,000 worth of airy promises a year, and Sidney Kent was that genius. His salesmanship had an eerie quality of hypnotism. He worked it first on Adolph Zukor, after being emphatically told that there were no openings for a salesman. He climbed steadily on his record of results to the position of general sales manager of Famous Players-Lasky. He was the greatest leader of men I've ever known. He commanded fanatic loyalty—his sales force outdid themselves for him. He was the first man in the history of the company who rose from the ranks to the board of directors.

Walter Wanger and I would start in January to prepare Kent's ammunition for the July convention—a very elaborate brochure touting the superlative merits of features which were actually only titles to us, coined in the urgency of the moment, and almost certain to be changed, if indeed the pictures were ever made at all. We always had a few honest titles to go on—books and plays we had purchased, such as H. G. Wells's *War of the Worlds,* which I bought in 1924 (but which remained dormant in Paramount's story stock pile twenty-eight years before George Pal filmed it in 1952). Zane Grey's books were especially serviceable for mock-ups because we had made a deal for his entire output and could therefore ballyhoo a Zane Grey book before it was written and without even consulting him, since the plots were fairly predictable and interchangeable. We could simply make up a Zane Grey title if we didn't have one and announce it for one of our contract players—probably Richard Dix because he was the outdoor type and good box-office bait. At one point we got so far ahead of Grey that we actually had pictures made and in the can before he started writing the books they were supposed to be taken from! It's understandable if there were some wide discrepancies between the two versions, but the books did follow their picturizations pretty closely, reversing the usual order.

The pressure of getting that damned convention book to the printers, as the deadline for copy sneaked up on us, panicked us into hasty and ill-considered purchases of plays and books, as well as making directorial and casting assignments before scenarios were written.

After *The Covered Wagon* we tried to have one superspecial or road-show attraction every year. I say tried, because inspirations for epics aren't easily come by, and we were usually still tearing our hair for one when it was time for the sales manual to go to press. The announcement of the road show for the year became the *pièce de résis-*

tance of our annual prospectus. One year the moment came when we couldn't temporize any longer and we were still out on a limb. We hadn't the foggiest idea for a superspecial.

"All we can do," I said to Wanger, "is take a double spread in the middle of the book, fill each page with a big question mark and throw a streamer over the top, 'WILL THIS BE THE GREATEST PICTURE EVER MADE?'"

On the first day of the convention in Atlantic City monitors distributed the books in sealed envelopes to the several hundred representatives from all over the United States, Canada, and Europe. I discoursed as usual on the incomparable pictures they were to have the privilege of handling during the coming year. I directed them to open their books and follow me as I soared to heights of verbal ecstasy over each cinematic gem. By the time I came to the double-page spread an hour and a half later, I had used every high-flown adjective in my vocabulary.

I paused significantly.

"Gentlemen," I intoned solemnly, "I am at a loss for words to describe the sensational dramatic spectacle shrouded in the mystery of these two question marks. But perhaps that is just as well, because it is to your advantage that we allow no advance information about it to leak out. We are protecting you from competitive attempts to cash in on the furor this picture is bound to create. We want you to have a clear field to yourselves. While your own loyalty is unquestioned, and I would trust every one of you with the secret, this is a very large gathering, and there may be spies from our rivals planted among you.

"So the crowning achievement of your company for next year must remain nameless for the present. No doubt you can guess who the director will be without my telling you. I can say this much about the author—he is known and loved the world over. The title, I might add, is a natural, but we're not going to announce it until this prodigious production goes before the cameras."

I raved on about the nonexistent work of art until I had to stop for breath. The men stood up and cheered. There's no denying that the film industry was a land of make-believe—especially around convention time.

When the tumult and the shouting subsided enough for me to go on, I expediently tacked in a different direction. "Boys," I said expansively, "we've all heard the vain boast that Metro-Goldwyn-Mayer is forging ahead and shows signs of becoming a real competitor of our organization. Well, I can tell you—and this is no secret—you'll never live to see the day when Metro can hold a candle to Famous Players-Lasky!"

Another cheer went up that lasted several minutes, and I doubt if any man in that assemblage would have admitted even to himself that any other company could seriously threaten Paramount's world supremacy in motion-picture production and distribution. But Metro had indeed been turning out outstanding features, and it wasn't long before that company, under the masterly guidance of Louis B. Mayer and Irving Thalberg, not only held a candle to us, but gave us an exceedingly painful hotfoot. Maybe *they* knew what pictures they were going to make.

The next day Sid Kent said, "Jesse, the boys are all talking about the picture you're keeping under wraps. They like it better than any super-special we've ever turned out. What's the name of it?"

I managed to stall him off.

Walter and I looked at each other when we were alone and said, "My God, what are we going to do?"

On the fourth day of the convention just before the closing banquet we were strolling disconsolately along the Boardwalk. As was always our habit, when we passed a secondhand bookshop, we stopped to look in the window.

Walter started and exclaimed, "What a title! What an idea!"

I looked where he pointed to a little book called *The Pony Express*.

Furiously we caught at flashing thoughts.

"One rider races against time and gives his pouch to the next one just before he collapses . . ."

"Indians, road agents, conspirators . . ."

"George Bancroft would be great in it!"

"I see Betty Compson as a pioneer girl!"

"Yes, and Ricardo Cortez as one of the riders!"

We knew when we sat down at the banquet table that night what the greatest picture of the coming year would be. We could have lifted our convenient ban of secrecy with an electrifying announcement. But the boys already liked our masterpiece so well we didn't bother. As it turned out, their blind and premature faith in it was completely justified. A story was developed around the dramatic role Pony Express riders played in saving the Union of States when California was threatening to secede, and James Cruze made a heart-warming thriller of it.

The next year when we faced the annual crisis of the convention book going to press with a big hole in the middle, we slapped in as the big road-show special a title we had bought from scenarist Monte Katterjohn. *The Greatest Show on Earth* was to be the story of P. T. Barnum and his circus, but our writers hadn't licked the story. So I had to ad-lib it in doubletalk at the convention.

"Well, here it is, boys!" I beamed with a reasonable facsimile of pardonable pride. "The show-stopper you've been waiting for! The picture of the century! The road show of all time! A sales leader that has everything! *The Greatest Show on Earth!*

"You have to see a truly colossal story like this unfold on the screen to appreciate its appeal to every picturegoer in the nation and in the world, so I won't attempt to detail it for you now. I have neither the time nor the storytelling talent to do it justice. But I'll give you just one incident and you can judge the caliber of the picture yourselves.

"Barnum meets a crippled boy in a wheel chair in a town where the circus is going to play the next day. He pats the lad on the head and says, 'Sonny, are you going to see the parade tomorrow?' The boy says wistfully, 'I've never seen a parade. We live too far from Main Street.'

" 'You'll see one tomorrow,' Barnum assures him as he leaves to intercept the circus train out of town.

"That night, as the train bearing The Greatest Show on Earth approaches a river, a storm breaks, the river floods, and the bridge to the boy's town washes out.

" 'I've promised a crippled boy he'll see his first parade tomorrow,' Barnum says grimly. 'We're going to cross that river!' And all night long, by the flare of torches in the torrential rain, the circus paraphernalia is loaded by his loyal circus hands. Then it lumbers precariously and agonizingly over a makeshift pontoon bridge thrown across the elephants' backs.

"We cut to a small frame house on a side street the next morning. It's a bright, sunny day and the little crippled boy sits by his second-story window. Suddenly down the side street comes P. T. Barnum on his white horse leading the parade right past the boy's house. . . .

"And remember, gentlemen—that's only a small incident in our road-show picture for next year, *The Greatest Show on Earth!*"

They got up and raised the roof with their cheers.

I refrained from telling them that that one puny incident was the only one we had. The story simply wouldn't jell. You may have millions of dollars on tap to pour into a picture, but if you can't lick the story, you're sunk.

We had to substitute something else and postpone *The Greatest Show on Earth*. But next year, there it was again in the featured spot

G*

of the convention book—"The story that Mark Twain might have written but only Paramount could produce."

I got up on the platform and went through the same song and dance with even more frills and fantastic flourishes, explaining that this gigantic undertaking was going to be such an epoch-making milestone in Hollywood's history that we had decided to lavish on it twice the preparation and production care that we had originally planned.

We didn't lick the story that year, either. Unfortunately Mark Twain was still dead.

We never did lick it. After ballyhooing the project for three straight years as the eighth wonder of the world, the theme was beginning to seem a little shelf-worn, and we abandoned it.

Cecil DeMille finally licked the story more than twenty-five years later, without using the crippled boy *or* Barnum—and it won him his first Academy Award.

I have a complete set of the books we put out for the convention each year, but they are of little use to me for filling in gaps in my memory about the thousand and more pictures made under my stewardship. The books describe pictures we never made at all, and stories which reached the screen under different titles and with different directors, writers, stars, and casts than the ones announced for them in the catalogues.

We never had any kickbacks or complaints of misrepresentation over the salesmen soliciting orders for peaches and then delivering bananas. Theatre men objected only when we substituted lemons.

Double Double Toil

and Trouble

Making pictures has in a sense enabled me to gratify all my early frustrated ambitions. In my youth I had been torn between various urges to become the world's greatest band leader, composer, novelist, and opera star. Eventually I lived the lives of a great composer, novelist, and opera star—by proxy. Making film biographies of George Gershwin, Mark Twain, and Caruso gave me an inner satisfaction that no other pictures afforded. I was preparing to add John Philip Sousa to that list when Twentieth Century-Fox stole a march-king on me, so to speak.

I had two other ambitions as a boy that cropped out later in celluloid form. I've already mentioned that my yen to be an adventurer and explorer found expression in sponsoring such pictures as *Chang, Rango,* and *Moana.* Finally I had fantasies of myself as one of Teddy Roosevelt's Rough Riders in the days when I blew my cornet in the escort bands that paraded down Market Street in San Francisco with regiments embarking for the Spanish-American War. The Rough Riders were the younger generation's symbol of high adventure then, as Hopalong Cassidy and Davy Crockett have been more recently. This led to my sister's and my wearing Rough Rider uniforms for the Army bugle-call number in our first vaudeville act. I had a picture taken of myself in that rig, looking as if I had just won the Spanish-American War singlehanded.

Jesse, Jr., ran across this picture when he was eight years old. His eyes got big with admiration and he said, "Daddy, you were in the war and you never told me!" So I told him what he wanted to hear—how I charged up San Juan Hill with Teddy Roosevelt. Often at bedtime after that he wanted to hear how *I* took San Juan Hill—with the help of Teddy Roosevelt and the Rough Riders. I made a good story of it. It was easy to tell—I probably enjoyed the fanciful recital as much as he did. At the time it seemed as harmless as any other fairy tale I could have spun for him. He took the picture to his room and practically made a shrine of it. I began to have some misgivings at that point, but rationalized, "It's no worse for a kid to believe in his father than to believe in Santa Claus."

But Jesse spread the tale among his little schoolmates, and it became quite a legend. The whopper may have served to stimulate his acute interest in American military history. He got appalling grades in nearly everything else, mostly because he spent so much time on history and collecting antique firearms. Then when he was fourteen, he was asked to prepare a composition to be read at a meeting of World War I veterans. Stuck for something to write about, he said, "Dad, I'm going to tell them about your part in the Spanish-American War!"

It was the day of reckoning. I had to explain that I had made up the story to entertain him when he was a little fellow, as Barrie entertained his grandchildren by making up stories about Peter Pan. He turned away, close to tears.

"What will I tell them?" he asked in a quavering voice.

I did some fast thinking. "Tell them," I said, "that your dad is going to produce a picture about the Spanish-American War—and they'll see exactly how Teddy Roosevelt and the Rough Riders charged up San Juan Hill!"

In recent years I happened to refer to Jesse's war record in the presence of his eight-year-old daughter, Jennifer, and was astounded to hear history repeating itself. She exclaimed, "Daddy, you never told me you were in the war!"

But there was a difference. After keeping an eye on as many as a hundred training-film scripts at once in the old Famous Players-Lasky studio in Astoria, and producing some himself, Jesse asked for an easier assignment—active duty. He served in New Britain, New Guinea, and the Philippines. In command of photographic coverage of the Leyte invasion he insisted on putting himself in the first assault wave that went ashore on D-Day. I would never have known from his own lips how he compensated for my absence at San Juan Hill, but Commander Robert E. Vining, whose ship he was on, was moved to send me a report of the landing, in which he stated: "In a wide experience in this war, I have never seen displayed more sheer guts, more commendable courage, such cheerfulness and poise as Jesse exhibited. He was an inspiration to us all. . . . Never before have I come to have more sincere admiration for any man."

Jesse's daughter will someday have a Legion of Merit medal among her souvenirs, but she doesn't know it and has never seen it.

"What do you do for bedtime stories?" I asked my son.

"Peter Pan," he grinned.

Naturally I put Teddy Roosevelt of the Rough Riders on my list of celluloid alter egos, and filmed the picture on the actual spot in San Antonio, Texas, where he assembled his band to train for the war with Spain. Our actor-soldiers were coached by some of the original Rough Riders themselves, and we also had the invaluable services of Hermann Hagedorn, the noted Roosevelt historian, as author and technical consultant. A film maker has a more potent genie at his command for wish-fulfillment than Aladdin's lamp, but the magic can go sour if it isn't kept on the right side of the ledger. Again I got a special budget of $500,000 but backed my confidence in the picture with more than twice that amount. It cost $1,200,000 before it was finished. You risk your job each time you overstep your budget, of course. No man can survive many mistakes of overexpenditure on such a scale when he's gambling with stockholders' money.

If we made such a picture as *The Rough Riders* today, we'd use the biggest-name star we could get and let the make-up department re-tread his face. Make-up artists can work miracles of transformation now that weren't possible in silent-picture days. We were obliged to find Roosevelt's double in actual appearance, without considering his dramatic ability, since he didn't have to speak.

We notified all our exchanges of our need. One of them sent in a photograph of a man named Frank Hopper, who bore a striking resemblance to Roosevelt. We sent him a contract to star in *The Rough Riders* and brought him from the Middle West to Hollywood. I noticed, as he sat in my office, that he seemed withdrawn, speaking hardly a word. I turned him over to the director, Victor Fleming.

A few days later, with the picture about to start, Victor said flatly, "Hopper won't do."

"Of course he'll do," I insisted. "He's a dead ringer for Roosevelt!"

"Only in looks," Victor said. "In every other way, he's the direct opposite. Roosevelt was aggressive, dynamic, stormy. This guy hangs his head. He trembles when you speak to him. He's so timid he's afraid to ask what time it is. If you've got a picture where he'd be working behind a ribbon counter, he'd be perfect—but leading the Rough Riders up San Juan Hill? . . . The audience would roll in the aisles!"

I was disturbed and asked Fleming to send him to me. Something obviously had to be done, but I didn't know what. We had given the man a contract—we'd be in legal difficulties if we dismissed him. Besides, it would cost a fortune to hold up the picture until we found a replacement.

Will Hays dropped in before Hopper got there, and I explained the difficulty.

"You know," Hays mused, "no person can help reacting to the way other people treat him. Let's try an experiment. I'll stick around and when he comes in, instead of telling him he's finished if he doesn't measure up to what's required of him, suppose you introduce him to me with the greatest deference and respect, and I act as if I'm meeting the President himself." Hays, of course, knew exactly how to stage such a scene, having been a Cabinet member.

We both jumped to our feet when Hopper appeared. It wasn't hard for me to counterfeit a glow of homage either. The man was the spitting image of Roosevelt, even to the teeth and mustache.

"General," I said obsequiously, "may I present you to Theodore Roosevelt?" From that time on we never used his real name.

"Sir, I am proud and happy to make your acquaintance," Hays said with a formal bow. "The resemblance is remarkable. I can see you have the same character, the same undaunted courage—and your eyes reflect a passionate love for your country." Then Hays turned to me. "This is a profound pleasure, Mr. Lasky. I am indeed indebted to you for the opportunity of knowing this man."

The man was so dumfounded I thought he was going to collapse. Then gradually, as we continued the treatment and he lost the suspicion that we were making fun of him, he was standing more erect. As he left my office, there was just the suggestion of a swagger in his gait. I grabbed the phone before he could get back to the set and told Fleming to give orders for everyone up and down the line to treat the fellow as if he were dealing with royalty, and to feign absolute sincerity in order to build up his ego. It's the only instance I can recall when grips, juicers, cameramen, assistant directors, and everyone else in the company except the star of the picture were acting to the hilt.

Before it was over Mr. Inferiority Complex came so far out of his shell that he got almost unmanageable. But *The Rough Riders* was a smashing hit as the big road-show special of its year.

Hector Turnbull and Ben Schulberg were responsible for two types of films which are still in vogue today. Hector thought of teaming Wallace Beery and Raymond Hatton in a series of slapstick feature comedies. They set a pattern for hysterical war satires with *Behind the Front, We're in the Navy Now,* and *Now We're in the Air.* Then they made *Wife Savers* and *Fireman, Save My Child.* All were sensationally successful, and other companies lost no time in developing comedy teams. Beery and Hatton comedies were the prototypes for the avalanche of Dane and Arthur, Wheeler and Woolsey, Laurel and Hardy, Abbott and Costello features which followed in their wake.

Schulberg touched off a cycle of gangster films by recommending that we buy the Ben Hecht story, *Underworld.* It was so sordid and savage in content, so different from accepted film fare, that the sales heads were afraid that no amount of effort could drum up business for it. But the picture was one of the most tremendous hits we ever had, and elevated George Bancroft to immediate stardom. It was so widely imitated—and still is—that it would seem like a stereotype if you saw it now.

The End of an Era

John Monk Saunders, a strikingly handsome graduate of the University of Washington and a Rhodes scholar, who had been a pilot in World War I, looked more like a potential screen star than a writer. But when George Palmer Putnam—the publisher who was later to marry Amelia Earhart—introduced Saunders to me, he said that the young man had an idea and a title for a picture he wanted me to hear.

Saunders outlined the tale of a lad you know is born to be a flier from the moment you see him as a young boy in the opening scene, lying on his back watching an eagle in flight. The picture was to take him through ground school, overseas training, and into aerial battles, treating every phase of flying.

I was immediately so excited with its broad sweep of dramatic possibilities I told Saunders I'd buy the idea, give him a contract as writer and technical adviser during the actual shooting, and a percentage of the profits. I thought he could write a better air picture if he started walking on air.

I didn't dare send him out to the Coast ahead of me. They would have thought I'd gone balmy, hiring a schoolboy just out of Oxford—with no picture or writing experience—to mastermind our big road show for the year. I was afraid they'd crucify him if he showed up alone with nothing but his youth and acquired English accent. There was still that unreasoning jealousy and suspicion of anything that originated in the East, and of anyone outside the charmed circle of Hollywood.

So I had Saunders wait about six weeks until I could go with him and run interference. I am fairly good with a glib sales spiel, if I do say so, and I presented the project and its designer with enough eloquence that no feathers flew. The fact is, Hollywood rather likes boy wonders, once somebody opens the door for them.

Ben Schulberg suggested as a possible director for the air epic a young fellow on the lot who had been a pursuit pilot in the Lafayette Escadrille, gone through many of the experiences that would be pictured in *Wings*, and been decorated for his bravery. His name was unfamiliar to me. But as soon as we called him in, it was apparent that Billy Wellman and Saunders talked the same aeronautical language. Wellman sparked to the writer's idea much as James Cruze had when I outlined the *Covered Wagon* story to him.

I had Wellman leave us for a few moments and asked Ben and Hector whether they really thought we could entrust the most stupendous venture we'd ever undertaken to a $200-a-week director whose Hollywood background was practically nil. (Directors who had proved themselves were making $1000 or $1500 a week.)

They pointed out that I had entrusted the writing of the magnum opus to a man even more youthful and inexperienced. But they had the utmost confidence in Wellman's ability to deliver, despite his limited studio apprenticeship, so I called him back in and told him it was in his hands. I added that if I personally liked the job he turned in—without waiting for the public reaction—I'd give him anything within reason that he wanted or needed. (I've never been above a bit of bribery to fan the flame of creative inspiration.) He said he'd like to have an automobile.

We not only gambled on an untried writer and an unknown director, but parlayed the risk by starring a novice actor, Buddy Rogers, fresh out of our talent school and his graduation screen play, *Fascinating Youth*.

The Army co-operated magnificently in the interests of a faithful picturization of military aviation, and we secured the use of Kelly Field, San Antonio, for location shots. The company entrained to Texas—and sat there. Wellman stubbornly refused to start shooting until there were clouds in the sky. There were days on end of perfect sunshine, and our $200-a-week director wouldn't turn a camera, while overhead mounted at thousands of dollars a day. I confess that we were almost ready to yank him off the picture and replace him with someone who would be more amenable.

If we had done so, *Wings* would not have been the great film it was. A moving picture of an airplane in a cloudless sky looks like a fake, as though it were taken on the ground against a painted backdrop. (This was in a day before process shots and rear projection could pass for the real thing.) It was only a detail, but Wellman was a perfectionist on every detail. He hired the best stunt fliers for the dogfight scenes and risked his own life in the camera plane.

One sequence, reproducing the St. Mihiel drive, called for such elaborate preparations and was to be so spectacular that an event was made of it, with top Army brass invited to witness it. A banquet was arranged to top off the occasion in the evening and I was urged to be there to represent Paramount's upper echelons.

I arrived by train and was whisked to a hotel and then to the field where weeks of work had reproduced the whole topography of the battlefield—trenches, shell holes, and all. Wellman, working with his first assistant and some of the cameramen on a hundred-foot tower at one end of the field, had left word for me to join him there.

From the tower I looked down on an impressive sight. Several thousand extras in army uniforms waited on all sides of the field for the signal to charge. Wellman pointed out assistant directors in officers' uniforms, spotted where they could lead and keep a rein on the required action. The whole field was mined with explosives. Several cameras were positioned at strategic locations to film the simulated battle from every angle. We were not yet using public-address equipment, and the director's megaphone was so inadequate for such large-scale maneuvers that Wellman had arranged for all units to launch the charge and blow up the field on cue.

"When I wave this red flag," he explained, "you'll see $60,000 go up in smoke. You can only have one take on a big scene like this."

It seemed to me all of San Antonio had turned out to watch the excitement from behind the camera lines. When we learned that the mayor and his thirteen-year-old daughter were in the crowd, we invited them to watch from the tower. They climbed up the ladder and I found a canvas-back seat for His Honor. Wellman had gone below to make final preparations with his men. I repeated for the mayor the things Wellman had explained to me. The conversation lagged. There was nothing to do but wait.

It was a hot day and the girl got restless. She kept leaning over the rail of the tower, looking for people she knew in the crowd below. Then she saw a chum and called blithely to her but couldn't attract her attention.

"Yoo-hoo—Mildred!" she shouted several times, but her voice was lost to the milling throng. She grabbed up the red flag and waved it, still shouting, "Mildred! Mildred!"

All hell broke loose. Amid thunderous explosions and clouds of smoke the army charged into battle, bewildered planes took off in confusion—and not a camera was ready for it. As Wellman had promised, I saw $60,000 go up in smoke.

The banquet was an embarrassed fizzle and I went back to Hollywood. It took several days to prepare the battlefield again.

The picture suffered another major affliction on the very day of its New York premiere. It represented a record outlay of $2,000,000 gambled on unknown quantities from the theme to the writer to the director to the star. Some of the business heads were still smarting over the disappointing reception of the costly *Old Ironsides*, which had dealt with war. Worry and suspense over what the public reaction would be to our new road show, which also dealt with war, reduced them to distraction. One of them thought this episode should be in a different place; another favored cutting out that scene entirely and tightening a whole sequence. They went through the entire picture finding big and little faults they were sure were going to affect its chances of success.

You can do that with any picture. It's like a book manuscript or a play being tried out on the road—you can keep fretting over it, editing, and changing things long after you've finished it. A film sometimes undergoes drastic revising in the cutting room after one or more "sneak previews" in theatres around Hollywood.

Such a tempest was stirred up that I sent for Lucien Hubbard, the picture's very able supervisor, who was in town for the opening, and installed him in a dressing room just off the stage of the Criterion Theatre with the cans of film, a pair of shears, splicer, and a list of the beefs from the unhappy boys in the home office. He was there recutting *Wings* behind the scenes while out front an audience sheathed in mink and tuxedos watched its glittering world premiere. With festoons of clipped film strung all over the dressing room Hubbard managed to put it together again and keep one reel ahead of the projectionist.

We needn't have worried quite so much about whether it would make the grade. It turned out to be the last great silent picture and won the first Academy Award ever given for best production.

Buddy Rogers' career was air-borne with *Wings*, and the picture boosted Clara Bow's popularity to the skies. It also established Richard Arlen, who had got a lucky break—a broken leg—while working as a messenger boy. He had fallen off his motorcycle while delivering film from the lab to the studio, and some bright diplomat had dangled an offer of extra work while he was laid up in the studio hospital, to keep him from thinking about suing Paramount.

But *Wings* was even more propitious for a bit player who appeared in only one scene, with Arlen and Rogers. The studio began to get letters asking the name of the tall lad who portrayed so briefly but so effectively the young lieutenant who quickly sized up his new rookie tentmates, put them in their place with a few trenchant words, took a bite out of a chocolate bar, and walked out—to his death.

The sales department reported that exhibitors were also commenting about the unknown actor who in less than two minutes on the screen had left an unbearably poignant impression.

Such things bear looking into. I asked Schulberg who the fellow was. He didn't know and called the casting director, who didn't know either. But we got hold of the assistant who had cast the extras and located the young man. I sent for him.

He came into my office and stood fidgeting with his hat, shifting from one foot to the other. A gangling cowboy from Montana, uncommunicative and ill-at-ease, he was the last person in the world you'd pick out on the street for an actor. About all I could get out of him was that he had been open for any kind of work and had taken the extra job because it was the first thing that turned up. But I knew that one scene had hinted at some hidden quality to which the camera's discerning eye was sensitive. The public had already discovered it, and it's the public that makes stars.

"How'd you like to become a regular actor, Gary Cooper?" I asked.

He fiddled with his hat and was silent. "Well, I don't know," he finally said in a burst of loquacity. "I don't know if I could." He hemmed and hawed and seemed anxious to escape.

We almost had to bulldog him to get his name on a five-year contract.

When he tried to act, he was very bad. When he didn't try to act, he was sensational. He has made a career of being himself, a career which has continued to flourish while hundreds of actors more gifted in dramatic ability fell by the wayside. Gary Cooper opened up a new concept of film-acting technique, that of no technique at all, substituting simplicity and sincerity for acting tricks. He never did a scene twice the same way because he couldn't blueprint it beforehand. He just had to get into it and let it happen. That used to drive the cutters crazy. But because he didn't develop acting patterns his style couldn't become outdated.

Two early pictures that established Gary securely in his niche were a remake of *The Virginian*, which we had done earlier with Dustin Farnum, and *Seven Days' Leave*, from the J. M. Barrie story, *The Old Lady Shows Her Medals*. Many years later, in Hemingway's *A Farewell to Arms*, Gary was terrified at the thought of playing opposite

Helen Hayes, considered by many astute critics the greatest actress of
the day. He went around wailing, "I can't act. How can they expect
me to play in a picture with someone like that?"

And Miss Hayes was just as terrified of facing Gary Cooper. What
gave her the jitters, she confided to friends, was, "When I act, I'm
pretending. He'll show me up. He *feels* what he's doing!"

The Sound and the Fury

While we were engaged in our superproduction effort of *Wings*,
Warner Brothers and Fox had been sponsoring experiments in synchronized sound and RCA was also working in that direction. We
watched developments, but many of us were skeptical that it would
amount to anything. Others had tried it before. In fact Edison mar-
keted the Kinetophone, which showed movies with synchronized
sound, to peep-show parlors in 1895. The sound was even better than
the picture, yet there was no noticeable demand for the combination,
so he went back to perfecting the silent-motion-picture camera. My
vaudeville act "The Pianophiends" had played the Colonial Theatre in
New York on the same bill as a talking picture in 1907, and there had
been many other abortive exploitations of eye-ear films. So the idea of
sound in pictures wasn't new in 1926. It had been kicking around for
over thirty years. We saw no reason to think it would catch on at this
late date.

I thought I had flattened the arguments for sound with irrefutable
logic when I pointed to Bessie's oil painting of trees blowing in the
wind that hung back of my desk in the Paramount Building and observed patronizingly, "Do you have to hear the wind to appreciate the
artist's intention?"

In truth, when Warner Brothers presented *Don Juan*, which had
a synchronized score, on a program with short subjects of singers,
instrumentalists, and a speech by Will Hays in 1926, there was no

stampede to the box-office. It was *The Jazz Singer*, in which Al Jolson sang his rafter-shaking, show-stopping "Mammy" and spoke a few lines of dialogue, that is generally credited with turning the tide the following year. I attended the opening, not because I was smart enough to know it marked the beginning of a new era, but because I went to every big picture premiere in town unless there were two on the same night.

I also visited the Fox New York studio and saw the sound shorts they were making. But even then it wasn't easy to see the straw in the wind. I was still clinging to my trees in the wind. And I wasn't alone. Men like Joe Schenck, Zukor, and Chaplin were being quoted to the effect that a cool, peaceful theatre was a relief from the turmoil of life outside and people wouldn't go in a boiler factory to rest.

We thought a bellowing screen was a novelty, as it had periodically been before, and we waited for the ruckus to die down. Not until Warners continued to draw crowds with any kind of picture as long as it bruised the eardrums—while the best silent pictures we had ever made began to slip—did we know the trend for what it was.

I think I first realized that sound might be here to stay during a train trip to Atlantic City for our sales convention in 1928. While I was marshaling my broadsides for the salesmen, my secretary, Randy Rogers, showed me an article in the *Hollywood Spectator* by Welford Beaton, a highly respected observer on matters pertaining to the film industry. He had staunchly opposed the idea of talking pictures before but now reversed his stand and called on the producers to wake up to the fact that silent pictures were doomed. It was such a discerning analysis of the new development indications that it gave me pause and caused me to alter the tenor of my speech.

There was no mention of sound in our 1928–29 convention book, but I told the salesmen it might well be that some of the pictures they found listed therein would come to the screen with sound effects and dialogue.

We had already made one concession to sound, but it was only a stunt inspired by the drum-beating Warners were doing before *The Jazz Singer* came out. Our special-effects man, Roy Pomeroy, had recorded some sound effects that would pass for the chatter of machine guns and various other noises. They were amplified on a set of three turntables during the dogfight sequences of *Wings*. It enhanced the realism of those scenes so much that each of a dozen road-show units of the picture carried turntables and a prop man to watch the picture from the wings of the theatre and turn on the records at appropriate times.

We had discovered Pomeroy as a struggling artist with an inventive mind, who had some exceedingly original and useful ideas about the employment of miniature sets and background projection to effect enormous budget savings in picture-making. I hired him and he did some fine creative work on tricks and special effects. He was the first specialist in that field and there has never been a better one. The techniques he devised are still being used.

For the Exodus scenes in DeMille's first version of *The Ten Commandments,* Pomeroy created the most famous special-effect sequence ever filmed, the opening up of the Red Sea to let the Israelites pass and closing it on the pursuing Egyptians. He also performed other miracles to order and wrote the Ten Commandments in letters of fire. Perhaps it isn't strange under the circumstances that he came to feel he was God. His universe was a tiny stage used for miniature settings and was known as The Pomeroy Department.

Glowing reports from our salesmen at the Atlantic City convention left no doubt that our first earsplitting contribution to sound, the popping of machine guns in *Wings,* had merely served to whet a voracious appetite for articulate movies. We could no longer ignore the handwriting that was gradually appearing on the wall with a plainly audible screech of the slate pencil. In fact the issue assumed such vital importance that Walter Wanger proposed that we retroactively add sound effects to Richard Dix's just-completed silent picture, *Warming Up,* a baseball story. He rushed a print of it to Camden, New Jersey, where Victor Talking Machine engineers embellished it with the crack of the bat against the ball, and the roar of the cheering crowd when the hero hit a home run. These two noises qualified it for scarehead advertising as "Part Sound" and enormously increased the financial returns. This "goat gland" operation, as it was called, rejuvenated many a silent picture which otherwise would have died with few mourners at the box-office.

Uncompleted portions of silent pictures already in work were finished in sound, so that the screen was apt to snap, crackle, and pop at any point, and then go dead quiet a reel later. *Shopworn Angel* was ballyhooed with "One Reel of Dialogue Plus Nancy Carroll Singing!" To the silent reels Gary Cooper contributed his natural mute reticence. It was really something to crow about when you could announce "Most of the Picture in Sound" or "Talking All the Way Through." (That was no exaggeration—some of those eager early talkies didn't let up on the frantic yakking for a second.) M-G-M proclaimed "garbo talks" in thunderstruck billboards that didn't even bother to mention the name of the picture.

In the meantime Roy Pomeroy had been sent East to look over methods of recording at Western Electric and RCA. He returned to Hollywood as something of a sacred oracle, the only one in our company who knew anything at all about the new science.

Things were moving so fast we had to plunge in over our depth, ready or not. A logical choice for our first 100 per cent talking picture was *Interference*, a current stage hit we had bought and scheduled originally as a silent offering. It might better have been called "No Interference," for Roy Pomeroy took complete charge, insisted on directing it himself, a function he had never performed, and demanded a salary raise from $250 to $2500 a week. He knew that he had us where he wanted us.

So our first talkie was directed by a special-effects man who became a sound engineer by virtue of a trip through the laboratories of Western Electric and RCA. We couldn't have treated him with more awe and homage if he had been Edison himself.

He sat with his earphones on in his little domain, monarch of all he surveyed, while terrified silent-picture stars without stage experience were ushered into The Presence for voice tests to determine whether they could talk. Then they fled to a church to pray, or to a voice coach, or signed up for some little-theatre work, and came back intoning, "Good mawning!" and "Hel-low Bill" in pear-shaped tones all over the lot.

Pomeroy shot the whole picture on that tiny stage, which would hold only one set at a time. It resembled a padded cell. The walls were upholstered with batting to cut down resonance, the floor was carpeted, and the actors' shoes were oiled and soundproofed with special material so extraneous squeaks and clumps wouldn't interfere with the dialogue. Later the first director to tear off the shoe pads and use the sound of footsteps dramatically was hailed as a genius.

Pomeroy allowed no one into his mysterious cloister but the crew and cast, which included Evelyn Brent, Clive Brook, Doris Kenyon, and William Powell. When the doors rolled shut and a musical auto horn heralded the commencement of black magic, everyone played living statues. A cough or a sneeze could cost hundreds of dollars by a ruined take. Not even studio manager Sam Jaffe or I could invade the chief's sanctum sanctorum without asking permission. We resorted to a Trojan-horse stratagem in order to keep in touch with what was going on. In the guise of a gift we sent William DeMille to be Pomeroy's "assistant." It flattered the self-elevated director to have such an important man working as his underling.

Pomeroy overplayed his hand by demanding $3500 a week after his first talkative movie. By then William DeMille, who now had an imposing background of both stage and screen directing, had surreptitiously picked up enough knowledge of the new methods to be able to direct the next picture himself, and we had organized a "racket squad" of telephone-company-trained sound engineers who were happy to carry on at salaries not exorbitant for technical experts in their field. By the time *Interference* opened at the Criterion on November 16, 1928, Pomeroy was dethroned, a fallen despot.

Silent pictures had reached a high degree of fluidity and artistry. The progress represented by sound was at first only mechanical. Artistically films had been set back ten years by the limitations imposed on them by the first crude recording apparatus. Moving pictures almost stopped moving. Until the microphone became portable on a cranelike boom which pursued the actors above the camera line of vision, a player had to deliver his utterances into a flowerpot, then pause until he could flit to a lampshade where another microphone was hidden for his next sentence.

The camera itself could do very little moving either, as it now had to be incased in a huge soundproof booth with a window to insulate its loud clicking from the microphone. This contrivance was sardonically dubbed the "icebox" because the poor cameraman emerged from its airtight confines after a long take, parboiled and gasping for breath, into an atmosphere only a little less stifling, thanks to the intensely hot lights and lack of any ventilation.

The "sound mixer" worked in a small monitor room of his own behind a glass panel at the back of the studio. With his telephonic training he balked at every line of dialogue that didn't come over his headset with clearly enunciated syllables in the slow, deadly "ny-yun, fy-yuv, thuh-ree" cadence of a long-distance operator. This unnatural yardstick for dramatic interpretation made the director blow his top, and whenever anyone raised his voice, a delicate light valve blew out, putting the recording apparatus out of commission.

Regiments of new personnel brought in from outside to handle the recording had to learn the picture business, and *everyone* else—not just the actors—had to learn it all over again. Nothing could be done in the same way as it had been before. Electricians had to convert from hissing arc lights to an incandescent system. Cameramen had to master the intricacies of motor-driven cameras synchronized with a sound track. Art and construction departments had to experiment with new materials to eliminate echoes. The wardrobe department discarded fabrics that rustled. Cutters had to start learning how to cut and edit a sound track. But I believe no one had to make a more drastic adjustment in their working methods than the directors, for they could no longer direct from the side lines while a scene was in progress.

It had been an accepted practice in the very recent "old days" to keep a violinist on the set to help key the players to the moods of their scenes. Now the actors had to emote without the customary obbligato, but whole orchestras were hired to key the moods of the audience with specially composed and brilliantly scored music on the sound track. Los Angeles Local 47 of the American Federation of Musicians prospered mightily. Tin Pan Alley moved to Hollywood to custom-fit theme songs to picture titles and heroes' and heroines' names, and too often the theme song occurred—too often.

Scenario writers found themselves suddenly called on to write good dialogue, and plenty of them never had and couldn't. We met this situation by bringing playwrights and novelists from the East to collaborate with our screen-play writers who knew more about telling a story through movement and camera angles but less about writing for the ear.

Before long a dialogue director was added to the staff, to help the no longer speechless actors better interpret their lines.

Two more all-talkies were filmed on Pomeroy's small excuse for a stage while a bank of four spacious, acoustically perfect, rock-wool-insulated stages scientifically engineered for sound-film production was rushed into construction in one mammoth building. William DeMille directed *The Doctor's Secret* with Ruth Chatterton and H. B. Warner. Rowland Lee handled George Bancroft in *The Wolf of Wall Street*.

Ruth Chatterton was a renowned legitimate actress who was characteristically cast as a highborn lady of culture and poise, and we gloated over our good luck in having signed her even before sound reared its domineering microphone. She had proved an asset as a silent star, and now we were sure her talents would be doubly valuable. Poise was quite a novelty in the days when another queen of the suave manner, Gloria Swanson, was having such a bad case of mike-fright that her lines had to be written on the shirt front of her leading man.

But Ruth's poise was almost poison in the hinterlands. Those who had never had the opportunity of hearing a cultivated, well-modulated voice thought she was putting on airs. Whereas New York play-goers loved her impeccable diction, many ears throughout the country weren't attuned to good diction. That's hard to realize, now that motion pictures, radio, and television have accustomed the whole nation to hearing English as it should be spoken. But when our audiences got the first dose of it, they complained bitterly. Our salesmen demanded, "No more accents. The public don't like accents."

Ruth Chatterton, born in New York City, didn't have a trace of an accent. She had merely learned to speak flawlessly in the best traditions of the stage. But she had the misfortune to be the first distinguished actress millions of movie patrons had ever heard.

We were worried about this hostile reaction. But the public was plainly wrong, so we put Ruth Chatterton in other pictures. She turned in marvelous performances and, in time, even the rural audiences began to appreciate her—after they got used to her faultless English.

A scant three months after I had told the sales convention we *might* make some sound pictures, I had issued orders that no more silent pictures were to be made beyond those already in work. We were committed to a full program of sound and were waiting only on the completion of the new sound stages to go full-speed ahead. Then, just as the first one was finished, before a single foot of film had been shot in it, a fire broke out and completely destroyed the building.

It would take four months to rebuild the stages. We had to begin turning out a steady stream of talkies immediately, and we couldn't make them on regular stages, which weren't soundproofed. Or could we?

Sam Jaffe had an inspiration. Late at night, with an air of mystery he wouldn't explain, he dragged me into the deserted studio to the burned-out stages. It was a disheartening sight.

"Listen!" he said, bright-eyed, expectantly.

I strained my ears. "Sam, what the devil are you talking about? I don't hear a thing!" I said, wondering for a moment whether the shock of the disaster had affected our studio manager's sanity. I knew from his brother-in-law, Ben Schulberg, that Sam had been brooding and losing sleep since the night of the fire.

"That's just it!" he exclaimed. "At night you don't *need* sound-proofed walls. You can work in the ordinary stages because everything is quiet outside. There aren't any noises to penetrate the building and spoil the takes!"

All shooting schedules went on a night shift for the next three months, the companies reporting for work at 9 P.M. Blankets were hung where they would keep the sound from reverberating too much in the cavernous stages. We made a dozen pictures at night while the din of pounding and sawing for the new facilities and for set construction filled the daylight hours. With an all-out effort the sound stages were ready ahead of schedule.

Our Long Island studio, which had been shuttered for a long time, came in very handy just then, particularly as most of the vocal talent was in New York. It was promptly reconditioned to the requirements of sound. Claudette Colbert and Edward G. Robinson, both from the stage, made their screen debut at Astoria in *The Hole in the Wall*. It was the first of his long series of gangster roles in films. Fredric March was introduced to the screen in *The Dummy*, and Jeanne Eagels, her triumph as Sadie Thompson in *Rain* still fresh in everyone's mind, was starred in another Somerset Maugham story, *The Letter*. Walter Huston, Miriam Hopkins, Helen Morgan, Jeanette MacDonald, Tallulah Bankhead, Kay Francis, and the Marx Brothers likewise had their celluloid baptism at Astoria. So did Rouben Mamoulian, who had been directing opera in Rochester, New York. On his recommendation I also gave George Cukor his first screen assignment.

We made a series of one-reel sound shorts at Long Island, too, but they were accepted with apathy because the names of the performers didn't mean anything to screen audiences—Ethel Merman, Burns and Allen, Ginger Rogers, Charles Ruggles, George Jessel, Willie and Eugene Howard, Jack Benny, Eddie Cantor, Lillian Roth, Rudy Vallee, Ruth Etting, Gilda Gray, and Harry Richman, among others.

However, in the course of only a few months, a whole new crop of personalities with engaging vocal qualities and stage training were registering strongly with the fans, while top favorites of the silent era had dropped out of sight. George Bancroft, who had been worth $5000 or $6000 a week to us until he had to open his mouth, made a few talking pictures, but his fans weren't pleased with them, and he went into a professional decline. Clara Bow found the strain too much for her nerves and voluntarily retired. Jack Gilbert had to abdicate as king of romantic stars at the top of his orbit. There was actually nothing wrong with his voice, but it seemed to belong to someone else, someone more refined than the dashing, tempestuous lover represented by his screen image. Norma Talmadge, Colleen Moore, and Florence Vidor were cut down in their glory, while Marie Dressler came out of retirement and zoomed to the heights again at the age of sixty-one (having been a Mack Sennett star in 1914), and Conrad Nagel, who hadn't done anything much in silents, found himself in demand for practically every sound picture made.

Sound killed off the career of our dapper, clever Silk Hat Comedian, Ray Griffith, who couldn't talk above a whisper because of a throat affliction. Vilma Banky, a ravishing Hungarian beauty who had been imported by Sam Goldwyn and given a tremendous exploitation build-up, couldn't overcome her accent and had to retire at twenty-five. One of the greatest silent stars of all, Emil Jannings, was packed off on the next boat, holding the Academy Award for the best acting of the year—his performances in two of our pictures, *The Way of All Flesh* and *The Last Command,* the latter an all-time screen classic that is still playing in art theatres. You could scarcely say his downfall was caused by an accent, because he had never got that far. He couldn't even speak English. Although born in Brooklyn, he left America as a child and was Germany's greatest actor when I brought him back.

The switch-over to dialogue and music took place within six months. The studios had retooled and converted long before all theatres were equipped to show sound pictures. Therefore, since silent films as such were no longer being made, we had to serve up dumb versions of talkies for a while, substituting printed titles for the sound track. I don't know who but a lip reader could have enjoyed them, but they kept the smaller theatres open until they could get delivery on sound projectors and install them.

Joe Mankiewicz got a foothold in the picture business by writing subtitles for these muted talkies. It would be nice if I could say we recognized the ability that was to win him four Academy Awards within two years, but the only reason he got that job was because his elder brother Herman, one of our top-notch writers, promised to be a good boy and stay on the wagon until he got a script for Claudette Colbert done, if we would put his nineteen-year-old brother on the payroll.

Trying to hold the foreign market, too, we made five extra versions of our American pictures in our Paris studios, using foreign actors. That idea failed in five languages—the foreign audiences wanted bona fide Hollywood stars, not their own countrymen. So the art of dubbing was born, using only the voices of the foreign language actors to make a substitute sound track, and matching their words as much as possible to the lip movements in the picture so our American actors would seem to be speaking French or Spanish, for instance. In some cases bilingual stars did their own dubbing or made two versions.

The "iceboxes" were replaced at first by camera hoods or "blimps" which muffled the sprocket noise in rubber without suffocating the cameraman. In due time silent cameras were developed. Microphones, too, became more adaptable and reliable. Pictures regained fluidity and perspective.

Within a year things were running smoothly again, but with many more craftsmen and auxiliary mechanical devices, less teamwork, more complex organization, less pioneering spirit, more expense, less inspiration, more talent, less glamour, more predatory competition, less hospitality, more doing, less joy in the doing.

Hollywood would never be the same again.

Talent-Scouting in Europe
and Brooklyn

At the beginning of the sound era Josef von Sternberg took a leave of absence from the studio and went to Germany to direct Emil Jannings in *The Blue Angel*. He kept raving in his letters about a girl in the picture and urging me to bring her to America. Sid Kent was going to Europe and I asked him to check into it and find out whether Joe's enthusiasm was professional or personal. Sid cabled back: "SHE'S SENSATIONAL. SIGN HER UP."

So I gave her a contract to star in Paramount pictures without seeing so much as her passport photo. I was never sorry I did. And, judging from many thoughtful gestures on her part since then, neither was Marlene Dietrich. Von Sternberg directed all her pictures for more than two years. The first one, *Morocco*, with Gary Cooper as her leading man, was a smash hit. For *Shanghai Express* exteriors were shot in San Bernardino, California, tricked up with Chinese banners and signs. Joe was shouting through a megaphone, the way directors had always handled crowd scenes. Sam Jaffe procured a microphone and loudspeaker for Von Sternberg, who had never used a public-address system and was as fascinated with it as a child with a new toy. A few days later the company was back in Hollywood. As I entered the stage where they were working, I couldn't even see the set at the far end, but I could hear the booming voice of the director reverberating through the enormous structure like a train announcer's in Grand Central Station. Joe was staging an intimate close-up of Marlene and Clive Brook, almost breathing in their faces as he gave them directions, but still using the microphone!

Critical historians have evaluated Von Sternberg's pictures as things of beauty but not a joy forever. His artistry with a camera was rarely surpassed, but he sometimes allowed pictorial effects to overshadow the story he was telling. Perhaps for this reason—or perhaps because *An American Tragedy* was twenty years ahead of its time in a day when audiences demanded happy endings—the first film translation of Theodore Dreiser's classic literary work had a disappointing reception. Audiences have grown up since then, and the remake of *An American Tragedy* under the title *A Place in the Sun,* directed by George Stevens, with Elizabeth Taylor and Montgomery Clift, was highly acclaimed.

My most pungent memory concerning the original version is of Dreiser's anxiety over the sale of the film rights. I negotiated with his astute publisher, Horace Liveright, who also acted as his agent, for some time without getting anywhere. Dreiser was as annoyed with Liveright's delaying tactics as I was, but I didn't know that. Finally Liveright consented to bring us together for lunch at the Ritz. I remember saying hello to Arthur Brisbane at his customary table as we entered the dining room. We enjoyed ourselves over small talk until the plates were cleared and the waiter brought coffee. Then I came to the point and said we wanted to close a deal for the film rights, and named the figure we were prepared to pay. As I recall, it was $90,000.

With quiet firmness Liveright said, "Mr. Dreiser won't accept that."

Dreiser delivered an explosive oath characterizing his publisher as an unmitigated liar, and threw his coffee in Horace Liveright's face.

It was a horrible moment, dripping with shocked embarrassment. And coffee. Liveright wiped away the fluid that was dribbling down his face and shirt front as though he habitually and profusely perspired coffee.

The negotiations were temporarily disrupted.

After its purchase (at my price) the Dreiser novel was first assigned to Sergei Eisenstein, the Russian director who had been hailed as a genius for his *Potemkin.* I had seen that picture in Paris and been immensely impressed with the vigorous directing and keen dramatic sense it displayed. As Eisenstein was also in Paris, I lost no time in signing him and bringing him back on the boat with me. He studied American film techniques for several weeks and then wrote a frighteningly unwieldy adaptation of the immense two-volume Dreiser novel. We thought he had better begin over again on something else, and shifted *An American Tragedy* to Von Sternberg. Eisenstein next chose the book *Sutter's Gold*, and again wrote such a ponderous script that our estimating department calculated it would cost many millions of dollars to produce. Perhaps it would have been the greatest picture of all time—I don't know. But we couldn't chance it, and regretfully let Eisenstein go without putting any of his ideas on film for us.

He then attempted an epic panorama of Mexico for other financial backers, but the picture suffered the same fate as Von Stroheim's most ambitious efforts. Financing ran out after he had spent two years shooting, and Eisenstein went back to Russia. Three different pictures were cut from his interminable but unfinished footage by various other hands, none of whom knew what grandiose design the master had in mind, since there had never been a complete original script.

No problems of handling *genius* or literary *works of art* were involved in bringing *Abie's Irish Rose* to the screen. It held the record for the worst critical notices and the longest run in the history of the stage—until *Tobacco Road* got still worse notices and had an even longer run. Practically every major studio in Hollywood was bidding for *Abie's Irish Rose*. In order to grab the plum for ourselves I finally offered the highest price we had ever put out for a play or book—$500,000 against 50 per cent of the profits. Even that wasn't enough to clinch the deal. After weeks of negotiations I let the author, Anne Nichols, and her manager hog-tie us with so many restrictions that we had to get their approval on everything—cast, screen play, wardrobe, advertising. I submitted to these autocratic demands because I was afraid some other studio might snatch the prize away from us. If only one had!

Even with the drawing power of Buddy Rogers and Nancy Carroll the film was not a conspicuous success financially. That's a gross understatement. I can't understand why it didn't do phenomenal business, since the picture was every bit as bad as the play! I guess the answer is that after a play has had a five-years-and-five-months' run on Broadway, with six road companies touring this country and others abroad, there isn't anyone left to see it in a movie house.

And it was something no one in his right mind could take twice in any form.

I first saw Maurice Chevalier as the star of a revue at the Casino de Paris early in 1929, where Bessie and I and our good friend Margaret Miller were guests of the well-known French writer, Alfred Savoir. Chevalier sang a number of songs especially for the large proportion of American tourists in the audience, and they were so captivated by his bubbling good humor and broken English I couldn't help thinking this ruddy-complexioned blue-eyed singer with a straw hat and infectious smile would have the same appeal for Americans in Paris, Texas, as he obviously did for Americans in Paris, France.

I impulsively went backstage and asked him if he'd like to go to Hollywood and become a picture star. His first reaction, with a spreading grin, was: "Would I meet Doog and Mary?" I made an appointment to talk seriously about it the next day in the offices I used in the Paramount Theatre in Paris, the architectural hybrid built under Al Kaufman's supervision and which he now managed.

When I told Kaufman I needed someone from the legal department to prepare a contract for a great discovery I'd made and that it was Chevalier, he couldn't conceal a fleeting quizzical expression as though he were talking to someone who wasn't quite bright.

"He's been around for years," Al said. "All the American producers have looked him over. Irving Thalberg and Louis Mayer saw him two months ago." His inference was that, if Chevalier was such a prize, why hadn't someone signed him up before?

I was suddenly deflated. Could I have been overly excited about him in the glow of an enjoyable dinner and evening? I wasn't committed. I didn't have to sign Chevalier. I wavered and might have called off the appointment if there had been time to do so. I didn't know what I would do—until he came in and his personality lit up the office. Then I knew I couldn't have been wrong, and neither were the other Americans who had been so delighted with his special brand of entertainment the night before. I gave him a five-year contract with options, starting at $1500 a week, and looked forward to the pleasure of his company on the boat returning to the States.

I cabled our New York office about my new find and had a prompt cable back begging me to lose him, reminding me that the public had shown definite antagonism to even the suspicion of an accent, that we were already stuck with Ruth Chatterton, and insisting that a full-blown French accent would be ten times as bad.

I was nettled but determined to brazen it through and get myself off the hook. I postponed Chevalier's departure for a couple of weeks so I might precede him and make sure his arrival was attended with full fanfare. I cabled Charles McCarthy of our publicity department to get started immediately on a whirlwind flurry of press releases on our acquisition of the famous French star, and to organize a gala reception-banquet for him the night after his arrival.

At the boat train in Paris, Chevalier turned up unexpectedly with a large bouquet of roses for Bessie, kissed her hand, and wished us *bon voyage*, beaming his radiant smile. Doting French fans looked on enviously as their idol enslaved another feminine heart.

The moment we arrived, I gave my full attention to the banquet details. We invited three hundred of New York's most distinguished people. The Crystal Room at the Ritz-Carlton was draped with American and French flags, the French Consul for New York City and the French Ambassador from Washington were there—a real hands-across-the-sea affair.

I had a moment of panic when I introduced Chevalier to the discriminating audience and begged him to favor us with a few "impromptu" songs (I had planned it for the night after his arrival so he'd have plenty of time to rehearse the pianist). But I needn't have worried. Although virtually no one in the room had ever heard of him, he captured the audience with his first song and held them spellbound through encore after encore. Even Zukor and Kent, who hadn't been happy about my impulsive commitment, were impressed.

The next day Flo Ziegfeld, who had been at the banquet, phoned and implored me to let him have the sensational artist for his *Midnight Frolic* on the New Amsterdam Roof. I told him that, as a special favor to him, I'd postpone Chevalier's first picture long enough to let him appear on the Roof for six weeks if he wanted him badly enough to pay $5000 a week. His gratitude was touching.

I refrained from mentioning that the Coast had just informed me they were rushing work on a script called *Innocents of Paris* but that it would be at least six weeks before they could hope to start shooting. Chevalier's contract salary started from the time he arrived in this country, but, instead of losing $1500 a week waiting for the script to be written, we made $3500 a week—and we couldn't have got a better publicity build-up for the picture if *we* had paid *Ziegfeld* $5000 a week to put him on the Roof.

One of the first things I did when he arrived in Hollywood was to give a dinner at my beach house and seat Chevalier between his idols,

Mary Pickford and Douglas Fairbanks. I could have sold him an autograph book right then and turned another bit of profit. He and "Doog"
became warm friends.

In *Innocents of Paris* Chevalier was a happy-go-lucky ne'er-do-well
whose side-kick was an appealing street waif played by David Durand.
Although made rather hurriedly it caught some of the magic of the
Chaplin-Coogan masterpiece, *The Kid*, and the public took it to their
hearts. A lilting, airy tune written for the picture by Leo Robin and
Richard Whiting has been identified with Chevalier ever since—his
cherished "Louise."

We might have been satisfied with that type of sentimental whimsey
for him for a long time, since the fans ate it up, but I felt we could employ his unusual talents in a more distinguished way. Except for his
intriguing accent a hundred actors could have played his part in *Innocents of Paris*. I sensed that in a musical comedy of Continental
sophistication he would have no peer. But for that he would need a
leading lady with youth, beauty, and a superb voice—and we had no
actresses who sang, since talking pictures were still so new we hadn't
done any exploring in the field of musicals. Our first tentative step in
that direction was a revue called *Paramount on Parade*, and Chevalier
was one of its chief virtues.

I began to look around for the right girl to team with him, and I
made a point of catching a Shubert show featuring a new singer one of
my assistants had told me about. I liked Jeanette MacDonald so well
I secured her as Chevalier's leading lady and turned the pair over to
Ernst Lubitsch, my imported director with an unequaled instinct for
Continental sophistication and wit, at the Long Island studio. This
absolutely unbeatable combination of talents in *The Love Parade*
and *One Hour with You* and the celebrated "Lubitsch touch" in
Chevalier's *The Smiling Lieutenant* made those pictures, to my mind,
the best screen musicals ever turned out.

I first heard Nino Martini at about the same time and under much
the same circumstances as when I met Chevalier—singing in a Paris
night club. And my reflex action was the same in calling for a lawyer
to draw up a contract. But on this occasion the night club had been
rented by our Paris manager for one night during my holiday stay and
turned into a makeshift audition hall for all the talent they wanted me
to look over. I watched a continuous parade of it from nine o'clock
till two in the morning, and of it all Nino was the only person I
thought we should do something about. He couldn't speak a word of
English so we had to use an interpreter. I signed him and arranged for

him to come to America about six months later, on his promise to learn English in the meantime. He did, and we put him, along with Chevalier and all our other stars, in *Paramount on Parade*. It was easy to spot a Venice canal scene in that and have him do an effective serenade in Italian (after he had learned English), but what to do with him after that stumped everybody, and he just waited around drawing salary until his first option was up.

The studio advised me to drop him.

I felt very bad, having made him learn a new language and perhaps changed the course of his life—having given him a hope and foretaste of fame, only to snatch it away from him. Such a disappointment can be crushing to a sensitive young artist. In order to soften the blow if possible I insisted on breaking the news to him myself. I invited him to my home and explained that our failure to cast him should not discourage him in the least, and that he would no doubt reach the heights through other channels. He left for the East and I could only hope I had not broken his heart.

We acquired another singer about this time who remained a top Paramount star for twenty-five years. I can't say we started him in motion pictures, because Bing Crosby had made a few slapstick one-reelers for Mack Sennett, but I hadn't seen them. Sam Katz told me there was a young fellow who had been held over in the Paramount Theatre stage show for twenty-nine weeks because the audiences seemed to like him. I went downstairs and caught his act, then sent for him—but he didn't answer the summons. Instead his brother Everett came in his place to handle the sordid business details. Bing has always held himself aloof from crass financial matters. I can assure you that Everett has done all right by him through the years as his fiscal mouthpiece.

I could have caught Bing's act five years earlier by taking the same elevator. I didn't realize when I signed his contract that he had previously played the New York Paramount with Paul Whiteman's band, when his singing had been so poorly received that Sam Katz requested Whiteman to remove Bing Crosby from the act—and the engagement finished without him.

If there's anything more unpredictable than the vagaries of show business, you name it.

I set Herbert Marshall and Charles Laughton on their movie careers by signing them after seeing them in plays in New York. Marshall was a very reluctant convert and it took a lot of persuasion to win him over. In Laughton's case it took a lot of persuasion to convince Schulberg and the West Coast studio that I hadn't pulled another boner worse than when I'd signed Chevalier. They thought that it would be impossible to cast a beefy character actor with an English accent in top roles. Cecil DeMille had just returned to Paramount to make *The Sign of the Cross* and I suggested that Laughton would be ideal as Nero. Everyone but Cecil thought it was a crazy idea, but after that performance Charles Laughton was on his way up.

The Four Marx Brothers were playing in their first big Broadway hit, *The Cocoanuts*, and their agent, William Morris, convinced us that their screwball antics would be a novelty on the screen. We bought the picture rights to the show, which they owned, for $75,000 and a percentage of the profits. It was made at Astoria in the early days when monk's cloth on the walls served in lieu of proper soundproofing, and the brothers' characteristic rapid-fire delivery rendered the dialogue unintelligible on the sound track at times. Besides which, all our directors being tied up on other pictures, we had assigned it to Joseph Santley, who worked at the studio in various capacities but had never directed a feature. It happened that the print previewed for the Marxes was a mess and the sound was projected carelessly. They were so disgusted they wanted to buy back the negative and destroy it, and they put up quite a howl about it. They could easily have afforded such a luxury, but—protected by our contract—we ignored their protests.

Even after it was released, we had all kinds of complaints about patrons coming back to see the picture two or three times, trying to understand what it was about.

It made something like two million dollars' profit, I guess because so many people kept seeing it over to try to figure it out. Kay Francis made her screen debut as the feminine foil in the picture, and soon became a star in her own right. The Marx Brothers—mollified by a resounding success after they had expected the mishmash to ruin their stage reputation—made four more pictures for us: *Animal Crackers, Monkey Business, Horse Feathers,* and *Duck Soup.*

This brings me to Kay Francis's first starring picture, made at Long Island, the title of which escapes me. I mentioned earlier that we pioneered in the Technicolor field. On this Kay Francis picture we pioneered at the opposite end of the chromatic scale. It was the one and only attempt the industry has ever made to produce a Nocolor picture. Walter Wanger, like every other brilliant person who is full of ideas, occasionally came up with a colossal dud. He conceived a plan which would have saved the studio untold expense if it had worked. And the irony of it was that it worked beautifully from a technical standpoint.

Wanger reasoned that, since the end result of a studio's endeavors appears on celluloid in black and white and intervening tones of gray, it's a waste of effort to bother with color anywhere along the line—in the sets, in the costumes, or in the props. You cover a ceiling with gold leaf and it can only show up gray in the picture. Your dressmakers create lovely harmonies of color, but they are likewise reduced to unimaginative grays. If the painters used mixtures of black and white for their entire palette, Wanger speculated, it would simplify and expedite their task. Moreover, everyone from the director and cameraman to the art director and lighting engineers would be better able to evaluate pictorial effects, as the live scene would appear to their eyes in the same values that would later fill the screen.

Without consulting anyone Wanger ordered a set painted entirely in tones of gray. Kay Francis unwittingly heightened the sepulchral effect by showing up for work dressed in a big black picture hat and a long black satin gown. The cameramen began to set up in an uncomprehending daze. They must have felt as though they had suddenly gone color blind. Wanger stood back beaming over his inspiration when Monta Bell, who had just been put in charge of the studio, hurried in preoccupied with other things and didn't notice the strange tableau immediately. When it hit him full force, he let out a cry of pain. He was already plagued with assorted troubles, this being his first sound picture, and Walter's brain storm was one too many. He wanted to quit his job right then and there.

A hurry call was put through to me that the company was on the verge of mutiny. All shooting stopped for the day, and the painters worked through the night at overtime rates to have the set shining with nice, bright colors by the next morning. But Wanger's complexion had turned to a monotone of gray that I can only describe as ashen.

He hadn't taken into consideration that actors are so sensitive and responsive to their environment that on a set drained of color and reality they would have given colorless and unreal performances. That's why Erich von Stroheim had been so obsessively exacting in such details as silk underwear embroidered with the crest of their mythical country for the soldiers in *The Merry Widow*. At no time was the extravagant finery in view on the screen, but he felt it would show up in the bearing of the soldiers who were conscious of wearing it.

There's No Place like Home

As I came into our New York apartment one day I heard the two younger children bickering.

"It's my turn!" Betty cried shrilly.

"No, it isn't! Let go!" Billy demanded. "It's my turn!"

I followed the commotion to its source in Billy's bedroom and found the kids pulling on opposite ends of a six-foot boa constrictor, squabbling over whose turn it was to feed the serpent. Billy had a technical advantage in the argument. He was in possession of the feeding end.

It was one of two such pets he kept in his bathroom draped over the crossbar of his shower. He had started collecting snakes at about the age of five, I think bringing the first one back from a walk in the park with his governess, who was afraid to take it away from him. The way he remembers it is that he settled on snakes for pets because we objected to his keeping a dog or cat. If you're a parent, you can't win.

His mother had been bitten by a dog as a child and still has an uncontrollable fear of even tiny animals. She's afraid of snakes, too, but it's easier to stay out of their way if they're in somebody else's bathroom. At any rate Billy was always coming home with a new reptilian love interest, and perhaps a bad case of poison ivy acquired in the pursuit.

I remember a frog he had that hopped in the large brandy snifter of a distinguished guest who never came back. Another time, investigating a box in the hallway she thought had been delivered for her, Bessie was nipped on the finger by a baby alligator. There was also an owl. And later kangaroo rats, giant moths, and falcons. While we would be entertaining very formally in the drawing room, little Billy might come in to say his good nights with a snake wound around his arms and neck. When he made a trip with me, I was afraid to open my own luggage after the time he smuggled one of his viperous friends aboard.

Once in Hollywood, Bessie phoned me at the studio in considerable agitation. "Jesse, you've got to come home at once," she pleaded. "The rattlesnakes are loose in the house and I'm locked in my room." The maid had accidentally tipped their box over while cleaning. Such occurrences were so common I didn't take this one very seriously. The police and neighbors were frequently up a tree looking for Billy's escaped protégés. Bessie insists that on this particular occasion I responded gallantly, "I'm in a conference, Bessie—I'll call you back later."

Billy kept his three rattlesnakes in a box by his bed and they hissed menacingly when anyone but him entered the room. They recognized him as their lord and master.

Frankly I don't like snakes and I didn't think it was cute of Billy to play for attention by parading his menagerie before guests. He was supposed to keep the pests—or pets, if you will—in his own quarters. Each of the children had a suite—bedroom, study, and bath.

By mutual understanding each member of the family was deemed an individual, entitled to pursue his own interests in his own way. Bessie had her artist's studio, as she has had in every home we have lived in since she started to paint, and if she felt like holing up in it for days at a time, there were enough servants so the rest of us could manage until her creative mood spent itself and she rejoined us. The same tolerance prevailed if, at intervals, I felt I wanted to substitute a trout stream for the swift stream of business and social affairs. I might disappear for three or four weeks to pack a canoe on a mule up to a mountain lake at a thirteen-thousand-foot elevation where no boat was likely to have sailed before (there being no folding boats then), or shoot some rapids no one had previously attempted (invariably smashing up a canoe on the rocks in the process and having to be fished out of the boiling eddies a couple of times), or descend a natural rock formation that no one else had ever been so foolhardy as to risk. I tried to work in a long trip on horseback, afoot, or in a canoe every year. Bessie and the children went along on several of the early Sierra Nevada camping trips, and Jesse, when he was old enough, accompanied me on some of the more rugged expeditions. Billy may have got his love for nature from my love of the outdoors, but it certainly took a different form.

Betty inherited her mother's musical ability and spent all the time she could at the piano. She also played the flute in the Beverly Hills High School Band.

Jesse, Jr., in his younger years lived in a dream world of campaigns, breastworks, and reimplacements of thousands of lead soldiers. He and his friend Billy Buckland, son of our first art director, staged battles that lasted for days. Our Billy, when he tired of being ignored by the older boys, would make his presence felt by wiping out a regiment with a swipe of the hand. Whereupon Jesse and young Buckland would notice him enough to give chase and hold him by his feet out the window or throw him in the swimming pool. One time when vengeance was close at his heels, he grabbed up a snake and Generalissimo Big Brother promptly fainted, having previously had some scares on exploration trips with me and in the snake-infested hills around our Hollywood home. From then on Billy had a secret weapon that would bring Jesse and Buckland to terms whenever he wanted something from them. But by the time these childhood war games were replaced by dead-serious military duty, Jesse had learned to control his fear of danger.

It was not a normal family, unless you use for a norm the Sanger family of *The Constant Nymph* or the Vanderhof family of *You Can't Take It with You*. We all went our separate ways, but there was strong rapport and affection among us. We might not come together until bedtime, in a huddle at the top landing of the stairs, when a spirited interchange could go on for hours.

While Jesse, Jr., was away at prep school in Princeton and at college in France, I wrote him long letters every few days so the warm family feeling wouldn't get lost in the shuffle. An excerpt dated New York, April 13, 1925, typical of our scattered activities, reads: "On Thursday, Dody, Robins and the babies leave for the Coast. They will stay at our beach house. Saturday morning at 1 A.M. Mother sails on the *Olympic* for Paris and the following Monday I leave for Hollywood." The "babies" were otherwise known as "Bugle and Little," because Billy cried with brassy virtuosity and Betty was small for any age.

Once when we all happened to be together with our retinue on the train to Hollywood, we trouped into the dining car about twelve strong and someone asked, "What show is this?"

Jack Hewson, one of our chauffeurs, said with a straight face, "*Uncle Tom's Cabin*," and pointed out Betty as Little Eva, my valet as Uncle Tom, and the rest of us as various other characters.

"What show is this?" became a family spoof.

Our Hollywood home was sometimes referred to as "The Snake Pit," not entirely because of Billy's hobby. He kept snakes by his bedside, it's true, like a child who can't go to sleep without his favorite Teddy bear, but the rest of us had our quirks too. I kept the mouthpiece of my cornet within reach when I went to sleep; Bessie had her palette and brushes handy in case she had a Technicolored dream and had to get up in the middle of the night and transfer it to canvas. Jesse, Jr., had a notebook and pencil always ready for nocturnal inspirations, after he passed the lead-soldier stage and turned to writing.

Betty was the only sane one. All she kept on her night table was a book and a glass of water.

Near our Hollywood home was an unspoiled remnant of old California history—an undeveloped tract of eleven acres containing The Hangman's Tree, a huge oak from which horse thieves and bandits had been hanged in the early days, and an ancient adobe house that Bessie had a yen to restore and preserve as a private museum. I was more interested in building a mansion that would reflect our prosperity, but there would be room for it among the stately sycamores without disturbing the picturesque landmarks. So at Bessie's urging I bought the property, paying $60,000. The Hollywood real estate boom was on, and before we could even get blueprints drawn for our new house, I heard that an apartment house was planned for the adjoining property. Feeling I had made a mistake in not choosing a more restricted area, I put the property back on the market, and it sold overnight to C. E. Toberman. The mistake doubled my investment. The tract, known as Outpost Estates, today contains three hundred homes.

Our twenty-room New York apartment was the whole tenth floor of 910 Fifth Avenue, at Seventy-second Street. We paid a rental of $36,000 a year to have the dividing walls knocked out of two ten-room apartments. Bessie made several trips to Europe to collect furnishings for it—rare furniture, rugs, silver, marble mantels, linens, art objects and books from England, France, Italy and Morocco, Madonnas from Toledo, Spain, and old crucifixes from Madrid. Religious relics dominated the decorations and distressed Bessie's orthodox father no end. I confess I can't get excited about antiques, especially about sleeping in a Charles the Third bed and pulling my shirts out of a converted altarpiece. But Bessie not only has a true appreciation for traditional period pieces—she had a curator's fervor and impeccable taste in assembling a collection that the Metropolitan Museum later appraised at $250,000.

At the same time we were spending another quarter million renovating a third home, a beach house at Santa Monica. We had started with a small weekend place and then bought a larger one from Mrs. Langford Stack, mother of actor Robert Stack. We sold the first bungalow to William Randolph Hearst, who acquired adjoining beach frontage and built the fabulous Marion Davies mansion (now a hotel) on the site. We enlarged our new beach house to twenty rooms and ten baths, with a sun-deck gymnasium and a convertible solarium-theatre. The larger of our two swimming pools, built to supplement the ocean, saw the flowering of a memorable Hollywood romance. Douglas Fairbanks, Jr., and Joan Crawford used it to escape the disapproving eye of Doug, Sr., whose house was a block or so down the beach. Louis B. Mayer and Sam Goldwyn built homes on either side of us and other close neighbors included Irving Thalberg and Norma Shearer, Pola Negri, Bebe Daniels, Harold Lloyd, and Myron Selznick.

Weekends overflowed with guests, and there were always private showings of the latest pictures, exchanged among Mayer, Fairbanks, Goldwyn, and myself, all of us having projection rooms. When we really threw a party, the roster of entertainment would have done credit to a charity benefit. I remember one we had with Abe Lyman's band playing for a ballet by the Albertina Rasch dancing troupe on the beach against a background of breakers, and Eddie Cantor emceeing impromptu numbers by Maurice Chevalier, Charlie Chaplin, Jeanette MacDonald, Elsie Janis, and Eddie Goulding among others. During the evening I missed Bessie and went looking for her. She was propped up in her New England four-poster, reading a book!

She had been much in evidence earlier, making the guests comfortable. (She was apt to forget a face the whole world knew, or call a famous actor a director or introduce a husband to a wife who had a different professional name, but she was such a charming hostess that nobody minded.) Then when she thought she could slip away without being noticed, she left the servants to carry on and retired for some *real* enjoyment.

"Don't ask me to change, Jesse," she would say, "I just *can't* fit in. I really have tried. But what I want are the things money can't buy. Someday you'll understand."

But I didn't then. I was absorbed in company business and making money to the exclusion of any real personal life. I sometimes think that's an occupational disease of executives. The more things I gave my wife and the more successful I was, the more she withdrew. The way to heal the breach and bring her closer to me was very simple, as I eventually found out—all I had to do was make less money!

Sometimes she'd say, "I don't like money! I hate it! I wish we had nothing to do with it!" It made me furious to have her talk like that. The only money I ever took a dislike to was the $50 in paper marks that Gilbert Miller and I had to lug in a suitcase around Berlin for small purchases.

I don't mean to suggest that Bessie was a recluse. She enjoyed having house guests like the great sculptor Boris Lovet-Lorski, who modeled heads of each of our family during his stay, and writers like Joseph Hergesheimer, Somerset Maugham, H. G. Wells, Bruce Barton, Edward Knoblock, Guy Bolton, and Fannie Hurst. Bessie could sit up all night after a party discussing art with George Gershwin, whose hobby was painting. Some of her best friends today are former film stars and intelligent women of the theatre world. But there has never been a time when she wouldn't rather stay home and paint a picture or write a poem than attend a glittering premiere.

Bessie was particularly fond of Amelia Earhart, a shy, gentle, uncommunicative person who frequently dropped in, wearing her customary breeches. I remember the night she and her husband, George Putnam, came over to tell us, before they announced the plans publicly, that she was going to fly around the world. Bessie was a little annoyed. She said, "Why are you letting her do it, George? She's had glory enough."

"*Letting* me!" Amelia laughed lightheartedly. "It's *his* idea. But I'll do it to please him."

"It will be her last trip," George said half apologetically.

We had three Rolls-Royces and our basic ménage included two butlers, lady's maid, valet, French governess, two cooks, two chauffeurs to cater to Bessie's and my divergent needs, and athletic trainers. I went two rounds every morning with the middleweight boxing champion, Kid McCoy, and Terry Hunt gave the children daily exercises and the boys boxing lessons. At times during those Roaring Twenties there were a dozen on the household staff. Some of them were with us fourteen years. My secretary, Randy Rogers, has been with me for over thirty years.

I don't tally these totals as something to brag about. Perhaps I would have something to brag about if I had managed to stay in the position where I never had to consider the cost of anything but only whether I had time to buy it. However, the memory of those brimming-over years is interesting in retrospect as an Arabian Nights adventure of an erstwhile cornet player who as a child had an allowance of ten cents a week and was trained to save pennies but was never trained to save dollars.

You never completely outgrow the training of a frugal childhood. I used to wait until my valet had left the room and then I'd sneak out the clean breast-pocket handkerchiefs he had removed from my suit and thrown in the laundry hamper. I'd put them back in the dresser because I couldn't help feeling it was wasteful to launder unsoiled linen. And to this day, even in a hotel or a locker room at the golf course, I absent-mindedly fold and hang a sopping towel up carefully after a shower so it will dry and be ready for use again.

Douglas Fairbanks and Mary Pickford told me one night when Bessie and I were having dinner with them that they were each putting a million dollars into an annuity. They urged me to do the same. But I thought I'd play it smart and wait until I could stash away $10,000,-000. The interest on one million wouldn't have done much good, the way we were living it up at the time.

Artie Stebbins had insured my life for $3,400,000. The premiums amounted to $40,000 a year. I was getting a $2500-a-week salary and 7½ per cent of the net earnings of Paramount Pictures.

One time when my financial adviser broke into a conference to bring me a check for half a million dollars—my share of company profits— I was annoyed at the interruption and chided him for bothering me! There was also the stock market. In a letter to my mother I told her how I had just made several hundred thousand dollars by buying some stock at sixty-five and selling it at eighty. That didn't indicate any shrewdness on my part, since the same adviser handled my investments and I hardly knew what was happening to them except when he annoyed me with checks.

The letter was written in a luxurious private railroad car loaned to us for a trip to Palm Beach, Florida, by William English, president of the Empire Trust Company and also on our board of directors, who had offered it in the offhand manner that a person might say "It's raining—here, take my umbrella."

It was a trip I'll never forget. We had several guests with us. Bessie was in the midst of shaping up a book of her poetry for publication, and invited her editor to come along so they wouldn't have to stop working on it. I took my valet so I wouldn't have to pick out the ties I put on. Our car was shuttled to special tracks alongside the Breakers Hotel, with a dozen other private cars. We were entertained by the Philadelphia and Palm Beach social leader, Mrs. Edward T. Stotesbury, at her Florida estate, "El Mirasol," and by other society people who were completely out of our class—they had *hundreds* of millions. The way they entertained made our Hollywood parties seem like clambakes. Our own sham and pretense and delusion paled by comparison. Sometimes you can't recognize your own vainglory without a magnifying mirror. The house that will accommodate a hundred people for dinner or five hundred for a party is a white elephant on the real estate market today. It's a relic of an era that has passed from the American scene—and good riddance. Who can get chummy with five hundred people in three or four hours?

Back in New York after our incredible Florida vacation Bessie plunged into her painting again, registering at an art school in order to work from live models. Her driver always had instructions to keep the Rolls at least a block away from the school, so her identity wouldn't be disclosed to her younger classmates. Neither did the bewildered grocery clerks know, when she shopped hours for perfect specimens of carrots, turnips, onions, and cabbages, that she was gathering the makings for a still life instead of a stew.

I wanted the children to appreciate the value of money, and perhaps because I was setting a poor example myself I undoubtedly leaned over backward in order not to be too indulgent in the matter of allowances. If they wanted something special, they could ask and would probably get it, but they weren't much inclined to ask. Billy's idea of an extravagant weekend was a trip to the desert to collect snakes.

Jesse sold papers at the corner of Hollywood and La Brea to get money for a football helmet. Then, when he was about twelve, he saw a seventeenth-century flintlock pirate pistol he wanted for his gun collection. It had a price tag of $30. He wormed his way into a crowd of extras applying for work in Douglas Fairbanks' *Thief of Bagdad*, and under another name got a job at $5.00 a day leading a camel. Doug spotted him after he had worked four days, thought it was a huge joke, and had a press picture taken that appeared in the bulldog edition of the evening paper. I should have been proud of Jesse, but I was embarrassed and had the story killed, pulled him out of the picture, but gave him the $10 he still needed for the gun.

When he started to write, he wanted a typewriter. Thinking it might be a passing whim, I had a usable but battle-scarred typewriter sent out from the studio. Jesse found "William Desmond Taylor" scratched on one corner of it, and that nearly ended his literary career before it began. He wouldn't touch the thing for months. He thought it was haunted.

The creative urge eventually triumphed over fear of ghosts and you could have knocked me over with a cup of coffee when Boni & Liveright published *Songs from the Heart of a Boy*, by Jesse L. Lasky, Jr. I hadn't even known my fifteen-year-old son was writing poetry.

At the same time he was becoming something of a prodigy of letters

Jesse was augmenting his $5.00 weekly allowance while he was at Blair Academy by writing love letters for less articulate schoolmates at fees ranging from $1.00 to $3.00, scaled according to the degree of passionate embellishment, and peddling "personally autographed" movie-star photos from the studio to his friends at $1.00 per pin-up.

I was unaware of these extracurricular activities as well as the problems Jesse had in trying to keep up with scions of the Mellons and the Lorillards, not to mention a new acquisitive interest in rare books that kept him broke. I was gullible enough to take at face value the school's guidance manual for parents when it counseled: "Do not spoil the lad with a big allowance. Five dollars a week is sufficient for all his needs."

When I found out about the brisk trade in fan photos, and that my indulgent secretary Jeane Cohen was furnishing them and becoming an expert forger by writing intimate inscriptions to the schoolboys and signing the stars' names (keeping samples of their real signatures in her desk for guidance), I put a quick stop to the traffic—after allowing Jesse one more batch to let him fulfill any commitments already made.

Jesse had a second book of poetry published when he was seventeen, and has done another and three novels since then, besides the screenplay writing that is his livelihood.

Billy continued to follow his natural bent. While in the Army he made an important mosquito survey singlehanded, trapping and identifying twenty-nine thousand mosquitoes and eight thousand larvae of eighteen varieties, and published a paper in a scientific journal on the work. He wrote, directed, and produced two nature-subject film shorts, one of which, starring a bald eagle and a rattlesnake, was nominated for an Academy Award. He built up a respectable reptile collection for the Griffith Park Zoo, where his duties as curator included force-feeding a cobra for two years. He recently made a lecture tour of the country, enlightening school children about falconry, hawks, and conservation, with the assistance of some of his pets, trained falcons and an owl.

Save the Pieces

There's a "Lasky Drive" in the heart of Beverly Hills. It is perhaps a fitting designation for a place where Lasky used to drive his specially built sports cars 110 miles an hour. I was a stockholder and director of the race track that flourished during the twenties where the Beverly Hilton Hotel is now located, and I liked to speed around the track by myself just for the thrill of it. When it later made way for a subdivision (doubling my investment again), one of the new streets was named after me. There was a twelve-hundred-acre "Lasky Ranch" near Universal City, leased and used by our company for sagebrush scenes even before the twenties. There was also a "Lasky Sandwich," sometimes found on menus around town as well as those of our own commissary. And a popular bartender's guide describes a "Lasky cocktail" as equal parts of grape juice, Swedish punch, and gin.

My associates in the company had decided, after we moved from the Lasky Studio on Vine Street to what is now the Paramount Studio on Marathon, that an undistinguished street (Lasky Drive hadn't yet acquired the gold-plated shingles of some of the leading doctors), a desolate stretch of barren ground, a sandwich, and a cocktail were collectively not sufficient recognition of my contribution to film-making. In as much as the Lasky Studio had been one of Hollywood's first landmarks, they proposed that the whole site, which we had rented for $150 a month, then bought for $150,000 and was now appraised at $2,000,000, be used for a monument to the birthplace of Hollywood's first feature film in the form of a "Lasky Theatre" that would outdazzle Grauman's Chinese and every other film palace in the West. Plans for the theatre that would bear my name were prepared and completed without consulting me. The first I heard of it was when our president's son, Eugene Zukor, walked in and laid a set of blueprints on my desk.

"The new Lasky Theatre!" he announced, and proceeded to point out architectural details after I had got my emotions under control.

"The horseshoe mezzanine of boxes will each bear a name plate of a famous star. The center box will be permanently reserved for the personal use of yourself and your friends, Mr. Lasky."

"So this is how it feels to be sitting on top of the world!" I thought to myself. In 1927, *Variety* had estimated my fortune at $20,000,000, the eighth largest in show business. I'm sure that was an exaggeration, but I felt secure enough to think I'd never have to worry about money again. My company had just granted me a new seven-year contract—and now this overwhelming homage of having a new theatre, Hollywood's finest, built and named in my honor. What a far cry from the maple-syrup-machinery and newspaper-route days, I reflected.

I could hardly believe that this personage to be so honored was the same Jesse L. Lasky who had once come back from Alaskan gold fields empty-handed, who had sailed to Hawaii in luxury and returned broke, who had made a fortune and lost every cent of it on a cabaret. But before long I had good reason to believe it was the selfsame Lasky, running true to form. In a few months I was out of the company I had helped found, which no longer bore my name, and I was actually broke again. The site of the projected monumental Lasky Theatre is now a monument to the National Broadcasting Company.

In retrospect it is easy enough to understand how and why the little world I had been sitting on top of was pulled out from under me.

Theatre attendance had not been too seriously affected by the stock-market crash at first. In times of trouble and stress people turn to cheap entertainment for relaxation and relief. Aware of this, I was convinced that we could ride out the downward trend, but I overlooked one important factor. Our Achilles heel was in the theatre chain.

To acquire these theatres, in the years preceding 1929, Publix had bought into partnerships with other circuits at a time when Paramount stock was at its highest. Many of these theatre purchases were made with part cash and part stock, which stock was to be redeemed, after a certain period, at a fixed price. After the crash our stock went down, way below the promised fixed price, but we had to live up to our contracts and redeem the pledged stock at many times what it was worth in the current market. This drained the company of capital, and the stock kept plunging and the creditors kept clamoring. We were keeping up our picture schedule, but no amount of production could halt the futile financial spiral our theatre IOUs had thrown us into.

The stock-market crash, followed by the long depression, finally caught up with the picture business. As our gross receipts fell off and personal fortunes melted, everyone got jittery. A feud between our sales and theatre departments that had at first seemed to me more silly than serious erupted openly and began to threaten the company's solidarity. Sam Katz, for some years head of our expanding theatre department, had been appointed president of our subsidiary Publix Theatres, now one of the most powerful theatre chains in the nation. In the meantime Sid Kent still headed what was unquestionably the strongest sales department in the industry, but had also been elevated to the position of general manager of Paramount Famous-Lasky.

I had consented to that corporate name change to emphasize to the salesmen that we all belonged to the same company. But the feuding continued. Kent claimed that Katz refused to pay as much for rentals of our pictures as competitive chains did, and Kent couldn't give our theatres discount rates without losing good-will and business from other circuits. Katz, on the other hand, maintained that it was his business to supply product for our theatres as economically as possible, whether they were Paramount pictures or other brands.

The attitudes of these aggressive executives infected the personnel of their respective departments and the two groups were barely speaking to each other. In some instances we had the absurd situation of our sales division refusing to sell our own pictures to our own theatres, and our own theatres refusing to play our own product! And this at a time when we needed the greatest co-operation among all our departments in order to cope with depression doldrums!

Zukor called me and told me of the difficulties, which he feared would wreck the company. Caught in the middle of it, he was becoming ill under the pressure. I rushed to New York and had conferences with both Katz and Kent. There seemed no way to bring them together. I stayed awake all night trying to figure a way out of the dilemma.

In the morning I went to Zukor and proposed another corporate title change—to Paramount-Publix. That way Kent's and Katz's departments would have equal billing in our company trademark.

"You'd eliminate your name from the pictures you make?" Zukor asked me incredulously.

"I'm not fighting anyone for top billing," I said. "And if it averts a crisis, it'll be worth it."

"We'll also give them equal rank as vice-presidents," Zukor said. "That plus the sacrifice you're making should preserve the balance of power and give us a little peace."

A mass meeting was called. It was held in the Paramount Building, with all our theatre managers, salesmen, and top executives from all departments present. Adolph Zukor announced that I had volunteered to remove my name from our corporate title, Paramount Famous-Lasky, in order to restore harmony in the ranks and loyalty to the parent company, and made an impassioned plea that we all pull together under the banner of Paramount-Publix.

I knew, of course, that the stock crash had deflated my investments, but I didn't realize the extent of my losses until my financial adviser told me I needed $250,000 to cover stock I had on margin and other immediate needs. I had bought twenty-five thousand shares of Paramount stock and had also invested heavily in important building operations. Harry Warner heard a rumor that I was in financial difficulties and sent a message that he would be glad to loan me enough to tide me over the current depression. A check for a quarter of a million followed, and I gave him my Paramount stock and, as I wanted him to have ample security, offered him my beach house and contents as well. Later I asked him to sell both to clear my obligation to him. The stock, which I had bought at $1,550,000, brought only $37,500. My investments in the building enterprises were a total loss.

While this was happening, powerful Chicago friends of Sam Katz— John Hertz, the Yellow Cab magnate, and Albert Lasker, the millionaire advertising executive—were elected to our board of directors. Almost immediately Hertz, who was the means of bringing badly needed new capital into the company, was appointed chairman of our finance committee. Katz was suddenly in the driver's seat of a Hertz Driv-UR-Self.

Sid Kent saw the handwriting on the wall. "Jesse," he said, "I'm getting out of this mess before they shove me out! Between you and me, I've been offered the presidency of the Fox company. You'd better come with me—you can be in charge of all production at Fox, the same as you are here."

But I couldn't bring myself to walk out of the company I had helped found, even though it was in dire difficulties.

Kent had no sooner announced his resignation than John Hertz suggested that I take several weeks' leave of absence.

"I've got work to do in Hollywood," I protested.

"We prefer you stay away from Hollywood for the time being," he said evenly. "You need a rest and change. Later we'll talk things over."

I remembered that Kent had tried to warn me. It was obvious now that they wanted to break my contract. I thought things were as bad as they could get, but at home Bessie handed me a telegram. "Your sister is very ill," she said quietly, trying to prepare me for the shock. Blanche had been suddenly stricken with pneumonia. Her husband, Hector Turnbull, advised me not to try to make the trip to her bedside in Hollywood. In a few hours she had passed away.

Bessie was a tower of strength in my grief over the loss of my sister and my distress over the turn things had taken with the company. I dreaded telling her that we must close our Fifth Avenue apartment and move to the beach house in Santa Monica. But she accepted our change of circumstances as though she actually welcomed the promise of a simpler, less complicated life and took complete charge of dismantling the apartment and packing furniture for storage in her usual calm, cheerful way.

Artie Stebbins reminded me that my insurance policies had considerable cash surrender value—the first good news I'd heard in weeks. He suggested that I accompany him on a steamer trip to the Coast through the Panama Canal. Bessie insisted that I do it while she went ahead with the children and their governess by train, to have the beach house ready for my arrival. And so I left my office in the Paramount Building for the last time on April 30, 1932, and after a floating rest cure in company with Artie was back in California.

They gave me the usual press reception. Our publicity department, not realizing what was in the wind, had assembled reporters from all the newspapers, as they habitually did whenever I arrived from the East, to get statements on my plans for Paramount's new season. I didn't want to tell them that I had been virtually forbidden to set foot inside the very walls I had ordered built. But I could have told those reporters, had I chosen to, that at long last I knew how Sam Goldwyn and Cecil DeMille must have felt when they had been eased out of the company the three of us had helped to launch. The wheel had come around full circle. Sam and Cecil had both gone forward to even greater glories in the business. Would I do the same, I wondered—or did my best work lay behind me? My mind was filled with apprehensions.

Jesse, Jr., still tells the story of a day at the beach, shortly after my arrival. Newsboys were shouting the headline: "'LASKY BANKRUPT!'" He says I paced back and forth on the sand all that day, looking at the waves, as he and his mother kept a wary eye on me. They were thinking of the many, many people, some we had known personally, who had taken their lives after the market crash. They knew that Blanche's death weighed heavily on my mind, that I wished I could have been with my mother to comfort her at the time, and that the crushing accumulation of events had taken their toll of my own health. Without daring to put words to it Jesse and Bessie shared the ominous feeling that, if I once turned toward the ocean, *that was it!*

I kept pacing till daylight began to slip away. Then they were horrified to see me pause, turn abruptly, and plunge through the waves toward the sinking sun.

"Go to your father," Bessie screamed, and Jesse ran for all he was worth.

For all their certainty of what was in my mind I had no idea what was in theirs. When Jesse reached my side, weak and winded, I exploded with fervor, "Jesse, I've got the greatest idea for a picture I've ever had! I've been thinking out all the details—I'm going to call it *Zoo in Budapest!*"

I practically had to drag the poor kid up on the beach to keep him from drowning. I think that he and Bessie had been seeing too many movies!

Independent Producer

My mother used to say when I'd suffered a defeat, "Jesse won't stay down. He's like a bouncing ball." Just knowing that she felt like that gave me confidence when I needed it. But if I morbidly contemplated the number of times I've been down and therefore obliged to bounce, my confidence might suffer a severe jolt.

There's one nice thing about "staging a comeback," though. It gets easier the more times you've done it. The path is familiar—you've trod it before and don't have to grope your way along. You have the advantage of hindsight—you know where some of your mistakes were. If you're a movie producer, you have the friendship of those you've helped along the way. Some of the ones you put on the first rung of the ladder to fame have reached the top and haven't forgotten who gave them their chances. Some of the highest-priced players and directors will go out of their way to help you get going again.

Sidney Kent made a place for me as an independent producer at Fox. He hadn't been able to hold open the post of studio production boss, which he had first offered me, but he built a special building on the lot for me and my staff with a private projection room, and arranged things so that I had to answer to no one but myself. Winfield Sheehan was in charge of all production except my six pictures a year. My deal was for $3000 a week and a percentage of the profits of the pictures I made on a three-year contract without options.

George Palmer Putnam wisecracked, "I hear the Laskys are cutting down. They only have two butlers now." I don't expect any sympathy for the inconvenience we suffered in the retrenchment necessary to adjust our living standards to a $3000-a-week salary. We adjusted to it so precisely that at the end of my three years as No. 1 producer at Fox I hadn't saved a nickel.

Zoo in Budapest was the first of eighteen pictures I made there. It opened at the Music Hall and the critics called it one of the most beautiful pictures ever put on the screen. Directed by Rowland V. Lee, it starred Loretta Young with Gene Raymond in his first important part—although I had snatched him from *The Cradle Snatchers* on the stage and made him a member of the Paramount stock company. (I did another good turn for Gene later—I introduced him to Jeanette MacDonald.)

The pictures I made on the Fox lot included *Berkeley Square* with Leslie Howard, and *The White Parade* with Loretta Young, both with excellent screen plays by Sonya Levien, then a Fox contract writer, whom I had started as a scenarist in the early days of Paramount, and who developed into one of the best-known and most skilled craftsmen in her field.

At Fox I also made *The Warrior's Husband, I Am Suzanne, The Power and the Glory,* in which a comparatively unknown actor, Spencer Tracy, made a smash hit, Nino Martini's first starring picture, *Here's to Romance,* and a flop I'm ashamed to acknowledge, *Redheads on Parade.* I mention the latter only because it was Dixie Lee's last picture before retiring to domesticity as Mrs. Bing Crosby, and because Don Hartman, later production head of Paramount, got his start in the industry by writing the lyrics and parts of the book for that musical. He also collaborated on another screen play for me, *The Gay Deception,* starring Francis Lederer and Frances Dee, and directed by William Wyler, whose great talent was just beginning to be recognized.

I brought Hector Turnbull to Fox as my story editor and associate producer. While in Europe scouting for material Hector found an American writer he thought had possibilities, Preston Sturges, who had authored the play *Strictly Dishonorable* and had an idea for a picture, though, to my knowledge, he had never written for pictures.

I sent for Sturges when he returned from abroad and asked him to tell me the story that had intrigued Hector.

"It isn't a story I can tell very well. It's too episodic," he said, "but I'll write it."

I raised my eyebrows at that. He obviously wasn't wise to the ways of Hollywood in a day when so many original stories were sold in ad-lib form over a luncheon or in a conference before being committed to paper. But I had no objection to reading the idea instead of listening to it. I knew that if it had any merit I could put a team of two or four or a half-dozen skilled film writers on it to develop the basic idea in a manner suitable to the film medium.

Preston Sturges went away and wrote his story. And he didn't even know enough about screen-writing to know that the first step is to do a *treatment*, or narrative story line. That's what I expected him to bring back, a few pages synopsizing the plot. Instead he brought a screen play of proper length, complete to every word of dialogue, the action of every scene blueprinted for the director, and including specific technical instructions for the cameramen and all departments.

He told his story in flashback, starting with the death of his subject, an unprecedented screen technique then but later used with powerful effect by Orson Welles and others. The manuscript crackled with its originality of conception and craftsmanship.

I was astounded. It was the most perfect script I'd ever seen. I dispensed with the usual practice of having other writers go over a finished script "with a fresh mind" to make improvements. I wouldn't let anyone touch a word of it. The director, William K. Howard, shot *The Power and the Glory* just as Preston Sturges wrote it.

I've heard Spencer Tracy tell people he wouldn't be a film star today if it hadn't been for me. He might not have become a star so quickly if I hadn't given him one of the year's choicest roles in *The Power and the Glory*, but with a talent like his I'm sure he would have reached the heights just the same. I make no claim to discovering him. He had given a notable performance in *The Last Mile* on the stage and impressed the Fox people enough that they put him under contract. I did, however, help him get his career started off on the right foot by being a little tolerant and giving him a second chance after he muffed his first one.

I had slated him for the starring role in *Helldorado*. Just as the picture was ready to roll, Spence disappeared. The studio gumshoed all the bars but couldn't find him.

Postponing the scheduled starting date of a picture is sometimes prohibitively costly if not downright impossible because of interlocked commitments geared to a timetable. In this case we couldn't even shoot around our star until he showed up because he had to be in almost all the scenes. We slapped Richard Arlen into the part, which didn't fit him at all, but there was no time to tailor it to his personality.

The studio rounded up Tracy a few days later and I sent word to him that I would never ask him what happened but that it might have happened to me instead of him and I was glad it didn't so I was willing to forget it. I added that there were plenty more good parts and I wanted to see him, but not till he had taken a little vacation and pulled himself together. He went to Honolulu and then reported back to the studio scared stiff, but not stiff.

"Spence, you look great!" I greeted him. "I've got a hell of a part for you!" And we put him in *The Power and the Glory*.

I'm not suggesting that the best way to become a movie star overnight is to forget to report for work on your first assignment. There are clauses in contracts by which the studio can drop a player like a hot potato over such an incident. Holding up production is the unforgivable sin in Hollywood. Players have been suspended, well-launched careers have been cut short by undependability and indiscretions. And Tracy's career was just beginning. The studio could even have sued him for damages.

I don't know to this day whether it was exuberance, lack of confidence, or personal problems that caused his lapse, because I never asked him. But I knew somehow in a way I can't explain that if I overlooked it it wouldn't happen again.

He's one of those who would go out of his way for me. Nino Martini is another.

When I was readying the musical *Here's to Romance* but didn't know whom I was going to use in it, I turned on the car radio one night on the way home and cut into a magnificent lyric-tenor voice. I had no idea who it was but made a note of the time and station and had my secretary check it the next morning. "That was Nino Martini," he reported.

I should have recognized that glorious voice, but it had been several years since he had auditioned for me in Paris, learned English, and come to Paramount in Hollywood, only to be dropped at the first option because we couldn't find parts worthy of his talents. He had sent me a wire when he made his debut at the Met in *Rigoletto*, wanting to let me know that my confidence in him had been justified, and that he was glad I had been responsible for his coming to this country.

As soon as I learned that the voice I'd heard on the radio was Martini's, I called his manager in New York and told him I had a picture I would like to use the tenor in.

"Oh, I'm sorry, Mr. Lasky," the manager said firmly, "but Mr. Martini wouldn't be available for a picture. He has a concert tour planned."

I was terribly disappointed because, while a great lyric tenor is hard to cast when you don't have a part for him, a part for a great lyric tenor is just as hard to fill when you don't have a singer for it. I was in a spot where I needed him very badly, but it looked as though I would have to find someone else. I asked the manager to give Martini my kind regards and hung up.

Within an hour the singer called back and said, "Mr. Lasky, it is so good of you to want me. If you think you can use me, I will be ready."

"But, Nino, I haven't talked terms with your manager," I reminded him.

"Never mind the terms," he told me. "Whatever you think is fair I will make my manager agree to."

The picture garnered much prestige and kudos for its artistic merits, which means it didn't make any money. It featured the lovely Anita Louise, the incomparable Spanish dancer Escudero, and for the part of the singing teacher who gave the young hero his first voice lessons I had called on Mme. Schumann-Heink, one of the greatest operatic contraltos of all time. It was the only picture she ever played in. When she first arrived and I took her to the sound-recording room, Nino and the members of the sixty-five-piece orchestra gave her a welcome that brought tears to her eyes. She was the most spiritual, courageous, wonderful character I've ever met in show business.

After *Here's to Romance* was finished, I started planning to star Schumann-Heink in a picture as a character actress, surrounded by young people. I thought I had discovered a new film personality of the caliber of Marie Dressler, and with a celestial voice besides.

M-G-M thought so, too, after they saw her in my picture. While I was on my way East to offer her a starring contract, they signed her. But they never used her in a picture and she died a year later.

With my penchant for singers you wouldn't think I could have passed up Judy Garland. But I did. She sang for me in my office in 1934, with her mother accompanying her on the piano, and I wasn't blind to her talent, but I thought it would be too difficult to find starring vehicles for a twelve-year-old. M-G-M beat me to the punch there, too, signing her up the following year.

My three-year contract expired the same month a merger was consummated between the Fox company and Twentieth Century Pictures, which had recently been formed by Joseph Schenck and Darryl Zanuck. I was asked to continue under the new regime, but I chose instead to accept an interesting offer from Mary Pickford to become her partner in a new corporation to produce at the United Artists Studio, of which Mary owned about 50 per cent.

The Path to Fame Is Paved

with Chewing Gum

While Pickford-Lasky Productions, Inc., financed by Eastern capitalists, was an association of only a year, it was a very pleasant one. Our first picture, *One Rainy Afternoon*, starring Francis Lederer and Ida Lupino, was not very successful. The other picture I made in partnership with Mary Pickford was my third attempt to popularize Nino Martini's sublime voice. This time we hit the jackpot with a musical satire, *The Gay Desperado*, featuring Leo Carrillo as the bandit with a soul for music. The story line was so colorful and unusual and Rouben Mamoulian's direction so distinctive that it is still considered his masterpiece. Every studio in town tried to make a picture like it. I even tried to follow it up myself with another Martini film. But in spite of Nino's good looks and brilliant voice he never acquired the devoted following among moviegoers that he did in the highest musical circles.

My final Nino Martini picture, *Music for Madame*, was made at RKO, where I also put Lily Pons in *Hitting a New High* and her husband André Kostelanetz to the trouble of commuting to Hollywood every week to supervise her music. He had a radio program originating in New York, a program that had made him a national figure, a household word.

The sorcery of radio began to fascinate me. Cecil DeMille was achieving a personal contact with the public through his Lux Radio Theater that he couldn't have had from pictures alone. Stars like Bing Crosby and Bob Hope who doubled in radio and pictures were bigger stars than they could have been just in the movies.

So I thought I'd have myself a fling in radio. Nobody had made me any offers. I just thought I'd work up a radio show because it was the only branch of show business I hadn't tried. It never occurred to me that I might have trouble getting a sponsor. Fools step in when they don't know where an angel is coming from.

I did have the prudence to map out a format that would take advantage of my seeming knack for and insatiable enjoyment in turning a spotlight on unrecognized youthful dramatic talent. I called my program "Gateway to Hollywood" and developed an elaborate formula for talent-scouting the whole nation, holding auditions in numerous key cities and bringing the cream of the discoveries to Hollywood. The ambitious young performers would be "screen-tested" on the network, a boy-girl team *starred* each week in specially written radio playlets, with people like Claudette Colbert, Joan Crawford, Edward G. Robinson, and Cary Grant supporting them in secondary roles. The youngsters would have the benefit of professional coaching before their appearances on the air and qualified picture people would judge their performances.

I would coin two fictitious names to serve for a series of dramatic playlets, and the "Gateway" entries would successively try on those names like Cinderella's slipper. The winners, of course, would be privileged to keep the highly publicized names permanently and pick up waiting contracts with a major studio, already made out in the coveted names and guaranteeing immediate screen roles.

Armed with my brochure of the idea, I went to New York to find a sponsor as naïvely as I had gone to Alaska to find gold. I talked to a host of advertising executives and potential sponsors, but they either had all the shows they needed or they couldn't get desirable air time or they thought my show would be too costly or something else. When I exhausted the likely possibilities in New York, I went on to Chicago and tried others. It was the same story. Ready to give up, I headed for the railroad station, passing the Wrigley Building on the way. On impulse I stopped the taxi and went in to visit Phil Wrigley. The first thing he did was dig up a facsimile of the $100,000 check I'd given him for the use of Catalina Island when we made *Old Ironsides*. The second thing he did was agree to sponsor "Gateway to Hollywood." I was able to arrange the studio tie-up with Leo Spitz, president of RKO, giving that company the services of the winners as well as options on any of the runners-up they wanted.

Our broadcasts were made on Sundays from the Vine Street Theatre, opposite the site of the old Lasky Barn. Cecil DeMille and Mary Pickford volunteered to give my introductory program a send-off. Cecil was taken sick at the last moment but, knowing it meant so much to me, wouldn't let anyone else take his place, and his remarks were piped to the theatre from his bedroom. The program caught on reassuringly. I learned one weekend that Phil Wrigley was flying in to attend the broadcast. I wanted him to be able to look around and see some recognizable faces in the audience as well as on the stage. Movie stars can usually think of something they'd rather do on a gorgeous Sunday afternoon than watch a broadcast, but I got a few to promise to show up. I phoned Spencer Tracy among others.

"Any other time, Jesse," he pleaded, "but I can't today. I'm playing in a big polo match."

"Well, if you can't, you can't," I said, but my voice must have betrayed my disappointment.

"Do you need me that bad?" he asked.

"We need you."

"I'll be there," he said, and he gave up his plans for the day in order to come into town.

I like to think of "Gateway" as more than just a piece of radio fare that held a spot on CBS for fifty-two weeks, because it gave quite a few young people such as Rhonda Fleming, Charles Drake, and John Archer a chance at show business which might not otherwise have come their way. Many of Hollywood's brightest stars were generous of their time in giving encouragement and advice to my protégés. And out of the sifting process of the talent hunt came two vivid personalities that have decidedly brightened the entertainment world. One of them, strangely enough, wasn't even a final winner. I think the judges must have chalked up her sublime self-assurance as unbecoming in such a youngster. But in spite of the judges' decision I thought Linda Darnell was the loveliest, most exciting sixteen-year-old I'd ever seen, and her talent utterly refreshing.

My radio program also paved the way to fame for Josephine Cottle of Houston, Texas, who was henceforth known by the name reserved for the winner of the series in which she competed. She is Gale Storm, who went on from pictures to become television's "My Little Margie." A few days ago I had a letter from her husband, Lee Bonnell, the other winner in the same "Gateway" series, whom I brought to Hollywood from South Bend, Indiana.

"Since you were instrumental in not only our meeting but in helping us to embark on our careers in the motion-picture field," he wrote, "Gale and I owe you a debt of gratitude beyond repayment. We would love to have you meet our three sons and baby daughter, who I think you may take some credit for indirectly."

Safari to Bag a Hero

In a book of conventional length I can't, of course, describe in detail the planning, preparation, finagling, cajoling, pleading, needling, and bargaining involved in bringing a thousand pictures to the screen. But perhaps I should take the case of one picture and demonstrate that not all the histrionics connected with a film take place in front of the camera. The tragicomic prelude and aftermath sometimes provide just as good a show.

Many of you will recall Gary Cooper's performance as Sergeant York, which rated an Academy Award as best actor in 1941. The inspiring story of the conscientious objector turned war hero was a natural for filming. But for over twenty years I despaired of that living testimonial ever reaching the screen.

On May 22, 1919, I had leaned out an eighth-floor window of the Famous Players-Lasky offices at Forty-first and Fifth Avenue and watched through clouds of ticker tape and torn-phone-book confetti the hysterical demonstration that welcomed Sergeant Alvin C. York back from the First World War, where he had distinguished himself by wiping out a machine-gun battalion in the Argonne Forest, killing 28 Germans with only 28 bullets, capturing 132 more and taking 35 machine guns practically unassisted. The spectators went wild as the car with York and the young Representative from Tennessee, Cordell Hull, rolled by.

I got a hot flash of inspiration and sent one of my aides to the old Waldorf-Astoria, where York was to be a guest for his stay in town, with orders to buy the rights to tell his story on the screen, no matter what it cost. He did his best, but all he got out of the sergeant was: "My life is not for sale." York was a very religious man, not at all proud of what he had had to do, I think. At any rate he was too much of a patriot to commercialize on his bravery.

Twenty years later, after "Gateway to Hollywood" went off the air, I began hunting for a story or theme important enough to serve for my second "comeback" in the picture business. An executive at RKO suggested Sergeant York as a subject. It took only a minute to spark my old enthusiasm, and I put writer Harry Chandlee to work digging up books and research material about York at the library. The more I learned about the dramatic elements of his life and his legendary feat on the battlefield, the more I was convinced that here was the greatest story of all time. I would tackle the sergeant once again—and this time I wouldn't take no for an answer.

I can't make a picture until I reach that state of self-hypnosis, and when I reach it, I *have* to make a picture.

I wrote Sergeant York in the Valley of the Three Forks o' the Wolf, Fentress County, Tennessee. He didn't even bother to answer. Very impatient to get the ball rolling, I sent him a telegram, asking him to meet me at his convenience to discuss "a historical document of vital importance to the country in these troubled times." Germany was again on the loose and President Roosevelt had proclaimed a limited national emergency. Moved by my appeal to his patriotism, Sergeant York agreed to meet me at a hotel in "Jimtown," as the natives affectionately refer to Jamestown.

On the date he set I flew to Nashville, rented a car, and drove over dusty roads into the Cumberland Mountains. He arrived on the dot, a towering farmer with bushy red hair, so taciturn that I had to say, "You're Sergeant York. I'm Mr. Lasky," and keep dribbling the conversational ball myself the whole time, with that huge hulk blocking the goal. He didn't introduce me to the shy, quiet woman at his side whom he addressed as "Miss Gracie." (After they had left, I asked the clerk who she was and learned that she was his wife.)

We went up to my room, where he and I sat on the bed, and Miss Gracie took the one chair in the best accommodations I had been able to get. I gave him a terrific sales talk, got no response, and finally ran out of verbal ammunition. I could only ask him to meet with me again after he'd thought it over.

"I won't refuse that," he said impassively, "but I don't want you to be hopeful."

I went back to Hollywood and a few weeks later sent a wire asking him to meet me at the Andrew Jackson Hotel in Nashville, where at least we wouldn't have to sit on the bed. I told him I'd have my lawyer along, and asked him to bring an attorney too. I was sure I could persuade him the picture must be made, and the lawyers could work out an arrangement.

He did bring an attorney, but he still didn't want any part of an agreement until I said, "Sergeant, you risked your life for your country in the World War, and you'd do it again if your country needed you, wouldn't you?"

He nodded slowly.

"Sergeant York," I said in a melodramatic tremolo, "that need exists right now, and I know you're going to give your life to your country—through the powerful medium of the screen. This country is in danger again and the people don't yet realize it. It's your patriotic duty to let your life serve as an example and the greatest lesson to American youth that could be told."

He looked puzzled. "Maybe we do have something to talk about," he conceded.

We did nothing but talk about it for several days. That is, the lawyers did. I offered Sergeant York $50,000 for the exclusive rights to tell his story, plus a small percentage of the gross receipts from the picture. His attorney from Jimtown put up a fight over the contract that eclipsed York's achievement in the Battle of the Argonne. He protected his client's interests almost to the point of extinction. My lawyer, Pete Bruington, blew his top repeatedly and at one point advised me to call the whole thing off.

The arguments for the most part weren't over money. Sergeant York was interested in the financial arrangements mainly because they would enable him to finish a Bible-school building he had started in his small community. The chief bone of contention was whether the contract should be interpreted under California or Tennessee laws. Bruington told me it would have to be in effect a California contract signed in Tennessee, since I lived and did all my business in California. York's lawyer adamantly balked on this purely technical point, for what reason I've never been able to fathom.

We'd sit there, the lawyers glowering at each other and York and I trying to think of something to break the deadlock. Every once in a while he would get up without a word and walk out. We couldn't go on without the principal, and once when he didn't come back for a long time I went to his room, two doors away, and knocked gently. There was no answer and I gingerly opened the door. He was on his knees praying by the bed. I closed the door quietly and went back to my room. The sergeant would saunter back in his own good time, and the negotiations would be resumed.

On Friday night, after several days of futile jockeying, Bruington said to me, "We aren't getting anywhere and we're not going to get anywhere. We might just as well pack up and go home tomorrow!" I agreed to throw in the sponge if we couldn't settle matters the next day.

Saturday noon we were still at an impasse. I walked up and down the room, lit a cigar, looked out the window, and saw the State Capitol Building a block or so away. It reminded me that I had called on Governor Prentice Cooper on my way to Jimtown for the first meeting with York, and he had been very sympathetic with my purpose.

I excused myself and went to a phone in the lobby, where I called Governor Cooper and asked him if he would witness the signing of the contract with York. He said he'd be delighted to have us sign it at the Capitol and suggested we get there immediately, as he was leaving for the weekend.

I tipped a bellboy to come to my room in five minutes and say there was an important call for me from Governor Cooper. I pretended to take the phony call in the manager's office and came back to report that the governor, knowing we were nearing the end of our negotiations, insisted on giving us his blessing by witnessing our signing of the contract on his historic desk in the illustrious State Capitol of the sergeant's beloved home state.

"There'll be no signing of the contract with that Clause Eight!" the Jimtown lawyer stated flatly.

"I don't think it's wise to offend the governor," I said. "He's waiting for us right now. But we don't have to sign the real contract; we can let him witness a dummy contract. Then if we don't come to an agreement before Bruington and I leave tonight, there's no harm done. But if we *do* sign the contract while the governor's away for the weekend, we'll have a photograph of him as a witness. That would please him and incidentally be very good publicity for the picture and your state!"

Sergeant York thought about it. "We *could* tear up the photograph if we don't sign the contract," he decided. "The governor is a good man. Let's don't keep him waiting."

I was afraid the governor might spill the beans when I confessed we weren't *actually* ready to sign the *real* contract yet. But he didn't bat an eye. Instead he pulled an impressive-looking document from his desk drawer.

"Then you might as well sign this bill that I can't get through the legislature," he suggested. "I'd like to see *some* use made of it."

He gave a signal and photographers from the national press services and the local Nashville papers swarmed in. We took our stances for the mock ceremony, a barrage of flash bulbs went off, we thanked the governor, and went back to the hotel to argue some more. Then we went to lunch. More bickering. Back to the hotel. Still deadlocked.

The invention of the printing press turned the trick. Late in the afternoon we heard newsboys shouting on the street, "EXTRA! EXTRA! CONTRACT SIGNED FOR SERGEANT YORK MOVIE!"

Sergeant York for once in his life looked defeated. "I guess we'll *have* to sign it now!" he sighed.

I was a little ashamed of playing on the altruism of a simple and good man to maneuver him into doing something he really didn't want to do, but I figured that the purpose of bringing a great picture to the screen justified any means, and I was desperate. Just how desperate I was can be surmised from the fact that I kited a $25,000 check, a penitentiary offense in California.

I didn't have money in the bank to cover the postdated check I had given York as his first payment, much less the rest of the $50,000, due in sixty days. Moreover I didn't know how on earth I'd get the only person who was perfect for the part of Sergeant York—Gary Cooper. But if what I felt was a laudable purpose justified a little bit of trickery, it would probably justify a little bit more. Accordingly I sent a wire to Gary as soon as I got to the Nashville airport.

Gary Cooper had come up in the world a good bit since he dug his toe into the carpet at my office and didn't rightly know if he wanted to be a movie actor or not. He now lived directly across the street from me in Brentwood in a Georgian-style show place of several acres with a pool, tennis court, and gardens that made my own big house, confined to a single acre, seem like a shanty on the other side of the tracks. His working pay was the highest of anyone in the United States.

The wire said: I HAVE JUST AGREED TO LET THE MOTION PICTURE PRODUCER JESSE L. LASKY FILM THE STORY OF MY LIFE, SUBJECT TO MY APPROVAL OF THE STAR. I HAVE GREAT ADMIRATION FOR YOU AS AN ACTOR AND AS A MAN, AND I WOULD BE HONORED, SIR, TO SEE YOU ON THE SCREEN AS MYSELF. SERGEANT ALVIN C. YORK.

A man stopped me as I walked away from the Western Union counter and said, "Pardon me, Sergeant York, but I heard you dictating that telegram. Could I have your autograph so my kids will believe I really saw you?"

He obtained the "signature" of Alvin C. York with a lot less difficulty than I had.

I got back to Hollywood and borrowed $25,000 on my life-insurance policy the first thing Monday in order to cover the check I had given York. I would have to persuade a major studio to finance the production before the second payment became due. I offered the proposition to RKO first, since the suggestion that reawakened my interest in York came from there. They turned it down cold. I then took it to Paramount and the other major studios, and each one told me that war pictures were dead, that nobody had made a war picture for ages because the public didn't want them.

As a last resort I took it to Warner Brothers, first consulting Charles Einfeld about the strategy of presenting it there. Einfeld had been my studio manager at Paramount and was now in charge of publicity and advertising at Warners.

"I think Harry Warner might fall for it if you get him alone and play on his patriotism," Charlie advised, "but don't mention I told you that's his weak spot."

I saw Harry at his farm and told him the story (by this time I'd had so much practice I could tell it pretty well) of a simple mountaineer who was the best turkey shot in Tennessee and a rough character until he got religion and became an exemplary citizen. Then the same parson who had accomplished his conversion and taught him "Thou shalt not kill" sat as head of the draft board in the grocery store in Jimtown and told him he was going to be conscripted in the Army. He vowed he wouldn't go. They got him to camp but he clung to the Biblical teachings and insisted he wouldn't use a gun or bayonet on his fellow man. An officer explained to him that killing is sometimes justified and gave him a history book and a leave of absence to go back home and think it over. After a night of meditation on a hilltop with his dog and his Bible he found his answer in "Render therefore unto Caesar the things that are Caesar's and unto God the things that are God's." Whereupon his turkey-shooting marksmanship made him what General Pershing called "the greatest civilian soldier of the war."

Of course I didn't neglect to elaborate on how patriotic it would be of Warners to make such a picture. Harry got his brother on the phone at the studio and I heard him say, "Jack, I want you to make a deal with Jesse for a story he wants to do. I believe in it so do it for my sake."

With a contract signed giving me 25 per cent of the gross proceeds, after recovering the negative costs, my next worry was over story preparation. We had the darnedest time trying to whip it into shape. Between the situations which provided dramatic high spots our episodic story of York's life lapsed into dull stretches. I suspected that this was because we didn't know enough about either York or life in the hills, so Chandlee and I packed up and went back to Tennessee to fill in the gaps. We took my son Billy along.

We did manage to supplement our stock of York lore somewhat before returning to the Coast, but most of our inquiries about the sergeant's childhood among his backwoods neighbors elicited nothing more helpful than "Alvin, he's a good boy," or "Alvin, he'd never harm nobody." Maybe they thought we were "revenooers." However, in talking to Miss Gracie, who was sixteen when she married York, we discovered that his courtship had stirred up a feud between the two families. Her folks hadn't approved of her keeping company with a hell-raiser noted mostly for his capacity for corn likker.

The sergeant staged a typical turkey shoot at my request, so that Chandlee and I could study its visual and story values for our purposes. Hillbillies came from miles around to vie for the steers I offered as prizes. Billy Lasky photographed the whole affair with his 16-mm. camera, and when director Howard Hawks saw the footage later in Hollywood, he was intrigued by York's characteristic gesture of wetting his thumb and touching the sight of his rifle before aiming it. "What's he doing?" Hawks asked me, and I explained that moistening the shiny gun sight reduced halation, or reflection of the sun, on it, permitting more accurate aiming of the old-fashioned rifle. Hawks established this habit early in the picture as a symbol of a perfect shot and a dead turkey, and for telling dramatic effect in the subsequent battle sequences.

I worked with several writers until I had a script that satisfied me.

The final collaborator was John Huston, who contributed some wonderful scenes including the one where the sergeant went off to war.

To avoid possible lawsuits over invasion of privacy, we had to get clearances from every living person portrayed in the film. There were about thirty survivors of the battle in which York captured the multitude of Germans, and tracking down every one of them was a sleuthing project that took several months. The search afforded an illuminating study on the fates of war heroes. One was in jail; another was wanted by police and had to be approached by an ad in the paper and a secret rendezvous. One family was destitute, with seven children, and in their case a bigger check was written than the usual $100 gratuity. Cordell Hull, the Secretary of State, was very gracious in granting permission for us to portray his part in York's story. He had been the sergeant's companion and adviser throughout the public ceremonies on his return from overseas.

With the script finished and clearances obtained the next problem was to try to obtain Gary Cooper, who was under contract to Sam Goldwyn.

"You're crazy!" Jack Warner exploded when I told him no one else would do. "Sam Goldwyn doesn't keep Cooper under contract just so we can borrow him when we need him! Don't waste your time—look for another actor!"

"Cooper is the only actor who's right for it," I said, "and I'm going to get him if I have to remind Sam who made it possible for him to go into the picture business!"

I went to see my ex-brother-in-law, who had himself declined the Sergeant York story earlier. I was prepared for a battle, but Sam assured me with a quizzical smile that he had no objections to loaning Gary Cooper to me for my picture.

I rushed back with the good news to Jack Warner. He couldn't believe it had been that easy, knowing Sam for one of the toughest traders in the business, and picked up the phone to verify it from Goldwyn himself.

"Sam, I understand you're loaning us Gary Cooper for the York picture," he said. He paused and a pleased smile spread across his face. "That's wonderful, Sam—I can't express my appreciation for . . . I can? . . . How?" I saw his smile burst like a bubble. "You're kidding!" he said harshly. "Bette Davis is our biggest star! I can't do it!" He hung up abruptly and stared darkly at me.

Hal Wallis, then production head of Warner's, helped me over that hurdle. He had kindled to my enthusiasm for the York story and supported my request for Cooper, even though they'd have to loan Bette Davis to Goldwyn in exchange. (Goldwyn made the most of his bargain by casting her in *The Little Foxes*, an outstanding picture.)

Howard Hawks was set to direct *Sergeant York*. He had piloted some notable pictures after beginning as a cub writer in my Paramount regime. For the part of Miss Gracie I wanted Jane Russell, who hadn't yet been seen on the screen, but Warner's understandably wished to develop one of their own contract players, so we cast Joan Leslie.

Before the picture started, we paid a bonus to Sergeant York to come to Hollywood, read the script, and make suggestions. The first day of his visit I brought him out to my house, where Bessie served him tea—he now neither drank liquor nor smoked—and then I took him across the street to meet Gary Cooper. Gary came to the door in his stockinged feet and I introduced to each other two of the three most uncommunicative men I've ever met in my life. If we'd had Calvin Coolidge there, it would have been a three-ring wake.

Every conversational overture I made was greeted with huge blobs of dead silence. I was getting progressively redder under the collar, until I remembered having seen a collection of Luger pistols, old muskets, and other firearms in York's farmhouse.

"By the way, Sergeant," I volunteered, "Coop has a fine collection of firearms." We walked to the gun racks in Gary's trophy room. York sighted and hefted and fingered the weapons, and asked questions. Gary expanded and expounded. I don't know enough about guns to carry on a technical discussion of their relative merits and features, and for half an hour I was dumb as an oyster. Anyway I couldn't have got a word in if I'd tried.

There are plenty of problems that come up *during* the shooting of any picture, but I'll skip them, as this chapter was just to be an accounting of the *before*-and-*after* headaches.

Sergeant York came East for the world premiere. I sat with him as our fleet of automobiles paraded down Broadway to the Astor Theatre with an American Legion band, a drum corps, and a host of attendants. I knew that the cheers of the crowd were for Sergeant York, but I was as elated as I had been at two other high points in my life, once as a young producer and competitor of Ziegfeld, when I rode down Broadway dressed in white tie and tails with Bessie at my side, on our way to the bejeweled opening of my Folies Bergère Theatre on Forty-sixth Street, and again when I rode in state down Broadway two blocks past the Folies Bergère to the opening of the Paramount Theatre.

After each of those triumphal rides down Broadway, Broadway had taken me for a different kind of ride—to the cleaners. But now I was riding in a procession of honor once more, down that same street of dreams, to the doors of the Astor Theatre, the plaudits of the crowd sweet music in my ears.

So were the reviews the next morning. And that night we saw the picture again with Governor Cooper and his mother, who hadn't arrived in time for the premiere. Over refreshments later I heard York say in a burst of confidence, "You know, Mrs. Cooper—all that talk you heard in the picture when I said good-by to Miss Gracie was just what I said when I went off to war."

There isn't a more credible writer in Hollywood than John Huston. He had even made Sergeant York believe that throbbing scene!

The picture opened with great fanfare in Washington the following week. Senator Kenneth McKellar and Representative Estes Kefauver of Tennessee were among a group of congressmen and other dignitaries in the cortege of cars that carried Sergeant York, Miss Gracie, the eldest of their five sons, and myself through the avenues of Washington to a presidential reception. At the White House I winked at my old friend Steve Early, the presidential press secretary, who had once been in our employ at Paramount. We were shown into President Franklin D. Roosevelt's office. He greeted Sergeant York, Governor Cooper, and the others cordially. Then, turning to me and knitting his brows, he thundered in a voice of rebuke that shocked me numb, "Lasky, I saw your picture last night and you made one unforgivable mistake."

He paused for effect and with a roar of laughter added, "You should have got old Cordell to play himself."

I felt a tug on my sleeve and sixteen-year-old Woodrow Wilson York whispered, "Where's the bathroom?"

You don't go to the bathroom while the President of the United States is talking to you, even if you have a president's name yourself, and I tried to put on a visage severe enough to discourage young York without being so alarming as to precipitate a more serious breach of diplomatic etiquette. President Roosevelt gave a signal for the cameramen and correspondents to be admitted and the flash bulbs began popping, with the boy still tugging at my sleeve.

The President turned to me and said, "By the way, Lasky, did you ever find that scenario I sent you in 1923?"

I had been praying fervently that he had forgotten. While Assistant Secretary of the Navy he had written a scenario for a film biography of John Paul Jones, called *I Have Just Begun to Fight.* He submitted it to the studio, and, to our everlasting mortification, it disappeared without a trace. We were never able to track it down.

I could only say, "If we hadn't lost it, you might be a scenario writer now instead of President of the United States."

I read awhile back that Elliott Roosevelt had reconstructed the story from writings found among his father's personal papers, so we may yet be privileged to see it on the screen.

I recently walked into a meeting of the Association of Motion Picture Producers and Frank Freeman greeted me with: "Jesse, I was just telling the boys how I turned down *Sergeant York*." His eyes gleamed with such pride that I felt like saying, "That's no distinction—you were one of a mob." I was deterred by reflecting that I have myself boasted about my stupidity in overlooking a Judy Garland or passing up an "Alexander's Ragtime Band." I guess we all like to identify ourselves with a smashing success, if only by such a slight connection as letting it slip through our fingers.

Longhair Music Is My Meat

While combing the Tennessee hills for anecdotes about Sergeant York I had hit pay dirt of a different sort. When we took up our headquarters in the little hotel in Jimtown, some of the townsfolk volunteered to furnish me information about their beloved hero.

The first to appear was an old mountaineer who told me that he had spent all of his eighty years in that section and been neighbor to the Yorks for three generations. I offered him a cigar and watched him take a few puffs as I phrased in my mind the first question about Alvin York's boyhood. But I never got a chance to ask it.

"You know Mark Twain's father built this hotel," the old fellow said suddenly. "He lived here afore he moved over yonder to Missouri." And before I could stop him, he was well launched on a succession of Mark Twain anecdotes.

He told me enough stories of Mark Twain to fill a book. After he left, I realized he had so fascinated me I'd forgotten to discuss Alvin York. Finally, when we were ready to return to Hollywood, the old hillbilly appeared again. He had brought me a faded newspaper clipping, which he said he had saved for forty years. I eagerly scanned it for some new bit of insight on Alvin York's family history. I should have known better—it proved to be a priceless article about Mark Twain!

"You keep it," the old man said. "I reckon I hain't got much time left for readin' in my span, and with my eyes failin', too. But I hope I'll be around long enough to see your pitcher."

"I'll hurry it up," I promised, "and I'll send the first print to Jimtown!"

"That'll be just dandy," the old fellow said, grinning. "There hain't a man, woman, or child in these here parts that wouldn't want to see a pitcher about Mark Twain!"

"Mark—Mark Twain!" I stammered. "Who said anything about making a picture about Mark Twain?"

I had filmed *Tom Sawyer* and *Huckleberry Finn* at Paramount, but it had never occurred to me that the life of America's greatest humorist had the makings of a wonderful film biography—until that old settler of Jimtown bombarded me with those yarns about the immortal Twain. Needless to say, *The Adventures of Mark Twain* was my next production. Fredric March gave one of the best performances of his career, aging through the picture from a young river-boat pilot to an old and famous author, and the art of make-up had advanced so much since we made the Teddy Roosevelt picture that March's appearance might have fooled Mark Twain's own mother.

I had acquired the Sergeant York and Mark Twain subjects myself, and produced them both for Warner Brothers within a year. My income from that pair of pictures was as great as that from my balmiest year at Famous Players-Lasky when I had charge of 126 productions. I had indeed made another "comeback."

I then took a brief leave of absence from the studio and produced a legitimate comedy at the Guild Theatre on Broadway. It was F. Hugh Herbert's first play, an amusing satire on movie producers called *Quiet, Please!* It got so quiet in front of the ticket window that the play folded after two weeks. It was the costliest dramatic flop of the season. Why couldn't I have waited and backed one of his later plays, say, *Kiss and Tell* or *The Moon Is Blue*?

For my next picture assignment Jack Warner gave me a choice of several subjects Warners already owned. I was drawn irresistibly to a screen biography of George Gershwin. The frustrated cornet player who wanted to play in Sousa's band was still paying devout homage to the highest musical expression, and gratifying unrealized ambitions vicariously.

I was fortunate in having known Gershwin quite well in his early life. One of the pleasantest tasks I had in connection with the picture was listening night after night to all of Gershwin's music and selecting numbers for use in the film, before we started working on the screen story. I gave my list to Ray Heindorf, the conductor-arranger who was to score the picture. I had picked the *Rhapsody in Blue, An American in Paris*, the *Cuban Overture*, the *Concerto in F*; "Summertime" and "It Ain't Necessarily So" from *Porgy and Bess*, as well as his first song hit, "Swanee," and a dozen other of his most popular numbers.

Heindorf did some figuring and gave me a quizzical look. "Well, this will save writing a screen play," he said. "You've got one hundred and nine minutes of music right here!"

The toughest task I had in connection with the picture was the one I had then—with a blue pencil.

Because Gershwin's death had been recent enough that he was well remembered by the public, I insisted we find a new screen personality who resembled George in general appearance rather than use an established actor. I chose Robert Alda, and he gave such a fine performance in the part as to threaten his career for a time. There are very few roles in pictures for an actor who is "typed" as George Gershwin!

Oscar Levant, Gershwin's greatest interpreter and best friend, played the *Rhapsody*, cast as himself. We had much help and advice from Ira Gershwin, George's brother and lyricist. Ira broke down when he and his wife watched the tragic death scene on the screen at a private showing in the projection room. After they composed themselves they said the picture was a beautiful tribute to George's memory, to my great satisfaction and relief.

At the premiere of *Rhapsody in Blue* on June 26, 1945, at the Warner Brothers Hollywood Theatre on Broadway, a tall, handsome woman of about fifty who was seated directly behind me touched me on the shoulder and said how much she had enjoyed the picture. I looked a little bewildered and she laughed, "You don't remember me because you have seen me only once before—the day I married Enrico."

It was Dorothy Caruso.

I told her that I had often thought of doing a picture about Caruso (in spite of the fiasco of the two pictures I made starring the tenor) but that I had never got around to gathering research for a screen play on his life. She said she hoped she had saved me the trouble, in as much as she had just written a book called *Enrico Caruso, His Life and Death*, and would send me the first copy off the press.

I read the book as soon as I received it, and was overjoyed to find that it had a clear-cut and entrancing story line. I started negotiations at once with Dorothy Caruso's representative, Leland Hayward, being afraid that some other company would realize the picture possibilities before I could acquire the screen rights. I agreed to pay $100,000.

I needn't have worried so much that one of the major studios would outbid me. No one else in the industry believed that it would prove profitable to make a picture with an operatic theme. I kept insisting that the basic theme was not opera but rather the drama of a fascinating life and an extraordinary personality. Caruso's story would have contained the elements of a fine and entertaining picture even if he had not been a unique artist, the greatest singer of his generation.

It took five years, however, before I sold the idea to M-G-M and saw it brought to the screen, after everyone else had turned it down, just as in the case of *Sergeant York*. Even M-G-M's plans to produce it were canceled time and again as various executives got cold feet. Each time I had to battle for renegotiation and in the end was almost forced to sue them to make them carry out their agreements.

In the meantime I made two other pictures under the banner of Jesse L. Lasky Productions, released through RKO, who also shared the financing. I hadn't liked the story Jack Warner wanted me to produce after *Rhapsody in Blue*, so I chose, perhaps unwisely, to leave his organization. I took Walter MacEwen with me from Warners as a junior partner. Our first picture was a fast-paced comedy, *Without Reservations*, for which we wanted John Wayne and Claudette Colbert. But they both had reservations, it seems. They wouldn't commit themselves until I would promise them an outstanding director. Their first choice was Mervyn LeRoy.

It didn't surprise me that they wanted him. He was considered something of a boy wizard and his directorial touch was highly valued.

Two things gave me an edge in obtaining the services of one of Hollywood's most sought-after directors. For one thing, I had sent him railroad fare when he was a boy, stranded in New York, and given him his first job in a picture studio. Besides that, he happens to be my cousin! I've always thought Mervyn was emboldened by his older

I*

cousin's example to brave the family prejudice against show business and become a vaudevillian (he started out as half of quite a good act called "LeRoy and Cooper—Two Boys and a Piano") and later cast a covetous eye on Hollywood, also inspired by my success there. When he wanted to get in the picture business, I gave him the lowly job of stacking wardrobe in the Lasky studio at $16 a week. Before long his talent was cropping out all over the place and he became a well-paid gag man. Gag men were the court jesters of silent-picture days. They sat on the set with the director and ad-libbed ideas for comic situations or bits of business to put in the picture as it was being shot. Mervyn had gone on to become a director-producer himself at several of the other studios.

Without Reservations was a successful picture, but the next one didn't do too well. It was *The Miracle of the Bells*, taken from Russell Janney's best-selling novel. We cast Fred MacMurray and Alida Valli in the leading roles, and then I had a brainstorm and suggested Frank Sinatra for the important role of the young Catholic priest. Ben Hecht and Quentin Reynolds, who had done the screen play, looked at me aghast. Hecht finally conceded that such "off-beat casting" was good showmanship, but Reynolds insisted that it would be a mistake.

They were both right. It was good showmanship and it was a mistake. Frank gave a perfect performance, but bobby-soxers who had come expecting to hear their idol sing were so disappointed when he didn't that their word-of-mouth publicity undoubtedly discouraged others from seeing it. I was accused of wasting a good singer in a non-singing part. It's ironic that, after I did my own picture an injury by demonstrating for the first time that Frank's talent goes much deeper than light singing roles, his career should reach its zenith in his Academy Award performance in *From Here to Eternity* and other straight dramatic, non-singing roles in *Suddenly, Not as a Stranger,* and *The Man with the Golden Arm.*

Finally M-G-M bought the Caruso property and obtained the necessary clearances for arias to be used in it. I had heard Mario Lanza give a concert at the Hollywood Bowl and thought he would be a prospect for the part. Louis B. Mayer heard him sing the same night and put him under contract to M-G-M. So when M-G-M bought the story, I suggested Lanza as Caruso. At first Dore Schary thought he was too young, but I insisted on interviewing him.

I asked him if he would be willing to study Caruso's records carefully and try to imitate him. A world of devotion came into his eyes.

"Mr. Lasky, my father is Italian and a great lover of music," he said.

"I was brought up on those records since I was seven. I know them all by heart. I can imitate any of them right now, this minute. Just tell me which ones you want to hear!"

From that moment he was my man.

My friend Sonya Levien wrote the screen play in collaboration with William Ludwig, and I worked in association with Joe Pasternak as the producer. Contrary to all rumors and reports about his behavior, Mario Lanza co-operated beautifully and enthusiastically, displaying no unusual symptoms of temperament or tantrums. I attribute the success of the picture largely to casting him in the role of Caruso. I'm sure he is equally grateful for the influence that bit of casting has had on his screen career. The picture broke all records at the Radio City Music Hall.

My mother followed the long negotiations over the Caruso picture with a consuming interest, reading all the trade papers and clipping every item she found about me, as she had done all her life. I told her many times that the clippings were hogwash, that I paid a publicity man to write them. But she never believed me—she believed the clippings! Her greatest pleasure was to sit in her accustomed armchair in the lobby of the Ambassador Hotel, boring her cronies to distraction about her devoted son. I don't know why I hired a press agent to mention my name—she did a good enough job of it for me.

She was also delighted when she could have for her audience her three grandchildren and Bessie—whom she had come to realize, through the years, was a rare spirit in this world, a daughter-in-law for the fondest mother to be inordinately proud of and grateful for. She would regale them with stories of the early days in San Francisco and of our tours in vaudeville and with Hermann the Great, days of one-night stands and scrimping along in hotels grossly misnamed The Palace or The Grand. She passed away in her seventy-eighth year, before *The Great Caruso* went into production.

Well, she *did* have a devoted son, and no mother ever merited more devotion.

A few years ago, after the children all had homes of their own, Bessie and I sold our big Brentwood place opposite Gary Cooper's estate and built a less pretentious home for the two of us. Incorporated into it, of course, is a big studio with the proper north skylighting that every artist prizes. It is on the same street, half a block from the other house, but much further removed in essential values. Bessie still enjoys her studio and flower garden, but they no longer have to compensate for other things. These days she has a husband around the house more than a few nights a year. My wife has learned to cook and sew and drive a car, and we eat in the kitchen on the maid's night off. Late in life we have learned to live.

Bessie's painting has gone through various periods—landscapes, trees, still lifes, portraits, flowers. Her highly distinctive style, developed with scant formal training, has won praise from art critics. Six years after she started to paint, she was represented in a Paris salon, and thereafter had countless exhibits in Paris, London, New York, Boston, Los Angeles, and other art centers. Some of her works have been purchased for the permanent collections of national museums and have been reproduced in *Time, Life,* and other magazines.

She is proudest of all, with good reason, of a series of paintings she made of the twenty-one missions of California. She worked on the twenty-one exteriors and ten interior and garden scenes over a period of two years, traveling alone, stopping in motels, following the ancient trail, El Camino Real, of Father Junípero Serra, who founded these first settlements in California from San Diego to San Francisco and Sonoma. And just as the loving care with which she plants and grows the subjects of her flower paintings is reflected gloriously from the canvases, her spiritual awareness, searching soul, convent training, and love for the gentle nuns and kind priests who helped her seems to shine forth from the mission paintings. Someday, perhaps when Father Junípero is canonized a saint—as it is said he will be—Bessie's mission paintings will become historically important. And her indescribably lovely flower paintings will still hang in art museums. I know that her pictures will be remembered long after mine have been forgotten.

I do have a pet project of my own—a picture I want to make more than I have ever wanted to make any picture. It started out to be the story of John Philip Sousa, a fit subject to follow my other film biographies of Sergeant York, Mark Twain, George Gershwin, and Enrico Caruso. It had the endorsement of M-G-M executives, so I started doing research on it as soon as *The Great Caruso* was completed at that studio, and imprudently took my time about conferring with the Sousa estate. An executive at Fox, learning of this, phoned his New York office to contact Sousa's two daughters and sew up the film rights to his life. This was a cunning maneuver, but I didn't consider it exactly cricket, and I was depressed for a long time over having to abandon my plans to honor the memory of my boyhood hero.

Then one night Bessie was thumbing through *Great Bands of*

America, by Alberta Powell Graham, one of the many books I had
acquired when I contemplated my Sousa picture.

"Listen to this, Jesse," she said, and read aloud: "'A national survey reveals . . . seventy-five thousand bands in the United States . . .
and fully nine million high school boys and girls belonging to school
bands . . . The school band is recognized as one of the greatest agencies for teaching democracy and good citizenship, as well as inducing
a nationwide love for music . . .'"

Right then I saw a tremendous theme for my next picture. . . .
*Teach a boy to blow a horn and he'll never blow a safe . . . the an-
swer to* The Blackboard Jungle *. . . I'd name the picture* The Big
Brass Band *and dedicate it to the nine million kids who spend their
spare time practicing on their instruments instead of running with
juvenile gangs, making music instead of mischief.*

I sat up all night planning it. Why not an All-American High School
Band as a special feature, but a real one, not a mythical aggregation
like the All-America Football Team? I'd select, through auditions, a
band of 110 top young soloists, the cream of high-school-band instrumentalists from the forty-eight states, Alaska, Hawaii, and the District
of Columbia, bring them to Hollywood, and use them in the picture.
Later, at the suggestion of Don Sartell, adjutant of the National Baton
Twirling Association, I decided to add a corps of All-American Champion Majorettes as another feature, picked by auditions from the
million young people who practice the jaunty and colorful skill of
baton twirling.

I spent months touring the country, studying at first hand the part
music plays in our schools. With a gifted writer, Charles A. Palmer, I
saw band festivals in Florida, Oklahoma, and Illinois. We reviewed
innumerable school concert and symphonic bands, including the famous Joliet champion grade-school and high-school bands, and met
their conductors.

As news of my project spread throughout the band-music world, I
was swept into a whirl of feverish activity. I attended a convention
of the American Bandmasters Association at Columbus, accepted in-
vitations to address the College Band Directors National Association
in Chicago, the Music Educators National Conference in Philadelphia, five thousand high-school band members in Des Moines (while
a guest of Lieutenant Colonel Santelmann and his U. S. Marine
Band), and the Music Merchants National Association. I appeared
before James Petrillo and his International Board of Directors of the
American Federation of Musicians in New York. All these organiza-

tions promised support for my endeavor, as did Colonel George S. Howard, conductor of the U. S. Air Force Band, Lieutenant Commander Charles Brendler, conductor of the U. S. Navy Band, the music trade papers—*The School Musician, The Instrumentalist, PTM* magazine, and *The International Musician.* In Washington it was suggested that the All-American High School Band not only could serve the picture but, if later sent abroad on a summer tour, would be the greatest ambassador for America since Benjamin Franklin went to France.

Everyone, it seems, is enthusiastically in favor of *The Big Brass Band* except the men who say what pictures shall be made. But they didn't like my Sergeant York or Caruso ideas, either. I've worn the studio heads down before, and I can do it again. I don't give up easily when I believe in something. After two failures with Nino Martini I tried again and was vindicated. Two failures involving Caruso didn't stop me, and the third venture paid off handsomely. You might call such manifestations the triumph of faith over frustration. Or call it stubbornness. Or call it stumbling luck. Or optimism. Or incurable enthusiasm. Whatever you call it, I believe in it, and I believe it can shape events.

That's been a sort of guiding principle in my life. I think that, if you put enough enthusiasm into anything, it eventually bears fruit, possibly in some other form, but it's never lost. No kind of effort is wasted, even when its results are not immediately apparent, and even when it wears a mask of failure. As I've already related, my youthful zeal to become a composer, opera star, novelist, and adventurer found expression in modified channels many years later.

We get out of life what we put into it. You can't draw out of a bank something you haven't deposited. Timidity, inertia, paralyzing fear of taking the wrong step bear fruit too—their own kind of blemished, wormy, or unfertilized fruit. You get back from life what you put into it.

If you ask others what to do, you invite confusion and indecision because the sum total of their opinions will be that your proposed course of action is foolproof, doomed to failure, isn't bad, isn't good. If you listened to everybody, you'd always be so hamstrung you could never make a move in any direction. So I say do the things you believe in and keep believing in them even when the going gets rough. That kind of faith has worked for me and given me, I think, as full a life as any man could wish for. Let me recommend it to you as an effective additive that will increase the mileage from the fuel of your endeavors, whatever they may be.

But I don't mean to hawk my pet precepts like a sweet old lady I know who sent her harum-scarum grandchildren a subscription to something called *Serene Living through Faith* with the smug admonition that they would be sure to benefit if they opened their minds to its inspirational message. Deeply touched by her concern for their tranquillity of soul, they dutifully thanked her and sent her a subscription to *Hot Rod Magazine* with a waggish prayer that it would open a whole new way of life for her.

This brings me up to and a little past the dinner of the Screen Producers Guild on September 12, 1951, where my old friends Adolph Zukor, Sam Goldwyn, Cecil DeMille, Gloria Swanson, and Mary Pickford said nice things about me as I received the first annual "Milestone Award," the silver wreath inscribed: "To Jesse L. Lasky for his historic contribution to the American motion picture."

And that, my patient friend, is where you came in.

Index